From the Humblest to the Greatest

How Susannah Knight took Chorley's Great War to the World

Adam Cree

DEDICATION

For Martha Cree

CONTENTS

FOREWORD BY DR BARRY BLADES

WHEN Adam Cree first introduced me to the story you are about to read, I knew immediately that this was a history that had to be told to a wider audience. The vast bulk of the historical literature dealing with the British experience of the Great War of 1914 to 1919 quite rightly depicts 'Tommy' in the trenches of the Western Front. Rarely do historians stray beyond the familiar fields of Flanders to remember the other participants in a total war in which so many British citizens – men, women and children – served their King and country. In this remarkable book, however, Adam Cree manages to combine the story of service and loss on the battle fronts with the contribution of a single citizen on the home front. It is a record of how the men of Chorley in Lancashire fought and died for their country in the Great War, and how a local teacher, Miss Susannah Knight, recorded their individual contributions and sacrifices.

Miss Knight was not alone in supporting the men of her home town as they prepared for war, came home on leave, recovered from wounds or adjusted to the new realities of peace in 1919. Nor was she the only non-combatant to devote time and effort to recording the exploits and ultimate fates of neighbours and other local townsfolk. What set Miss Knight apart from her contemporaries was the extent to which she continued to champion the men of Chorley in the decades after the war. Her *Memorial Album* is both a testament to the 'Pals' and to her own astonishing endeavour in producing it. This combative and doughty schoolmistress was driven by a sense of mission which was underpinned by a deep religious faith and conviction. The *Memorial Album* served to record and to remember the casualties of war and, at the same time, act as a symbolic vehicle for the promotion of international cooperation and a more peaceful world.

Miss Knight was tireless in her efforts to publicise the album. She presented it, often in person, to the British establishment: members of the royal family, Prime Ministers and their Cabinet colleagues, and numerous

Members of Parliament. Their signatures were added to the album, as were those of field marshals and generals who had ordered the previously nameless and faceless citizens of Chorley – and those of every other village, town and city in Britain - into the killing fields of Europe and elsewhere. The story was then exported. Miss Knight travelled thousands of miles over two decades to gain the signatures and acknowledgement of European royalty, Allied wartime leaders, US Presidents and elected representatives, numerous foreign dignitaries, experts, celebrities, and even – perhaps especially – of the Holy See in Rome.

Important stories need champions. Adam Cree has championed the work of Susannah Knight and thus continued her memorialisation and promotion of the men of Chorley. History is far more than simply a record of the great and the good, the heroic and the iconic. The deeds of 'ordinary' people – and especially those who did extraordinary things in extraordinary times - also deserve the attention of historians. Often dismissed as micro history, such detailed individual case studies as presented in *From the Humblest to the Greatest* add to our 'accepted' knowledge, enlarge our understanding, challenge generalisations and stereotypes, and, collectively, modify the grand narratives. Adam Cree has spent many hours in the archives, and the depth of his research is most impressive. He is clearly sympathetic towards the subject matter but deals with sensitive issues with calm authority and appropriate empathy. His almost forensic analysis of signatures in the *Memorial Album* – their ownership, timing and circumstances, sequencing and pagination – allows us to witness the often incredible juxtaposition of major historical events with local and individual stories. In writing *From the Humblest to the Greatest*, Adam Cree has reminded us of the myriad faces of war, and why the Great War of 1914 to 1919 is still worthy of our attention and remembrance.

Barry Blades

August 2016

Dr Barry Blades is author of *Roll of Honour: Schooling and the Great War, 1914-1919*, published by Pen & Sword Books in 2015.

PREFACE

S USANNAH Mary Crossley Knight was a woman of limited means and apparently unexceptional connections who ordinarily would have led an unremarkable life. She was an uncertified primary school teacher, a devoted sister and a devout Roman Catholic. In 1916 however, she began to pursue what became a single-handed quest for world peace which endured through the remaining decades of her life: to record the men of Chorley, Lancashire who had died in the Great War. On 5 April 1919 a notice appeared in the *Chorley Guardian* under the heading 'Chorley and District Memorial Album' (Plate 4):

> Miss Knight desires the relatives of all who have made the Supreme Sacrifice for their country to please send in their names to her at Shepherds' Hall, Chorley, on any Monday night, from 7-0 till 9-30, or leave them with Mrs Mills, 74, Market Street, or Miss Balshaw, Market Street.

> Printed forms may be had on application at either of the above shops, and can be filled up at home. All names will be grouped with regard to the Churches they attended and it is desired that no name, from the humblest to the greatest, may be omitted, so that our heroes may never be forgotten, and their names may be revered and honoured throughout the future generations.

> The names will be inscribed in a *Memorial Album* and a full page in the *Album* will be devoted to each man. If his photo is sent in it will be pasted on the page opposite his name. The *Album* will be specially made and when complete will be on view before being presented to the Town.[1]

Susannah was imbued with a determination to address Chorley's sense of loss and became the chronicler of the wartime sacrifice of a small Lancashire market town. She independently traversed two continents, submitting the *Album* to those responsible for forging the peace. She became Chorley's ambassador, bringing together presidents, prime ministers and politicians; generals and admirals; monarchs and princes; pontiffs and prelates. She sought representatives of the social, religious and political establishments of the inter-war years.

To further her cause she berated the wife of the president of the United States but even in her own lifetime, Susannah's extraordinary labours slipped from the notice of the town that she so loved. At the dusk of her life, a correspondent writing in *The Chorley Guardian* contemplated her achievements: 'Forgetfulness of past service is a common trait in human nature'.[2]

This book is an attempt to understand one woman's quest for peace in the decades following the outbreak of the Great War.

ACKNOWLEDGMENTS

MY late history teachers, David Ramm and Lynn Martindale, inspired me to study the subject in depth and breadth. My own pupils have contributed their own insights over recent years and I hope they will continue to value the past. My parents have nurtured my appreciation through the telling and re-telling of family narratives. Joe and Jane Roberts have encouraged me throughout. Without these influences I would not have had the resilience to pursue this story.

It was a great joy to meet Jan Walmsley, Susannah's great-niece. The family letters have helped us to understand so much more about 'Aunt Susie'.
I must thank Dr Barry Blades. He engaged with Susannah's story from the moment I shared it with him. His support encouraged me to persevere in writing the fuller account of her life.

So many archivists and librarians have helped me build up a picture of Susannah's life. These guardians of knowledge work with such quiet patience and passion. I owe them a debt of gratitude. Archivist Janice Tullock has followed Susannah's travels with me from the beginning. Laurence Pround'homme at Rennes Archives helped me understand Susannah's visit to the city. My French friends on social media, many of them archivists, illuminated the lives of the two French casualties listed in the *Album* in a spirit of openness that crossed language and national boundaries. I have appreciated support in the USA, including that of Jerry Cohen of the Texas Fire Department. The Texas Folklore Society shared Susannah's story at their 2015 Convention. I thank the staff at Chorley Library who have located the most obscure material for me. The staff at Astley Hall in Chorley have supported me with every step. Marianne Howell and Simon Brotherton have offered invaluable editorial advice when reading my drafts. It has been a relief to be able to discuss Susannah with friends that have followed the full arc of her story. Thank you to Ryan Eccleston for the cover design.

Finally I would like to thank my friends and family for keeping me sane and urging me on. I have particularly Good Friends at St Michael's CE Academy in Chorley where I teach and I am indebted to them in so many ways. They know who they are.

I hope that my daughter, Martha, will continue to love learning new things.

1 BEGINNINGS

CHORLEY is a small market town in the South of Lancashire, not quite in the foothills of the Pennines and not quite on the plain stretching out towards the Irish Sea. Tucked away in the smallest of rooms in Chorley's Astley Hall is the town's *Memorial Album*, compiled by a teacher called Susannah Knight and dedicated to the local men who fell in the Great War. Sometimes the volumes are referred to as the 'Golden Books', but few people have turned their pages to let their story shine.

The books are bulky and bound by maroon leather which has seen better days. Imagine for a moment that you are cradling one of the volumes in your arms – you'd be feeling not just the weight of the books themselves but the memories of a lost generation.

Behind reinforced glass, two of the volumes are open to view. At any one time the lives of four men are permanently laid bare for anyone who cares to look. This simple gesture is the result of a choice made by one of the curators. The decision to remember these particular men might be because of a personal attachment, a resonant name, the composition of a photograph, or a poignant story. There are 764 stories to tell in total and it would take over a year to show each pair of men for a day.

The third volume rests like the lion beneath the feet of an entombed crusader and contains the record of a year-long pilgrimage to the United States to commend those recovering after the Great Depression.

Susannah would live an eventful and insightful life in the years leading up to this extraordinary expedition, and it was her experiences of wartime Britain and the role she played in it that would not only give her the determination to compile the volumes but also to see out their completion. Her story begins in Ireland, with the marriage of her parents.

The parents of Susannah Mary Crossley Knight were married twice in Dublin on the same day, in the Roman Catholic Cathedral and in the Parish Church of the United Church of Ireland. Whichever of these was the second ceremony was not only irrelevant but also illegal. William Alfred Knight and Elizabeth Bryan simply took it upon themselves to unite in an unconventional way by having a Protestant wedding in the south of the city and a Catholic wedding in the north. This little ecumenical conspiracy that bridged the divide between Catholic and Protestant was witnessed on both occasions by John Geraghty and Mary McDonald.[1] Susannah was born 10 months later.[2] She followed her mother's Catholic faith resolutely.

Elizabeth Bryan was born in Westmeath in Ireland, the daughter of a farmer, James Bryan. Life was hard in rural Ireland and some of the extended family headed for the United States.[3] In her own life, Elizabeth revealed a strength of will to forge her life in different cities and harsh circumstances. Indeed, her mark on both of her marriage certificates was made as a cross, an indication her illiteracy. Yet letters were addressed to her in later years.

William Alfred Knight was born in Ardwick, Manchester, in 1841. He was the youngest son of John Knight and Susannah Bright.[4] He came from a large family, and his father was a master at a day school during the year of William's birth.[5] He was also a Sunday school teacher and clerk at St Thomas' church in Ardwick.[6]

William made a journey to Russia with his mother and father in his youth, though when this took place and for how long is uncertain.[7] The family had had earlier connections with Russia and his uncle, also called William, was said to have been crushed by a falling baulk of lumber in 1815 whilst working as a timber merchant.[8]

On their return from Russia, the family set up a business at 99 Oldham Street, Manchester.[9] They established a stay-making business manufacturing ties for corsets or for military uniforms.[10] It is worth noting that a major source for the whale bone required in the manufacture of stays came from Russia. For his part, William began his working life as an agent for the family business.[11] His parents remained at Oldham Street for the remainder of their lives.[12]

The cotton famine years of the American Civil War caused great hardship in Lancashire in the 1860s and by 1861, the family business had encompassed drapery as well as stay manufacture. William was still living at Oldham Street at this time.[13] The Knight family were practical opportunists and, later in the decade, William crossed to Ireland as a commercial traveller. It was here that he met Elizabeth Bryan. The focus of the family business had subtly changed and William described his father's trade as both a cotton spinner and cotton manufacturer on his marriage certificates in 1867.[14]

Elizabeth and William were in Scotland by the time their first child arrived. Susannah came into the world at 1pm on 24 February, 1868 in Greenock, Scotland. Her parents were lodging in an imposing yet cramped tenement at 27 Holmecroft Street in Greenock. William was employed as spirit dealer's assistant, something which seemed at odds with his earlier employment, indicating that he had taken a step down the ladder of life. William was a newly-married man in a different job, a different city and different country, and now with a daughter to support.[15]

Despite their hardships William and Elizabeth had a second child. John was born on 20 July 1869, and became known as 'Jack' to the rest of the family as he grew older. It was a family that did not like to stay in one place for too long, however, and by the time Jack was born, the family had moved to 5 Wallace Street, Glasgow. Jack's father William was at the helm of the young family and both children had been given the names of his own parents. In terms of occupation, there had been yet another change – though perhaps for the better – as William had begun working in the more familiar role of stay manufacturer's cutter.[16]

The family moved again and settled near Liverpool. Elizabeth, Susannah and Jack made the then-Lancashire town of Bootle their home.[17] Tragically, William died soon after they arrived in England. We do not know when or how. His details have slipped out of historical sight. By the often unforgiving standards of the era, it was not unusual for a marriage to be cut so short by death and Elizabeth was not even 30 when she lost her husband, with Susannah and Jack barely 10 and nine years old respectively. Life was challenging, but Susannah inherited her resilience, a passion for travel and an unconventional spirit from her parents.

In 1881, the family was living at 16 Olivia Street. It was a comfortable terraced home, two up and two down, typical of both the period and the region. Elizabeth worked as a seamstress. The census shows that both the children were in school.[18]

At this stage in her life, Susannah was extremely fortunate. She was almost certainly educated by the Sisters of the Sacred Heart of Mary at their Marsh Lane School in Bootle; a product of chance which granted her a life-long linguistic skill. Three of the staff, in particular, were in a position to teach her French. This framed her outlook on the world. Sister Frances Granie had been born in Béziers and in 1881 she was head of the convent which had become associated with St James' Church, Bootle from 1872, providing a school for the poor children of the town.[19] Two lay sisters. Maria Gracieuse Candroza and Marie Sales were also from Béziers, as was Trino Scio, an 'orphan girl'.[20] Opportunities for educating the poor had been opened up by the Education Act of 1870 and at the very same time, the school at which Susannah spent most of her career, Chorley's Weld Bank School (Plate 3), was also opening its doors.

Susannah's time at the convent had a far-reaching impact on her future. She learned French and set down the foundations for learning a wider range of languages in later life. The Sisters placed a great emphasis on the vocation of teaching and the care of orphaned children. Susannah drew on this early grounding when war broke out in 1914.

The connection with Béziers led her to correspond with a family named Moreau in her later life. She received letters from the family whilst their son, Leon, fought at Verdun in early 1916 (Plate 10)[21]. It is a story which will be returned to below. Susannah visited Béziers in July of 1921 so that the Mayor and other local dignitaries could autograph the *Album* (Plate 11).

The French language was a passion for Susannah and it became a gift that she shared widely. She was able to speak and read it fluently. She learned Russian, Spanish and German during the course of her life as well as having a reasonable understanding of Italian and Latin.[22]

In all probability, Susannah followed the Sisters to Seafield House in Seaforth, Merseyside, when the community moved to larger premises in 1884. She almost certainly began her career there as a pupil teacher. She consolidated her linguistic skills here and there is evidence that she continued to pursue study for its own sake later in her career. In 1905 Susannah anticipated the results of an examination.[23] It is likely that Jack studied at the naval school of HMS Conway in Liverpool with a mariner's life in mind – the typical route for young men in Liverpool and its environs to take.[24]

The 1881 census identifies another point of change in Susannah's life. There were two additional residents recorded at 16 Olivia Street; Angus McInnes, a 25-year old joiner born in Glasgow and James Moran, as 16-

year-old dock labourer from Ireland. Both were lodgers. It is significant that McInnes topped the list of residents and initially 'Head' was placed alongside his name, to be corrected as 'boarder', with Elizabeth taking the role.[25] Angus McInnes was already a dominant figure in the household and indeed, he became Elizabeth Bryan's second husband in the summer of that year.[26] Elizabeth and Angus raised four more children, with Elizabeth (known as Lizzie or Lily), Ada, Mary and Angus being born between 1882 and 1889.

Susannah maintained her Catholic faith in the pattern of her mother, though Jack followed his father's faith as a Protestant. The family had rapidly become much larger. By 1891, they were living in a more spacious terrace house fronted by bay windows on the upper and lower floors of 16 Beatrice Street, not far from their previous address.[27] Susannah and John had left home by 1888. Susannah was making her own way in life as an uncertified teacher. John had cast himself out onto the oceans of the world as a merchant seaman.

2 TEACHER AND TRAVELLER 1888 - 1914

A T the age of 19, Susannah completed her training as a pupil teacher and took a post as an assistant teacher at St Mary's Catholic Primary School in Euxton near Chorley, around 1888.[1] In 1891 the census shows her lodging at 27 Chorley Road with the head teacher, Elizabeth Hargreaves and another assistant, Harriet O'Neil.[2] She was living just around the corner from the school.

Susannah maintained her links with Bootle. Her mother and step-siblings had moved to Beatrice Street in the town by 1891 but they were still a single train ride away.[3] Susannah was a young woman keen on novelty and in the same year that the 1891 census found her in Euxton. She and an uncle had the opportunity to see Buffalo Bill Cody perform in Liverpool.[4] Buffalo Bill's Wild West Show had caused a great deal of excitement when it made a brief excursion to Liverpool on 7 December 1887. The artistes took a day trip from their main showground at Salford racecourse to perform a matinee of *Shadows of a Great City* at Liverpool's Court Theatre. A crowd of 30,000 had met Buffalo Bill at Lime Street Station that year but the event that Susannah witnessed was on a far bigger scale. Buffalo Bill came to Newsham Park in July 1891, not far from where Susannah's mother and younger siblings were living. It was a spectacle that made a lasting impression on Susannah and inspired her in her later travels.

An advertisement in the *Liverpool Mercury* vividly set the scene:

> [See] the wonders of the plains, the peculiarities of the buck-jumpers, the skill of the men with the lasso and rifle, the marvellous horsemanship of the children — both Red and White — of the Wild West, and last, but not least, some of the 'medicine'

and 'ghost' dances which are peculiar to the red men of the States, will be set forth in the company of 240 people (including 70 Indians), 150 horses, 18 buffaloes, and other properties in all the reality of actual life. [5]

The adventures of Buffalo Bill, with re-enacted scenes from the Indian Wars, proved tantalising to the English audience. Annie Oakley and Johnny Baker showed off their phenomenal marksmanship and there was the famous 'Capture of the Deadwood mail coach by the Indians' and the ever-popular 'Cowboy Fun'.[6]

Susannah looked back on the event much later in life with clarity: 'I always treasured the memory of the visit and the Buffalo and the wonderful horses'.[7] Perhaps she had a lasting memory of a South American horse called Untamed, said to have killed four men, which captured the attention of the Liverpool audience. Susannah held a fascination for the Wild West in her later years and recaptured her youthful fantasies through her later travels in the United States.[8] As well as seeking out a cowboy hero Tex Cooper, she met the singing cowboy Gene Autry, many Texas Rangers, one of the officers who gunned down Bonnie and Clyde, and possibly even listened to tales from a veteran of Little Big Horn.[9] One of the riders in the show in 1891 went by the name of 'Texas', the US state where Susannah spent much of 1935-6.[10]

The spirit of adventure was an essential part of her character and at the age of 27, an arresting redirection in her life took place which took her away from Euxton. The *Chorley Standard* of 8 June 1895 reported 'A Presentation to an Euxton School Mistress':

> A very pleasing incident took place on Sunday last at St Mary's Catholic School, Euxton. Miss Knight, who has been assistant mistress at the school for the past seven years, has recently resigned and taken the position of governess to the children of a French Count and the children and parents deemed it a fitting occasion to present her with a substantial token of their regard and esteem. This took the form of a handsome silver watch, inscribed, 'Presented by the Children of St Mary's, Euxton, to Miss Knight on her leaving the school'. The recipient gratefully acknowledged the present. The departure of Miss Knight has occasioned deep regret among both parents and scholars, whose good wishes she carries with her.[11]

Susannah's employment in France had a significant bearing upon the eventual creation of the *Album*. The child she tutoured was a six-year old boy called Paul de Méhérenc de St Pierre, who had been born in Versailles in 1891.[12] Susannah headed to Paris to take up the position in the summer of 1895,[13] a move which was to be the beginning of a long-lasting bond with France.

Meanwhile her brother Jack pursued his career in the merchant navy with Nourse Shipping, a company which plied its trade between Calcutta, New York and Dundee with textiles. His visits to Calcutta and onwards to the Fijian Islands in 1896 and 1897 included the occasion when he saved the lives of two young Australians from a shark-infested sea for which he was presented with a gold medal from the Mayor of Sydney.[14]

Susannah's employment in France poses several questions. After all, she had left a secure position at St Mary's School in Euxton where she was clearly highly regarded. The de Méhérenc family retained an enduring relationship with Susannah for more than two decades after she left their service. It is unclear how long Susannah spent in France and though it could have been as long as five years, it may well have been less than a year. Correspondence from Jack suggests she was in Britain rather than France by September 1896 but she only moved to Chorley in around 1900.[15]

Jack's letters in this period are packed with tales of travel and adventure. They are also full of affection. Only Jack's half of the correspondence remains but it is clear from what is written that Susannah yearned for his return to the home port of Liverpool. There are anxious enquiries throughout the letters that reinforce the ties between ship and shore. Jack was generous towards his sister and sent her such exotic gifts as a cashmere dress, bananas and a rhinoceros beetle in a small box. In all his letters, Jack enquired closely about the welfare of other family members, neighbours and friends that asked well of him.[16] Susannah wanted adventures too. Jack's cherished gift of the Rhinoceros Beetle has survived to this day in its little box.

Susannah and Jack shared a concern that their step-sister Lizzie, aged 13, should have the same rigorous convent schooling as Susannah. It is not known where Lizzie was educated though one of the few mementoes which Susannah retained at the close of her life was a brochure for Notre Dame School in Southport outlining its termly fees.[17] Lizzie's education was a significant cost to the family. Jack responded to a letter from Susannah whilst he was in port at Calcutta in 1896. There was the excitement of promotion to Second Mate and a forthcoming voyage around the Fijian islands but Jack also discussed Lizzie's education arrangements with his sister:

I heartily agree with all that you are doing for Lizzie. I certainly shall do a share in what you ask. I am not in a position to forward any money on at present but six months from now. That is when I expect to return from here. I shall forward the amount to you in a lump sum.[18]

Despite Jack's promotion, all was not well with the Nourse line and he had become increasingly impatient with his employers. By September 1897 the *SS Rhine* was in such a poor state of repair that Jack and his crewmates spent most of their time anchored at Calcutta making repairs and fitting new rigging. James Nourse had died in April of that year and the executors, Hampton and Bromehead, took over the running of the company.[19] Jack's letter to his mother makes it clear that the employees, even far away in Calcutta, were aware that Hampton and Bromehead had no intention of attending to their commercial responsibilities with due care. He complained to his wife, Mary Louisa, that: 'Mr Nourse's will has been a curious affair not one of his employees has got a red cent. The people who filled his coffers have been entirely forgotten'.[20]

Indeed, Hampton cut the wages of the crews whilst they were still abroad, which was bitterly received, to say the least. Jack seems to have spoken as something of a ringleader saying that 'one and all' were not going to stand for this. He was in a determined mood when he wrote to his mother: 'In fact the employ now is going to the dogs all together. I see that his ships have been put up for sale to the sooner (people). The officers in the ships get into steam or some other firm' [*sic*]. The company was being run down and many of the ships were scrapped in 1907. The old Knight family instinct to move on was kicking in and Jack had decided on his future path in this letter with a warning of a promise: 'So don't be a bit surprised if you hear of me going into steam as soon as I pass for master which I hope will be next April if I get home then'.[21]

By 1899 Jack had managed to escape from the failing Nourse line and was employed by the Booth Steam Shipping Company. Steam power was the future and Jack was on *Huascar* in Madeira in March 1899.[22] This was Liverpool's oldest merchant company – Jack had chosen his new firm well.

He gained his Competency Certificate for being the Master of a steam ship in July 1899 but he needed to be patient and it was to be 15 years before he would command a vessel himself. Jack stayed with the Booth Stream Shipping Company for the rest of his career and the firm remained loyal to him to the very end of his life. His voyages on *Huascar* in 1899-1901 and 1905-1906 left a strong impression for the remainder of his life.[23]

Jack's letters give glimpses of the wider events which took place parallel to the lives he and Susannah led. In October 1899, war had broken out with the Boer settlers in the South of Africa. In March 1900, Jack was on *Huascar* and told Susannah a tale of a surprising encounter on the high seas. The story is of a chance sighting of a ship carrying troops to the Boer War on his outward voyage. On his return trip, he saw the ship again within three miles of where it was spotted on its outward voyage:

> Well what is the news in England now? I suppose that by this time they will have fought and won a few more battles. Let us hope it will soon be over. Yesterday we passed very close to the transport No.50 *S.S. British Princess*. And a very strange coincidence on our way home last voyage we passed just as close to the same vessel only she was now going out with troops to the cape And now she was returning empty. And within 3 miles of the same place according to our position … [We] looked forward to a cheer like what we got from her before from the troops who crowded her decks but as I said before she was empty. [*sic*][24]

This reveals a shared weariness of war. There is a sense of waste from a mariner's view – a profitable ship should always have its hold full, and an empty vessel is a lifeless soul. Jack's experience of war became far more direct when the Great War broke out in 1914 and Susannah, restricted to the Home Front, fought with equal determination in her own way for her community when the call was made.

The social impact of the Boer War had a resonance for Jack's new employers, Alfred and Charles Booth, the sons of the company's founder. It was at this very time that the younger son Charles was making a name for himself in a far more enduring way. Between 1891 and 1903 he used his position of wealth to investigate social deprivation in the East End of London and characterised poverty as a repeating cycle from which the poor could not escape, rather than a choice for the feckless and lazy. Low wages, poor health and incapacity in old age perpetuated the lot of the poor. It was for this study that Charles Booth would be remembered and his report, together with Seebohn Rowntree's study of poverty in York published in 1901 led the Liberal Government to embark on an ambitious social reform programme when it was elected to power 1906. The Boer War had put the issue of poverty sharply into focus because of the weak quality of the volunteers recruited to fight in South Africa, with many men rejected as unfit to serve.

Britain was in the midst of a crisis of confidence as the nation questioned its ability to sustain influence over its empire. The workforce was hungry and the army was unable to swell its ranks with the finest troops. Charles Booth shared some responsibility for the provision of school meals and the free medical inspections that were received by Susannah's pupils. The children who benefitted from these reforms grew up in better health, with greater opportunities for regular employment and the hope for a pension when they reached the age of 70. They were fitter to fight a war which was already looming closer to home in Europe.

Jack's letters described daily life on board his vessels as they coursed the Atlantic, the Pacific and the waterways of South America. He wrote of how he tackled the anxieties of the weather, disease and his relationship with his superiors. The letters reveal the range of Jack's experiences and perhaps the interests his sister shared. The matter of disease was addressed on more than one occasion and on 5 February, probably in 1901, from *Huascar* in the lower reaches of the Amazon, Jack recounted that:

> [In] Para the Medical Faculty are in great glee over the discovery by and English doctor of the Yellow Fever microbe. There were two English Doctors out here investigating this Yellow and one of them died a martyr to science. The other took the yellow fever and recovered. And I believe he sails for England with the fruits of his search. [*sic*][25]

Despite his enthusiasm for medical breakthroughs in Para, he was less keen on the measures to limit infection. There was frustration as he complained of having to delay his voyage at Ilha Grande off the Brazilian coast at a quarantine station. He also expressed a strong dissatisfaction with the captain of the *SS Basil*.[26] Relationships between crews were strained on occasions and a typical experience might be reflected in a wonderful anecdote that Jack recounted in 1901:

> Up to the present we have had a very bad fare. The individual we have here as a <u>cook</u> this voyage is a grand hand at spoiling food, we have hardly had a properly cooked meal for nigh on a month, and the more that we complain the worse he is. It is an old but true saying that <u>God</u> finds the food + Satan finds the cooks. Such is life'. [*sic*][27]

Jack's voyages with the Booth Steam Shipping Company were not short of excitement. Jack's Continuous Discharge Book begins aboard *Huascar* on 1 June 1901. He was Second Mate for the first time and it was *Huascar* that held his respect for the rest of his career. He was bound for Iquitos. It lay so far up the Amazon and its tributaries that it is actually over the border of Brazil and within Peru, nearly 2,000 miles upstream. On this voyage, at

Manoâs on 15 July 1901, he wrote: 'Up to the present, we have had an exceedingly warm voyage on the Amazon, here it is scorching through the day. Such a thing as sleep is out of the question altogether by day'. [*sic*][28]

He was the Second Mate whilst on *SS Obidense, SS Hildebrand, SS Horatio,* and *SS Jerome,* during a period in which his destinations were the USA, the Brazils, Manoâs and Para.[29]

In July 1901, Jack sighted the King and Queen of Portugal twice – In Lisbon and then in Madeira – and expressed surprise at the lack of deference and excitement shown by their own subjects:

> In Lisbon the day we left, the King and Queen of Portugal embarked on a man of war which was anchored very close to us as they passed we had a grand view of their Royal Persons. The Queen of Portugal without a question is one of the finest Ladies that I have ever seen. She is far superior to her Husband. He is just like your brother short and fat. And again upon our arrival in Madeira we had a very good view, again we were anchored right close to the Palace where they were staying. And were able to see them through our glasses on the veranda taking an airing also when they left for Manoâs on the Sunday morning the most unenthusiastic crowd that I have ever seen. There was hardly a cheer raised when they entered the carriage to go to Church which was only about 100 yards away from the Royal Quarters. And again after the service, plenty of onlookers but no attempt at any act of word to show their royalty. [*sic*][30]

By 1901, the core family had moved again and were living at 106 Benedict Street.[31] Elizabeth, Angus and the three younger children were living in the road that nestled between their old addresses of Olivia Street and Beatrice Street. Letters reveal a close bond between John, Lizzie and Susannah, who is referred to as 'Susie' or 'Dearest Sister'. In September of that year, Jack apologised for the slowness of the *SS Huascar,* much to the disappointment of the women of the family who anticipated his homecoming.[32]

Susannah took up her post at Weld Bank School in 1899 or 1900. The 1901 Census shows she was living at 6 Norris Street in the Roman Catholic Parish of St Mary's, Chorley.[33] It was a very short street comprising of eight older terraced houses squeezing off Pall Mall. She was living in the town by March 1900 when Jack wrote from Madeira: 'I live in hope of going to Chorley when I return' which suggests he had not yet had a chance to see Susannah at this address.[34] She was still an uncertified assistant teacher. She taught Class 1 throughout her remainder of her career.[35] The school later became more commonly known as St Gregory's School.

There had been a school associated with the Roman Catholic Church of St Gregory's since 1815 but it had been closed in 1843 and it was not until 1869 that it received pupils again. The creation of the School Boards following the Education Act of 1870 prompted a renewed effort to provide a school for pupils of all denominations in the south of the town, supported by the rate payers of Chorley. This area of Chorley was expanding at the turn of the century and provision of schooling was a pressing necessity for the new families moving into the area.[36]

A strong Irish contingent lived in the south and south west of Chorley and particularly in the area of Standish Street, Leigh Row and Leigh Street. Indeed, Standish Street came to be known as 'Little Ireland' but many Catholic migrant workers also set up home in the Pilling Lane and Weld Bank areas close to St Gregory's Church. Religion was an important feature of the community in this part of the town and the Public House situated between the school and the church is still called The Mitre. The nearest Public Houses to Susannah's own home also tell a story, neatly illustrating how Chorley was changing. The Plough stood at the end of the street where she lived between 1900 and at least 1911, whilst the Black Horse was a little further down the road. Both recall the rural landscape which had been eroded in the previous five decades. The Moor Inn, a little further out of the town, fell well within the boundaries of the growing urban landscape by 1900. The adjacent public house, The Colliers, underlined the industrialisation of the area and offers an explanation for Weld Bank School's expanding roll, coal pits having been developed in Chorley and Coppull since the early 19th century. Chorley Moor, Ranglet's, Burgh and Birkacre pits employed many of the working men in the south and south west of the town, though some of the pits were drawing their last coal by 1900.[37] Textile mills sprang up enticing a fresh surge of migrant labour. Mayfield Mill, Avenue Mills, Moor Mill, Weldbank Mill, Chorley Bleaching Works and Birkacre Bleach Works were all bringing more workers to the area with the necessary ranks of terraced housing needed to accommodate them. The men who worked at these mills and collieries went on to form the ranks of Kitchener's army in 1914.

Jack's relationship with his family was as strong as his sister's but had to stretch between continents and in March of 1900 he wrote in sadness of the family that missed him so much and that the moments of company snatched on leave were always bitter-sweet.[38] There are indications that Susannah was still settling into her home in April of 1901, as Jack asked if her crockery made it safely to Chorley.[39]

While Susannah was establishing herself in Chorley, Jack was forming stronger roots in Bootle. He married Mary Louisa Johnson on 28 May 1902.[40] Mary Louisa was the daughter of Henry, a carrier, and his wife Jane. Born in 1881, she was 11 years younger than Jack and made quite an impression on both him and the family.[41] Known as 'the Duchess' in later life, she was described as 'dignified' by family members and indeed, photographs of her from the 1920s and 1930s certainly seem to correspond to this image.[42] Jack had a series of addresses up to 1902 and when he married, he was at 20 Park Street, though by 1909 Jack and Mary Louisa had made a more permanent home at 28 Litherland Road. This remained their home until they moved to 79 Merton Road later in the 1920s.[43]

As well as marriage, there was promotion. On 30 October 1905, Jack returned to Iquitos in the Amazon Basin on *Huascar,* acting as Chief Mate. He served on *Huascar* again from 10 April 1906, on route to Para. He plied the same routes on *SS Bolivar, SS Domino, SS Augustine, SS Boniface* and *SS Aidan* up to 1914. *Huascar* figured so strongly in his memory that he would name his house in Merton Road, Bootle, after this most favoured vessel which remained the best ship of his career.[44]

Susannah's step-sister, Lizzie, was establishing a firm direction in her life as well. She had been enclosed in a convent environment for much of her childhood, and on 24 May 1904, she took her vows as Sister Mary Clement in the Society of the Holy Child Jesus at Mayfield in Sussex.[45] Jack and Susannah had helped see Lizzie through her education but Jack was on *Horatio* somewhere in the 'Brazils and USA' until July and had to be content to see her when he disembarked.[46]

In May 1905 Susannah travelled to Ireland. She sent her mother and Jack a shamrock as a gift.

> I can imagine how delighted Jack would have been to receive the shamrock and tobacco, it would cheer him up a bit, he must often feel very neglected being so far away from his friends and relations.[47]

It was a deliberate token for Elizabeth to recall her native shores, for she died in August of that year at the age of 57.[48] Angus McInnes, Susannah's stepfather, died in April of 1908 and was interred with his wife.[49]

Susannah's school in Chorley underwent a great deal of change from 1911 to 1914 and it is during this period that she moved from Norris Street. She was living at 57 Bolton Street above a fried fish dealer by 1914, though she had left this address by 1918.[50] The original structure of the Weld Bank

School was considered insufficient for its needs and it was threatened with closure in 1911, being served with a 'notice of defect' in the same year. The school was required to cater for the growing population working in the collieries and mills in the south of Chorley. Construction of a new two-storey building thus commenced in 1911 and the foundation stone for the expanded school was laid on 19 June 1913.[51] By this time Susannah's first class of 1899-1900 was employed by the likes of Birkacre Print Work, Birkacre Colliery and Ellerbeck Colliery.

In the midst of construction came a little excitement for Susannah's pupils. George V and his consort Queen Mary made a point of visiting the industrial north west of England in 1913 and visited Chorley on Thursday, 10 July of that year.[52] All the children in Chorley were given a day off school to see the reception, which was held at the newly created Coronation Recreation Ground on Devonshire Road.[53] The royal visit certainly made an exciting end to the summer term and the school broke up for the six-week holiday the day after the reception. Susannah was about to depart on her most distant adventure to date.

Susannah embarked for the United States on *RMS Mauretania*.[54] She was already an experienced European traveller but this was a particularly brave adventure. It was less than a year since *RMS Titanic* had been sunk on its maiden voyage. Susannah was fortunate to catch a second sight of the King and Queen at the start of her journey. George V and Queen Mary chanced to be in Liverpool on 14 July, still on their tour of the industrial north, to take part in the opening of the Gladstone Dock. They made a tour of *Mauretania* with Captain Turner and several Cunard officials.[55] With the speed of the telegraph, Susannah could read details of the visit later in the *New York Times*, which reported the arrival of *Mauretania* and recounted the royal excursion in Liverpool with some excitement:

> 'Their majesties inspected every part of the great ship, and were enthusiastic in their approval of her splendid interior [and] fitted with wonderful turbine engines'.[56]

This was certainly an exciting moment for Susannah, seeing the royal couple twice within a week, and on her first voyage across the Atlantic!

Susannah arrived in New York on 19 July, having crossed the Atlantic in four days, 21 hours and 45 minutes. Autographed etchings of the King and Queen were of great interest to the press and had been put on view when the ship arrived in New York. Susannah stayed with her cousins, identified as Miss Bryan on the passenger list and a 'Mary' with an indistinct surname. Annie Bryan, a member of his mother's family, was the initial contact.[57]

Susannah's full itinerary is unknown but her return journey had a significant connection with destiny. She was conveyed from New York by *Mauretania's* running mate *RMS Lusitania* in third class accommodation and arrived in Liverpool on 9 September 1913.[58] She may or may not have met Captain Daniel Dow, the commanding officer of this liner on this voyage. He later commanded *Mauretania* when it had its narrow scrape in 1915. That liner narrowly survived an encounter with a German U-boat, thanks partly to the vessel's superior speed. Susannah made a point of searching out the Captain in the 1920s so that his signature could be placed in the *Album*. *Lusitania* will feature further in Susannah's life.

During this time, building work on the new school had progressed and by 1914 it had been constructed to the 'newest and up-to-date principles'. A 10-foot wide corridor separated each of the two floors with the area below being for the Infant Department, where Susannah would teach, and the Mixed Department being upstairs. The building was designed to allow light to flood into all the classrooms from the outlook of Weldbank Lane and it still retains these bright and spacious qualities today. The rooms are high and the connecting corridor gives a reassuring sense of space when one enters. The new structure comprised a cloak room, teachers' room, store room and cleaner's room. It allowed for the intake of an extra 100 children.[59]

The school opened for 385 children on May 18, 1914. George Teebay, the priest of St Gregory's and the school's Reverend Manager, recorded in the school's *Log Book* that 100 people attended the opening. On 14 July 1914 the 'Form 14' confirmed that the school could have 235 pupils in the Mixed Department and 150 in the Infant department.[60]

There were three teachers in the Infant department. Miss Eccles had been Head Mistress of the Infant department since the early 1880s.[61] She was supported by two uncertified teachers, Elizabeth McClelland and Susannah Knight.[62] Despite her talent for languages, Susannah taught Class 1 for most of her career, caring for the very youngest children as they began their education at five years old.[63] The pupils were much engaged by Susannah's frequent 'Nature Observations' along Burgh Lane, as well as opportunities to walk through corn fields. Susannah also took her pupils to see the coal workers at the nearby mines.[64] She frequently took them out into the world beyond the classroom.[65]

3 PUPILS AND PALS 1914 - 15

SUSANNAH Knight was travelling through France on her return from a holiday in Switzerland when the Great War broke out in August 1914.[1] The *Weld Bank School Log Book* entry for the week beginning 10 August recorded that: 'Miss Knight Assistant Teacher [is] unable to return to school, detained in France on account of the war'.[2] She travelled close to Béziers and it is probable that she already had a connection with the Moreau family, with whom she later had a correspondence. She may even have visited the city. The German assault was not unexpected but still came as a shock[3]. The French army rapidly moved into position, initially expecting the main German force to punch through Alsace and Lorraine. There was passion, patriotism and fear in France just as there was in Britain. It was a matter of ill-fortune that placed Susannah in the path of Germany's Schlieffen Plan in August 1914.

Susannah was very much aware of the withdrawal of French forces towards Paris and the movements preceding the Battle of the Marne. Other residents of Chorley were also caught on the continent. Mr F.W. Henderson of Trinity Road was a teacher at Chorley Secondary School. He had been holidaying with his wife in Switzerland and was among 10,000 British subjects who were stranded when hostilities commenced. He gave an account of his experience of the French mobilisation in the *Chorley Guardian*. Mr Henderson and his wife were delayed until 21 August and then made a 73-hour journey from Finhaut to Folkestone by way of Geneva, Lyons, Montaries, Paris and Dieppe.[4] They saw the movement of fresh and wounded troops at railways stations as they travelled through France and it is entirely likely that Susannah made her way home by the same route. The *Chorley and District Weekly News* described how crowds of French passengers at Lyons had shared in the singing of the 'Marseillaise' and the British National Anthem with the English tourists.[5] W.J. Sandiford and two female members of his family were caught in similar circumstances, being in Belgium when war broke out. He described the overloading of their boat to Harwich by Belgian refugees to the *Chorley Guardian*.[6] He became the printer of the *Album* at the end of the war and his daughter, Ethel, helped Susannah in its compilation.[7]

Three young men from the Grammar School – Openshaw, Halton and Fowler – had taken up placements in France through the Modern Language Association. Fred Openshaw was working for a German firm that had premises in the Montmartre quarter of Paris. This report vividly recounts his observations of a city entering a war:

> One German grocer attempted to sell his eggs at one franc (10d.) each, but the shop was pillaged and the proprietor pelted with eggs. Everything about the place was wrecked ... Some carried off cheeses on their shoulders, and boxes of eggs were borne away heedless of the dripping mess running through the packages onto the carriers. Occurrences of this kind were frequently occurring ...[8]

Fred Openshaw was inspired to volunteer for the King's (Liverpool) Regiment in May 1915 and he died of wounds in France on 8 October 1918.[9] Susannah collated his details and included his photograph in the *Album*.

Susannah returned to her post during the week beginning 24 August.[10] These reports and her own experiences framed her own response to the outbreak of war.

Men in Chorley were volunteering even before war was declared on 4 August 1914. The first cohort of boys Susannah had taught at Weld Bank School were of military age when war broke. Inevitably some of her former pupils were included in the *Album*. James Dickinson, Michael Duffy, William Enderby, William Harrison, Edmund Hart, Joseph Nelson, John William Rogerson, Sidney Thexton, William Edward Tootell were all members of the St Gregory's congregation and passed through Susannah's classes. These men were recorded in Susannah's *Album* as well as on the Church's Roll of Honour.[11] Some of the girls who had been her pupils became young widows.

The Loyal North Lancashire Regiment was based at Fulwood Barracks in Preston, and formed a battalion from its Territorial Force. A significant number of men who attested in the first weeks of war were already in the Terriers, prepared for home service whilst pursuing civilian professions.

They volunteered to serve abroad and those who enlisted at Preston on the first Saturday of the war slept on the floor of its town hall awaiting further instructions. Chorley men tended to be in 'D' Company of the 1st/4th Battalion. By December almost 1,000 men had enlisted.[12]

The deaths of at least 24 of the men who joined on that very first day of the conflict were eventually recorded by Susannah in the *Album*. On the second day of the war, the flood of men had continued and of those that signed their commitment to King and Country that day, 10 more Chorley men would not see out the war to the end of 1918.[13] For each man who signed and did not return home, there were many more that returned physically maimed or mentally scarred.

The earliest death recorded in Susannah's *Album* was that of the Lieutenant Paul de Méhérenc de St Pierre of the French 33rd Artillery Regiment who died on 11 September at Ecury sur Coole on the Marne.[14] Once a boy, now a man, he had been the child Susannah tutored when she left Euxton for France in 1895. By 1914, the family had moved from Versailles to Lanvallon in Brittany. Paul de Méhérenc de St Pierre joined the French army at the age of 18 in 1909 and was involved in the desperate repulse of the German army as it closed on Paris.[15] He was posthumously awarded the Légion d'honneur. Susannah had retained a strong connection with the family, for she was later able to include a recent photograph of him in his military uniform alongside his entry in the *Album*.

John Thomas Burke, a sergeant of the Second King's Royal Rifle Regiment and connected to St Mary's Church in Leyland, was the earliest British casualty to be recorded by Susannah. He, too, was a professional soldier and had been recalled to duty on 4 August, 1914. He was killed 45 days later on 14 September 1914 after having been engaged in the Battle of Aisne.[16] Though neither de Méhérenc nor Burke were from Chorley itself, their inclusion underlines how the *Album* was a means for those who felt grief to give their loved ones a place to be remembered. It is not just a geographical accounting of casualties.

William McGowan of the Second Royal Irish Regiment was killed in the same action as Burke, two days later. He was also a reservist and had originally joined the army in 1902, subsequently serving in Ireland, South Africa, India and finally France. He had helped the French resist the German advance at the Battles of Mons, Marne and Aisne.[17] Burke and McGowan were typical examples of experienced men in Britain's small professional army of 1914. They were the 'Old Contemptibles' of the British Expeditionary Force who had already served as regular soldiers. They were recalled to provide 'backbone' to the repulse anticipated by the

British Expeditionary Force. Countless towns like Chorley lost many such men in the first months of the war and Britain's fighting potential was sorely weakened.

The death toll slowly gathered pace. Christopher Brooks of the 2nd Lancashire Fusiliers was killed at Aisne on 25 September.[18] On 22 September, Leading Seaman Thomas Feeny died in the North Sea on board *HMS Hogue*. He, like the 'Old Contemptibles', was a professional serviceman who had been in the Royal Navy for over 12 years and had only been assigned to the *Hogue* three days previously.[19] His ship was trying to rescue survivors from *HMS Aboukir* when it was torpedoed and sunk by the German submarine *U-9*.[20] Chorley had had a brief taste of the bitterness of war on land and at sea. Susannah was aware of the risks her own brother faced aboard the *SS Boniface* off the coast of South America. Jack Knight noted in a letter that a German warship had been patrolling whilst he was in port at Naval Rio Grande De Norte.[21]

Susannah's sense of duty compelled her to offer her skills as a linguist. She organised evening classes in French for the Terriers at the Chorley Depot from 19 September in order to prepare them before they went to support the British Expeditionary Force.[22] This is one of the few acts of devotion that Susannah is remembered for today and she is often more strongly connected with the later lessons she gave to members of the East Lancashire Regiment.

In October Susannah formed a close attachment with 'C' Company of the 7th (Accrington) Service Battalion of the East Lancashire Regiment, which became 'Y' Company of the 11th Battalion in December 1914. James Milton had begun to raise this Chorley Company from 3 September and was appointed Captain on 11 September, then promoted to major in January of the following year.[23] His promotion reflected the rapid growth of what became the 'Chorley Pals' and by October, around the same time that Susannah began to teach the company French, he had recruited 212 men, just short of the required 250.[24] Men from Blackburn built up the company to full strength and young men were under a great deal of pressure to join. The 11th Battalion, known collectively as the 'Accrington Pals' drew its men from Accrington, Blackburn, Burnley and Chorley.[25] The *Chorley Guardian* published weekly reports of recruits and used numerous opportunities to report on the East Lancashire Regiment and The Loyal North Lancashire Regiment to maintain the momentum. A typical exhortation came from Chorley's then MP Sir Henry Hibbert, who quoted a lady who had stated in the *Evening Standard* that: 'The young unmarried man who has no physical weakness, no serious domestic or other ties and who will not now serve his country in the hour of need, proclaims himself to be an abject coward, and deserves the contempt of every right-minded person'.[26] It was a difficult to refuse the call.

The town was encouraged to contribute in any way it could, either by responding to the call to arms, or securing the home front in the workplace. This came to be known as 'total war', where everyone worked towards victory and Susannah's pupils were as much a concern to the council as the men enlisting. Many main wage-earners headed off to the Western Front and the town needed to make sure that these men need not worry about their loved ones. The town councillors took a week to unanimously agree '... to provide meals for necessitous school children' on 27 August 1914.[27] It must be noted that the permissive legislation for this had been available since 1906 following the Education (Provision of Meals) Act and it is a matter of shame that the poorest of children of Chorley only gained this assistance as a consequence of war.

Weld Bank School was already playing its part in the war effort and when Chorley's Secretary of Education, Mr Roby, visited in the week beginning 25 September, the school was ensuring that meals were provided for children.[28] The *Chorley Guardian* reported that teachers were arriving early to make sure that their pupils could have breakfast at 8am and estimated that 12 per cent of children were being provided for. Everyone did their bit. Father George Teebay of St Gregory's Church sent a basket of apples to distribute to the children of Susannah's school in January 1915.[29] Everyone needed to pull together to keep the nation physically fit and strong.

In the week ending 30 October 1914, the Infants at Weld Bank School were taken to a farmyard to see a threshing machine at work but Chorley was about to reap a different sort of harvest in the fields of France. The winter was drawing upon the town and in mid-November snow had arrived early.[30] December however, was much colder for the families of Patrick Asleford, John Foy and Thomas Kelleher of the 1st The Loyal North Lancashire Regiment and William Rothwell of its 3rd Battalion. The first of these men was killed on 2 December, the other three on 6 December.[31] Foy had acted with particular valour and the *Album* records that he was 'killed whilst saving the life of a Belgian child. He was killed but the child was saved'.[32] Thomas Carr of the 2nd Border Regiment died on 18 December and was the first of three brothers from St George's Congregational Church who were eventually recorded in the *Album*. The cumulative effect on this family, their church and their community was not unique. The New Year had not broken when William Kerfoot of the 1st The Loyal North Lancashire Regiment, having been wounded in the area of La Bassée, died in captivity as a prisoner of war at Soligen near Cologne on 29 December.[33] Susannah Knight's *Album* recorded 20 men from Chorley who died in 1914. Some of the young men who enlisted knew Susannah as they were her former pupils. At least three of the six Roman Catholic casualties who are recorded in the *Album* had been at St Mary's School in Euxton when Susannah was in post. There are 36 casualties connected to St Gregory's Church in the *Album* and at least a third of these were in the right age range to have been taught by Susannah. Of course, the *Album* is only a record of those who did not survive the war. By the end of 1914, at least 42 men from St Gregory's enlisted. At her own church, St Mary's in Chorley, at least 78 men enlisted in the first months of the war.[34]

War drew even closer to home for some communities on the east coast of England. Yarmouth was bombarded by eight German warships engaged in minelaying on 3 November. These were engaged by the Royal Navy. Wright Boardman was on board the British submarine *D5*, attached to *HMS Adamant*. Of the 25 crew, *The Times* reported that only four survived and Boardman was not among them.[35] Two congregations in Chorley mourned his loss and he is listed in the *Album* with the men of St George's Church, whilst his name is also inscribed on the memorial plaque of Trinity Methodist Church.[36]

Through the autumn and winter of 1914 the Pals were polishing both their military and foreign language skills. Susannah conducting French lessons with the company for an hour every evening over a period of six weeks and on 21 November, the *Chorley Guardian* gave an extended report on their progress remarking on the skill of Susannah as a linguist and the enthusiasm of her uniformed pupils. They were learning phrases such as 'Do you know which way our soldiers have passed' and 'Madam, I want something to eat, as I am very hungry'.[37]

Susannah helped strengthen the comradeship of her French class and the rest of the Pals by organising social events, the Terriers having already left for front line duties. On 16 December she arranged a dinner for her class together with Belgian soldiers recovering in Chorley hospital. This event gave the Pals the opportunity to refine their skills with native speakers, as well as giving them a Christmas treat. The dinner also brought them into contact with men who were battle-hardened and gave pause for more sober thoughts. There was plenty of singing at the dinner and many local people lent their talents for the concert which followed. Susannah extended an invitation to the rest of the Company for another tea and concert at the Parish Institute on 22 December.[38] The men held her in high regard. The then-ranked Lieutenant Charles Gidlow-Jackson, Captain James Milton, and Second Lieutenant William Rigby sent a Christmas greetings card in 1914 which was later pasted into the *Album*. The three officers also gave her a unique grouped portrait of themselves which Susannah kept with her for the rest of her life. This photograph was used to model a painting of the three officers commissioned by Susannah in 1920. On 15 January, Milton was elevated to the rank of Major but in the photograph he is clearly still wearing his captain's uniform.

4 HOME AND FRONT 1915 - 18

THE Chorley Pals were still clothed in their blue uniform rather than the yearned-for khaki in February 1915. They continued to train at the Drill Hall on Devonshire Road and practised with their rifles at Common Bank, empty land outside the town. Susannah continued her programme of language lessons throughout this period.

On 8 February the Pals were invited to the Parish Church Institute for tea with entertainment and the *Chorley and District Weekly News* described the warm camaraderie that now held the body of men together.[1] It reported a relaxed atmosphere with liberal supplies of cigarettes provided which the men were allowed to smoke during the music. Robert Ernest Shipcot, a local music teacher, played the piano. A Belgian refugee, René Casteleyn, was the flautist for the afternoon. There was a serious edge to the entertainment. Castelyn had attended the French lessons and coached the men. His presence was a reminder to them that war was a shattering experience and had displaced people across Europe. A more pressing reminder of their own mortality was that the flowers from the event were taken to the grave of Private George Milton, the first of the Pals to die after he was taken by pneumonia on 1 February 1915.[2]

Susannah was presented with a leather travelling bag as a token of thanks for teaching French to the men and the *Chorley Guardian* reported that the gift had her initials marked upon it: 'The bag had been subscribed for by the Pals as a mark of appreciation for the interest Miss Knight showed in them … and voluntarily taught the men French ever since the companies had been formed whilst had done much in providing for their enjoyment…'[3]

The newspaper indicated her ability to teach, entertain and engage with the men. Susannah herself referred back to this farewell dinner when the surviving Pals held a reunion meal and concert at the Ambulance Hall in February 1935 to mark two decades since the men had prepared to leave home soil.[4] On 23 February 1915, the children of Chorley's East Lancashire Regiment recruits were given leave from school to see their fathers off at Chorley railway station.[5]

Susannah also used her linguistic skills to help civilian victims of the war. In the week beginning 12 February 1915 three Belgian refugee children were enrolled on the registers of Weld Bank School.[6] The first refugees had arrived in Chorley on 23 October 1914, the number described varying from 23 to 29 individuals.[7] Appeals were placed in the *Chorley Guardian* for aid including bedding and clothes even before the Belgians arrived, with the convent at Gillibrand Hall offering them accommodation.[8] Weld Bank was close at hand to accept their children on roll, regardless of any advantage that Miss Knight's language skills might have offered them.[9]

The presence of convalescing Belgian soldiers and refugee families in Chorley provided an additional incentive for the men of the town to enlist, and the famous 'Remember Belgium' poster of 1915 with a lone Belgian soldier glancing back to the 'atrocities' behind him was used, nationally, to motivate recruits. War became a part of everyday life in 1915, with the anticipated victory not having been achieved by Christmas 1914. Posters began to put much greater moral pressure on men to respond to the call of duty. The use of recruitment posters intensified and many became iconic images of the era.

The Pals of the 11th East Lancashire Regiment waited in anticipation for frontline action. On 23 February the snow blanketed the streets of Chorley. The Pals mustered at the Drill Hall at 11am and marched to the railway station. Their newly enlisted mascot, an Old English Sheepdog named 'Ned', was led by Lieutenant Rigby near the front of the column. At 11.50am they boarded their train to Caernarfon. There were months of further exercises ahead of them before they embarked for Egypt in December 1915.[10] Susannah was 47 years old on the following day.

Reports of casualties continued to filter home. William Farnworth of the Sick Berth Reserve was on *HMS Bayano* when it was torpedoed at 5.15am on 11 March 1915 by *U-27*. The former liner, which had become an auxiliary cruiser, sank within three minutes in the waters between Scotland and Ireland, 10 miles off Coreswall Point.[11] Harry Parker volunteered for the Royal Field Artillery on 4 May 1915 and joined the 170th Brigade. The *Album* records that he made repeated applications to leave his job as a Shipping Clerk for the Lancashire and Yorkshire Railway and had said:

'How can I stand back and let married men with little kiddies go? It is my duty to go!' He was wounded at Arleux and died in Nᵒ 13 Hospital, Boulogne just two days shy of completing two years of service.[12]

Chorley became accustomed to such tragedies. The Jackson family of 18 Arley Street suffered more than most in 1915. All the men of the family were colliers, so perhaps they sought better pay, better conditions and a measure of adventure. Joseph Jackson had enlisted in 1912 and was called up to the 2nd Coldstream Guards when hostilities broke out. He was killed at Cuinchy in Belgium on 12 February 1915.[13] The elder son, Robert, was killed at Festubert on 11 April later that year. He had enlisted in 1912 and was serving in the 2nd Northumberland Fusiliers.[14] The youngest of the brothers, Samuel, died at Festubert like his brother, but with 1st/4th The Loyal North Lancashire Regiment on 15 June 1915.[15] It had been a catastrophic year for the family and Jesse Forsyth their step-brother was killed in 1917.[16]

Their father, Robert, died in 1920 'as a result of sickness contracted whilst on active service' though this statement has to be measured carefully against his service record. It is true that he had a military career that took him to South Africa in the Boer War. His service in the Great War was rather shorter and he was discharged from the 3rd The Loyal North Lancashire Regiment as 'not likely to be an efficient soldier' on 8 December 1914. It is clear from his Service Record that he lied about his age in 1914. He claimed he was 44 years old, but he was 10 years in advance of this, something which became apparent to his officers as he began his training. He is the oldest individual to be recorded in the *Album*, whether or not he can be regarded as a casualty of the war itself. His age, a sustained career in the army and harsh labour in a colliery as a hewer may all have contributed to his death but the loss of all his sons must have dealt a blow which no surgeon could heal.[17]

The *Chorley Guardian* settled on a format that gave regular lists of recent recruits, rolls of honour and military decorations and there were weekly reports on the overall progress of the conflict in the different theatres of combat. Inescapably, there were the obituaries, memorial notices, and news of the missing or wounded. The *Chorley Guardian* made use of photographs for the first time to show the faces of the fallen. The format of the newspaper responded to the demands of reporting the war. The lists posted outside the town hall often brought news from the front before a telegram or letter.

There were weekly columns promoting local fund-raising events and initiatives related to the war. Susannah was party to many of these events right from the start. To some, these notices for dances and whist drives in aid of the servicemen and their families were a little distasteful and a bone of contention for such as C.E.H. Calvert in December 1916:

> There is, perhaps, no harm in dancing, but the advocates of it would scarcely suggest the time and place was at a funeral, and if the organisers cannot see that there is a constant interment of the finest manhood England had produced, because the knock has not reached their doors, it is regrettable.

> If the idea is to get away from the horrors of war it serves as no useful purpose because the only people who really matter and who desire to get away from the thoughts of war, are the mothers, wives, children and sweethearts of those dear ones who have made the great sacrifice, and also of those who remain on the altar.[18]

The Loyal North Lancashire Regiment regularly placed illustrated recruitment notices. Advertisements for commercial products made use of the war to their own advantage using patriotism and a fascination for war as a means to sell men's attire, self-medicating remedies and combat-inspired toys. The Euxton Cycle Company, perhaps a little tastelessly, made their strapline 'always at the front'.[19] Church, social and self-education groups organised talks on a regular basis that revolved around the war, its causes and the certainty of victory. The more light-hearted columns featured a weekly serial, a 'Wit of the Week' section and a 'Ladies Letter' which gave wartime fashion and cooking tips.

School life was routinely punctuated by the ever-constant presence of the war. In the month that the school accepted the refugee children from Belgium the *Weld Bank School Log Book* marked a concern for low attendance in one week and referred to the departure of the Pals in the following entry. Attendance returned to a normal level once their fathers had left. In the first week of March 1915 the children were taught a song called 'Merry Soldiers', making paper hats and wooden swords for marching. The school was doing its best to raise the morale of the children in their care and dispel any sense of fear, yet despite their efforts, the Inspector chastised the staff of the Infant department for their teaching methods in the following month. The Infant department was reprimanded for 'treating' classes as a whole, having 'massed games' and 'simultaneous answering'. The time for games was receding as the realities of war bit harder.[20] Albert Henry Clarkson of the 2nd King's Own Royal Lancaster Regiment was killed in action at le Toquet on 4 April. His son was born by the end of that week and Rhoda Clarkson named the child after her husband.[21]

Susannah's brother was on *SS Boniface* when war broke out and had been its Chief Officer since 21 March 1914. Booth Steam Shipping Company avoided transatlantic routes and redirected its trade in South America. He wished his family well 'Despite the upset over the war'.[22] He was discharged in New York on 21 October having completed this voyage to the Brazils. His previous journeys had returned him to his home port of Liverpool. He was to remain based in New York for some time, though he hoped to put in at Galveston and Barbados. Jack and the *SS Boniface* took three tours from New York to the Brazils with very little time for recuperation. Having arrived in New York in October, he was re-engaged as Chief Officer within two days and returned to port on 15 January 1915. He rejoined the ship on the 27 January, returning to Liverpool on 17 April.[23]

Seafarers like Jack were providing a vital lifeline of trade for Britain, as raw materials and foodstuffs were in short supply because of the actions of German U-boats. The *Chorley Guardian* regularly encouraged people to make prudent use of food and textiles. Susannah walked the streets of Chorley pushing a hand cart to urge the townspeople to collect and recyclable material. She told the journalist for Liverpool's *Daily Dispatch* in 1949: 'We seemed to have a lot of scrap iron then ... because nearly everyone could give me old clog irons'.[24] This was a war in which everyone had a role.

On 1 May 1915 Jack set to sea from New York. Another ship, the liner *Lusitania*, made its departure from this port on the very same day. Susannah had returned to Liverpool on this ship in September 1913 when it had been commanded by Daniel Dow. *Lusitania* sank on 7 May within sight of the coast of Ireland with the loss of 1,195. Paul Crompton, an American who was one of Booth's own directors, was drowned. Even more tragically, his wife, six children and their governess, Dorothy Allen, were also lost to the sea. In all, 128 Citizens of the United States perished. This event moved America much closer to its eventual entry into the war on 6 April 1917. The sinking of *Lusitania* caught the popular imagination at the time but the increasing tonnage of less iconic American merchant ships finding their way to the bottom of the Atlantic moved men like President Woodrow Wilson more convincingly. For Susannah, Jack's brush with disaster underlined the risks her brother was taking each day he was at sea, and she longed to see him after his near-exile in America since 1914.

Susannah was well aware that her brother was at sea. She had reason to recall her return from New York *Lusitania* in 1913. Jack was risking his life on every day of every voyage he made. Jack returned safely to New York on the *SS Orduna* but we do not know when as whilst his record is stamped, it is undated. The Continuous Discharge Book ends here because Jack was promoted to that position he had coveted for so long - Master of his own ship. We have not however, come to the end of the Susannah's connection with *Lusitania*, for its story ebbs and flows through her memory during the next two decades.

The *Album* records 26 of the 32 Chorley men who were killed at Festubert on 15 and 16 June, 1915. The 1st/4th The Loyal North Lancashire Regiment was in action at this village, taking part in an offensive that aimed to recoup the failures in May at Aubers Ridge. The number of wounded however, was far higher. John Thomas Rigby, a signaller in the Terriers was lucky to be injured shortly before his comrades saw action at Festubert. He had been hit by shrapnel in his right leg and was recovering in a hospital near Paris that had been a large hotel before the war. With plenty of food and in relative comfort, he was safe.[25]

It was by far Chorley's worst day for casualties since the war had begun. The youngest man from the town to die on that terrible day at Festubert was William Connolly, who was only 17 years old. He was Chorley's youngest casualty recorded in the *Album* but only by a narrow margin.[26]

Joseph Ainsworth was another man who fell at Festubert with the 1st/4th The Loyal North Lancashire Regiment. He was 22 years old. His brothers, Eli and Henry, had also been in uniform since the beginning of the war. Henry was the eldest brother and had rushed back from Canada 'at the first call of danger'.[27] He was killed two months later at Gallipoli in the uniform of the 5th Connaught Rangers. Eli Ainsworth's story will be recounted later, as Susannah had a particular affection for him. Mary and Joseph Ainsworth's only relief was that their youngest son, Jonathan, survived the war and returned to 4 Wellington Street.[28]

John Jackman was also killed at Festubert and had enlisted on the day that war was declared.[29] Jackman and Joseph Ainsworth both worshipped at St Lawrence's Parish Church, a congregation which lost eight of its sons on 15 June: Herbert Arnold Bleackledge, Richard Geldeard, Samuel Jackson, John Cleobury Leigh, Launcelot Morris and Adam Wharton.[30] All the larger congregations of Chorley had similar stories. St George's, St Mary's , St Peter's, Sacred Heart, and St James' all lost men in the action of that day. But this was St Lawrence's worst day of the war and accounted for almost 10 per cent of the men of the parish who were claimed by the conflict. The *Album* is a reminder of the unrecorded words of condolence shared between families at church doors or in the street in the weeks and months that followed.

John Thomas Rigby, the wounded signaller who had missed Festubert, returned to the battalion and died for his country on the 5 August of 1916 on the fields of Flanders.[31]

Susannah recorded that five more men of The Loyal North Lancashire Regiment lost their lives in France in that month. The *Album* contains 322 entries for the regiment – by far the greater proportion of casualties of any regiment that recruited from Chorley. In the week after the battle the children of the Infant department at Weld Bank School were taken for a walk to see the haymaking and to stroll through the fields. [32]

Every church had a response to the tragedy that was unfolding in Europe and Mrs Williams, Mrs Eastwood and Mrs Wilcock led Trinity Methodist Church's response. These three women introduced a service of intercession for soldiers and sailors at 1pm for a quarter of an hour each day from August 1915.[33] Mrs Williams was the minister's wife and her son, Alfred, was a news agency journalist in London who had enlisted in 1914.[34] He was sent to France in November 1915 with the Royal Fusiliers and was killed at Frezenberg Ridge, Ypres, with the 49th Coy Machine Gun Corps in August 1917.[35] Mrs Eastwood's son was in the Royal Garrison Artillery. He married Edith Parker on 17 July in 1918 and survived the war. The efforts of these women, and the work of others in the congregation, continued beyond the war whether or not they had sons to lose.

Chorley tried to keep some of the more familiar patterns of daily life and the children returned from their holidays on 9 August 1915.[36] They had an extended weekend for Chorley Fair in mid-September and All Saints' Day was celebrated at the beginning of November.[37] Life went on. There was 'a terrific gale of wind and rain all day' on 12 November and because only 20 pupils of the infants' classes returned after lunch, the school was closed for the afternoon. Jack, who had been able to meet Mary Louisa and his daughter in a fleeting visit to Bristol, experienced this very same storm out in the Atlantic. Now as the Master of his own ship, the pressures must have been enormous:

> Well quite we had a devil of a time indeed right from the beginning. As soon as we got to the Bristol Channel the wind changed and the bad weather set in. I am very much afraid that all that night from the Sunday there was a great many vessel wrecked on around the coast. As you know we passed through the War Zone and aimed very safely and dead tired out. [*sic*][38]

Jack was exhausted when he reached New York and Cunard, a close ally of Booth Steam Shipping, made every effort to recuperate him. His ship berthed at the Cunard-owned Pier 56 and he was installed in the Grand Union Hotel at the company's own expense. He managed to catch up with friends and family in New York, including Annie Bryan. Jack was able to convey the news that Annie was to be married to a Mr O'Connell on 28 November just after he had to leave port. Susannah had stayed with Annie in 1913.[39] Mary Louisa Knight maintained a correspondence with her.[40] He also caught up with the Hyland family who had expected him and had noted the arrival of his ship in the newspaper, which suggests that an on-going correspondence was sustained between the family in Liverpool and contacts in America.

While Jack was in New York he was given sealed orders that were to be opened once his next voyage was underway. It is not clear if these orders came from the company or elsewhere and the responsibilities of captaincy were compounded by the dangerous transactions of war. Jack shared this news in a letter to Mary Louisa and it is clear that he yearned to be home with his family, doting upon both his wife and his daughter.[41]

The weather continued to be wild in Chorley. On 19 November a 'serious snow storm' left the lanes in Chorley slippery and attendance was poor at Weld Bank School.[42] The storms of war continued to sweep around the wider world too, and 117 of the men who were to be recorded in *Album* were already dead. Thomas Rimmer and Joseph Miller of the 9th and 1st The Loyal North Lancashire Regiment, both members of St Lawrence's Church, were killed in action on the Western Front on Christmas Day of 1915. They were not the last to die in that year. Nathaniel Brindle of the 2nd South Wales Borderers were killed on 28 December in Gallipoli and John Jolly of the 2nd Royal Sussex Regiment was killed on New Year's Eve.[43]

Meanwhile, Susannah kept herself busy contributing what she could to the war effort. She organised balls and teas to raise money for injured soldiers and bereaved families. Her reputation for organising food parcels for the men at the front line was remembered by a former pupil in later life.[44] She made sure that children whose fathers had been killed were well-supported.[45] Indeed, Susannah Knight was actively involved in raising money for the aid of soldiers and their families throughout and after the war.[46]

In January of 1916, the nature of recruitment changed. Patriotic enthusiasm could account for much of the enlistment in August 1914. Some of the men who had joined the British Expeditionary Force at the beginning of the war had previously been in the forces or in Haldane's Territorials. A peak in Chorley's pattern of enlistment in early 1915 can be explained by a post-Christmas realisation that the war was going to last longer than expected.

A further year of advances, blunders and reverses had led to a decline in the number of recruits. Nationally, there had been a decline in volunteers and men who were physically fit and unattached were compelled to join the armed forces. In January 1916, conscription was introduced for young unmarried men. By March, this call came to married men. An analysis of recruitment patterns from the data available in the *Album* and associated information from the *Chorley Guardian* records increasing rates of enlistment in January and May of 1916 but this was neither a repeat of the surge of August of 1914, nor the more belated obedient response to the 1915 recruitment campaign.[47] At least 141 of the casualties were enlisted in 1916. Of those who are recorded in the *Album* 233 joined in 1914 but only 91 joined in 1915.[48] David Lloyd George, as the Minister of Munitions, was concerned that the burden of sacrifice should be shared and that essential industries should retain male workers who had the skills to maintain the momentum of production. Conscription combated a declining surge of enlistment and also allowed for a more controlled flow of replacements in the front line It also protected industry from losing the key workers in reserved occupations. Now the opportunity to die was held in common across boundaries of class.

In the Western Front the French were struggling in their defence of Verdun. Susannah was almost certainly the parishioner referred to in the May 1916 edition of *The Messenger*, the monthly magazine of St Mary's Church in Chorley. A 'French Soldier from the Fort of Verdun' wrote a vivid diary entry describing the horror of the German barrage. The writer was Leon Moreau of the 139th Infantry Division of the French Army. He was from Béziers. The passage is worth recalling in full:

> Verdun, 16 May, 1916. I will not speak of the terrible shelling we had to bear day after day and night after night. Heads, arms, legs blown off, and blood flowed down the slopes like water; and amongst the noise and the dust the poor boys shouted for their mothers. As for me, I took out my Rosary, and began reciting Aves. We may be very brave, but when we are face to face with death, we are thrilled through. Yes, God and Our Lady watched over me during that dreadful battle and protected me all through it. If I am spared to my parents it is only because God's finger kept the bullets away, and those dreadful killing machines, for over 25 days. I spent terrible hours which I shall never forget. We were bombarded with heavy shells for two weeks, day and night – the very earth was shaking beneath our feet. We had food only once each day at 7-0 in the evening. The weather was very cold, and most of us got our hands and feet frozen. We were in fever, and

our thirst was almost unbearable, and we only quenched it in eating snow from the ground. In spite of these hardships we remained in the firing line. Verdun is still in our hands, and I am yet alive. [sic][49] (Plate 10)

Weld Bank teachers did their best to raise morale on 24 May 1916 by getting the pupils to wave flags and sing patriotic songs to celebrate 'Empire Day' whilst out for a walk, but attendance was poor after an outbreak of mumps.[50]

The first day of July 1916 went unnoticed in the *Weld Bank School Log Book*. According to the *Album*, the opening day of the Battle of the Somme was Chorley's worst single day for casualties and thirty-two men lost their lives that day - most of them from the 11th East Lancashire Regiment, the Chorley Pals, at Serre. So much has been written about this infamous day but perhaps an account from a Chorley man is as good a summary as any. Corporal John Egan Morgan of the 1st/5th The Loyal North Lancashire Regiment described what he saw at the Somme to the *Chorley Guardian*:

> [The] attack commenced at 7-30 am ... the men showed great examples of cheeriness, pluck and fortitude, and gave some assuring reports as to the progress of the battle. About noon we went into the front line trenches. The sights we saw there were beyond description. What great sacrifices and what great slaughter! It was with mixed feelings of horror and revenge that we waited for the order to charge. [51]

Morgan had been a member of the choir of Hollinshead Congregational Church, also being its secretary and organist. He had also been well-known as an amateur entertainer. He was wounded at Poziers and was taken to Netley Hospital where he died on 31 July.

Three of the men that died on 1 July 1916 were William Tootell, Owen Thomas Parry and Seth Rollins.[52] Tootell and Parry had joined the Pals on the same day in September 1914. Seth Rollins, Tootell's cousin and a neighbour of Parry, had joined the following week. Parry was the organist at St John's Church in Coppull. Tight connections between families, friends and neighbours have been identified throughout the *Album*.

One casualty of the Somme Susannah almost certainly taught was James Dickinson, who was only 17 years old when he was killed in action, the youngest member of the Chorley Pals to die.[53] He had been on leave in the summer of 1916 when his nephew, eight-year-old Joseph Critchley, had been asked by his grandfather to take the young soldier to Chorley railway station by pony and trap to catch the train so that he could re-join his regiment in France. On this journey with his uncle, the conversation turned to the war and life in the trenches. The nephew recalled how his uncle, was clearly terrified of the impending battle, the 'Big Push' to drive back the Germans. He also realised the great danger ahead, since many of his friends and comrades had been killed in previous battles. During this journey Joseph believed that somehow, this teenager had a premonition of his fate. Only Joseph was at the railway station to wave him off. His lasting memory was of his uncle's sad, serious face as he boarded the train. How unfortunate that neither his parents nor any other member of his family were there at the railway station to say their final 'goodbyes'. This was the last time that this James Dickinson set foot in Chorley. A few days later, he and five other members of St Gregory's Church were consumed by the slaughter of the first day of the Battle of the Somme.[54]

A mundane entry in the *Weld Bank School Log Book* notes that Miss Elizabeth McClelland, an assistant teacher, was absent for most of that week as she prepared for her wedding. She married William Porter on 6 July. Despite the ever-present war, Chorley still needed to act out the familiar patterns of an ordinary life.[55]

Susannah was still fondly remembered by the Chorley Pals and she featured in a *Chorley Guardian* article on 9 September 1916, which reported that Mr and Mrs Harrison, whose three sons were in the Pals, wanted to show their appreciation for the French lessons she had organised. Corporal Harry Harrison's younger brother spoke on his behalf and read a letter:

> [Please] find enclosed a small cross. I have shaped it out of a piece of copper from a German shell, which was found near the scene of our attack on the never-to-be-forgotten day, July 1st Will you please get it gold dipped, and a small ring put in it at the top. Then I want Miss Knight to accept it as a souvenir of July 1st, because it was found in the very same trench from which her many Pals sprang to the charge.[56]

All the Harrison sons were fortunate to survive the war.

Jack Knight returned to Britain that summer for a brief visit, as he had to return to New York on 29 July 1916. Significantly, Jack was listed as a first class passenger on Cunard's *RMS Orduna*. His health was about to become a cause of great concern and he had been given some additional leave.[57] Whilst Chorley suffered the consequence of the Somme in the late summer and autumn, Susannah had reason to fear for the life of her brother by September 1916.

Jack faced a serious illness in the late summer and wrote to his wife that he had been close to death. On 27 September he was in a hospital in Barbados where his condition was critical. The years spent in the punishing climate of South America had taken their toll and his ample weight did no good for his health. He was confined for several weeks with near-fatal diabetes and rheumatic fever and was placed on a special diet to tackle his illness. The rheumatic fever caused him to lose mobility in his shoulders for a period. He was physical shattered. For a man so active and so courageous, he took it well and the Masters of Booth's vessels paid him the courtesy of making port in Barbados to pay their respects to him. In September he had managed to summon the strength to put pen to paper and write to his wife and child.[58]

Susannah had a further tragedy to face at this time. Moreau's description of Verdun had featured in the May edition St Mary's *The Messenger*.[59] In October 1916 the church magazine broke the news of his death at Chaulnes on the Somme on 11 September. He was only 21 years old.[60] His parents wrote:

> A terrible blow has fallen upon us. Our dear child, our well-beloved son, our Leo, is dead, from wounds received during an attack; and our poor child has left us for ever in this life, and never more shall we look upon him! – Ah yes in a world that will have no end! We must bow before this appalling trial, and ask our God to give us courage and strength to bear it. The loyal and frank character of Leo, his sincere piety, his generous affection for his friends, made him deeply loved by all – and now he is dead and there remains only for us the memory of his virtues ... Gallantly he died, a good soldier, a fervent Christian, a martyr to his duty shedding his blood for France.[61]

Susannah was described as 'a dear friend' of Moreau though it is unclear how she became associated with the family. Moreau's description of Verdun had appeared in *The Messenger* and became the text for his entry in the *Album*. He was described as having been a worshipper at Sacré Coeur in Béziers. It has already been suggested above that Susannah's education by the Sisters of the Sacred Heart of Mary in Bootle had a strong influence on her later calling and this Béziers was where the order had originated. A sustained correspondence with a family in Béziers over a period of two decades or more is not out of the question. The fact that Susannah chose to give the full quotation from his correspondence in the *Album* indicates the impact that the death of this young man had on her. It is strange that there is a misspelling of Sacré Coeur which suggests a lack of care on the part of the printer and ill-informed proof reading. His death may have been an additional stimulus for her activities later in November.[62]

Susannah had much to reflect on. She placed a prominent notice in the *Chorley Guardian* advertising a 'Solemn Requiem Mass' to be held at St Mary's Church in Market Street at 11am on 5 November. Susannah invited relatives of the Roman Catholic Pals of Chorley, Adlington, Brinscall, Coppull, Croston, Wheelton and Whittle and asked respondents to refer the names of those killed or missing, no matter what regiment '… to be sent to her by 3 November so that the names may be placed on the altar, and that they may share with the Pals in the privileges of this special Requiem Mass'. She concluded that she 'would like to ask all Catholics to offer up at least one Holy Communion for our heroes. They have given their lives for us'.[63]

The notice was repeated in the next two issues of the newspaper and other churches were making similar responses at this time. A notice announcing a memorial service at St James' Church was placed directly above that of Susannah's on 28 October.[64] It has already been noted above that the women of Trinity Methodist Church were engaged in work of prayerful compassion. There was a drive to organise a subscription to send parcels to the troops at Christmas in October 1916. In a Non-conformist parallel to Susannah's Requiem Mass, the regularity of deaths had led to the practice of the minister asking bereaved families to choose a suitable hymn to be sung in the following Sunday service. From 15 November 1916, Trinity Methodist Sunday School was commissioned to keep a roll of honour which was eventually used to form the church's memorial plaque that was dedicated on 15 May 1922. Every church was gathering its spiritual family together in sustained mourning.[65]

Susannah was prompted to arrange the Requiem Mass by her faith and her friendship with the young men she had taught. Her faith attracted wounding comments in the following months. She had a bigger project in mind. As well as the notice promoting the Requiem Mass, the *Chorley Guardian* carried an additional announcement on Susannah's behalf on 28 October, headed 'Proposed Memorial to Chorley Pals'. She planned a public meeting at the Shepherds' Hall at 7.30pm on 7 November, something which was to unleash a level of vitriol on this 48-year-old pillar of the community which is hard to comprehend.

The notice for the public meeting to discuss a war memorial was repeated on the front page of the newspaper the following week. A narrow range of reactive opinion was gathered by the *Chorley Guardian* – despite the fact that Susannah's meeting was yet to be held. As with all good character assassinations, the newspaper began by praising Miss Knight. It introduced her as '…a local lady who is well known for her kind and practical interest in the Chorley Pals' Company. The following editorial comment argued that her as yet unannounced proposal was 'particularly inappropriate' and that a 'permanent memorial, worthy of the noble and splendid lives that have been lost in the cause of humanity, and a memorial representative of the whole town, should be erected ...'

The editorial concluded:

> 'The subject is one which requires thought and consideration before final judgement is made, and in order to gauge the general feeling upon this matter we append a number of interviews which our representative has had with the leaders of all classes of the community'.[66]

These 'interviews' gave Susannah's unspecified proposals a savage mauling. Firstly Sir Henry Hibbert MP, wrote of how important it was that a 'permanent and worthy monument be erected' and that the matter should be taken in hand by a 'strong, fully-representative committee'. The Mayor, Mr J. Turner, assumed that a memorial should be built but that '... the matter should be taken in hand by the townspeople as a whole'. He magnanimously added: 'When the time comes I shall not object to taking a leading part in the matter'. Dr Harris agreed saying: 'I think the Mayor, who is the leading citizen of the borough, should take the lead in any scheme for the erection of a memorial to our dead soldiers'. In more reasoned language, Mr J.P.T. Jackson and Mr T. West (of the Weaver's Association) referred to some of the difficulties that might be presented when planning a memorial.

The representatives the *Chorley Guardian* had chosen as 'leaders of all classes' were all men. It is significant that all five made the assumption that the memorial would be an 'erected' memorial and Hibbert went one step further by referring to a 'monument'. A lot is betrayed in this language and the men had made clear assumptions about how the war should be remembered. It needed to be an object, it needed to be agreed by committee, it must not be an outwardly emotional response to war. Hibbert, Turner and Harris assumed that a memorial should have approval from those who led the community or those perceived to be chosen by the community which seems, in fact, to be them. Turner nominated himself. Harris nominated Turner. Hibbert underestimated and dismissed Susannah by saying that no individual should undertake the task. Only Jackson and West escaped with any scrap of honour but even they misunderstood the real nature of Susannah's yet-to-be-announced memorial. All five men believed that Susannah's proposal for a memorial was only for the Pals.

Miss Knight had a lot to organise in the first full week of November 1916. On the Sunday 5 November, she had arranged the Requiem Mass at St Mary's. Father Crank celebrated the Mass and gave the sermon pointing out that 'the men who gave up their lives formed a rampart in defence of those living in comfort at home'. The Dead March from 'Saul' was played by the organist Mr S. Beddoe. On Tuesday 7 November Susannah held her public meeting at the Shepherds' Hall, which drew an audience of 30 people. The event was extensively reported in the *Chorley Guardian* on 11 November. She seemed not to have been unnerved by the negative remarks in the previous Saturday's newspaper and gave an assured presentation. The report of the proceedings gives a rare insight into Susannah's voice and tone. She had a complex proposal which had been much misconstrued by the town worthies, and was misunderstood in many of the letters which were sent to the newspaper in the following weeks.[67]

There are several factors which probably motivated her first effort to create some form of memorial for the people for Chorley. The most obvious was that she was responding to the terribly high loss of life sustained by the Pals battalion at Serre in the Somme on 1 July. A connected concern was that the surviving Pals might be transferred to other military units to make up weak companies which had also been battered in battle. She seems to have been concerned to recall the integrity of the unit before it was cast adrift. Susannah wanted some form of recognition that the comradeships formed in August and September of 1914 still had significance even if the original body of men was subsumed into other regiments.

A more personal motivation was deeply rooted in her faith. By this time news had been received that her brother was through the worst of his illness and was recovering well. Susannah must have experienced both despair and joy in the preceding months and it is more than likely that her proposal also came from a deep sense of gratitude to God for protecting those she loved. A sense of calling to bring comfort to the servicemen who were less fortunate and to their families matched the pattern of mission which had been instilled in her by the nuns of Béziers.

About 30 people attended Susannah's meeting at the Shepherds' Hall. What she proposed did not match what her critics thought they had been responding to in the previous week's newspaper interviews. Her concern was more considered, and more life affirming, about the value of ties of loyalty, community, and of memory.

Furthermore, the memorial was not to be some static monument, but something far more purposeful.

What she wanted to have erected to the memory of the Pals was a home where 25 of the most seriously maimed soldiers of Chorley and district could be housed and cared for as long as they lived.

> Such a home was badly needed. When the war was over the hospital doors would be thrown open, and a large number of men who were sightless, armless, and legless would be let out. There was already one case of a widow, whose only son had lost both legs. There were worse things than death.[68]

Susannah was presenting a very different plan from the one assumed by her detractors, and she was offering something that really did need to be commenced immediately, rather than after the war by a committee of town councillors. She tackled her critics head-on. There is a wry sense of irony at work in Susannah's proposal, in that a project to create a cottage hospital for the wounded was to be organised by women alone. She had committed £10 of her own money and urged the women present to aim for the same: 'They should not be discouraged. Their work would reach up to Heaven. The dead did not want human praise – they had passed that'. To his credit, Mr J.P.T. Jackson, who had been one of those interviewed by the *Chorley Guardian,* had attended this meeting and Susannah challenged him to help her to carry out a house-to-house collection. Susannah was in a supremely combative mood.[69]

At the public meeting there were arguments made against her proposal. Mr R. Higham suggested that it was too big a task for the women and that they had no idea about the costs involved: 'The aid of men ought to have been called in, and a thoroughly representative committee ought to be appointed'. Susannah was fiery in her answer. She wanted the memorial to be the work of Lancashire women. If a man wished to contribute she hoped he would let a woman be a donor. There was still opposition. Dr Rigby had the death of his brother on his mind when he said a 'town's meeting' ought to make such decisions and that the Government had a duty to care for injured soldiers. Lieutenant William Rigby had been one of the three officers who had sent Christmas greetings to Susannah in 1914 but had fallen on the seventh day of the Battle of the Somme. Mr J.P.T. Jackson was more conciliatory and spoke up, saying 'everybody admired Miss Knight's womanly heart in taking up this work'. He suggested that the local Press 'throw open their columns for public expression of opinion and by that means ascertain the feelings of the public'. Jackson suggested that the scheme should be deferred and a meeting should be called at a later date when there had been further consultation of the public. Jackson admired Miss Knight's proposal but urged that consensus should be sought. His proposal for a public debate was to open up some bitter wounds within the community.

What happened to Susannah next was truly shocking. On 18 November five letters were printed in the *Chorley Guardian* that disputed her proposals in the strongest terms, or rather they made the same assumptions that the interviewees of 4 November had made. The first letter missed the point that Susannah's main aim was to create a hospital for the desperately wounded which was so urgently needed. The second letter suggested that it was 'odious that Miss Knight should step in unwittingly' and that she would 'create discord'. 'A Patriot' in the third letter expressed 'strong disapproval' and asserted that: 'It is the Mayor's duty. Miss Knight has usurped his functions, with the result that she has incurred the displeasure of the majority of Chorley people'. The fourth letter, from 'Jack' ignored the humanitarian thrust of Susannah's proposal and says 'do let us get on with the war'. The fifth letter, perhaps the most treacherous, contained anti-Catholic undertones saying: 'If Miss Knight is really anxious to perform some charitable duty, in accordance with Divine approval, there is ample scope to feed His lambs'.[70]

Her 'faults' throughout this humiliating treatment in the press can be summarised simply in that she was a woman, she was not from Chorley and she was a Roman Catholic. Her proposal seems to have wounded the pride of the men of authority. She had fought back in the public meeting and exposed their expectations as prejudicial gossip, poking fun at them with her emphasis that the memorial was to be the work of the women. As a woman alone, at this stage, she had incurred a heavy punishment for this act of resistance but was ultimately be undeterred.

Jack returned to Liverpool in the midst of Susannah's battle, having had to wait several weeks until he was well enough to be discharged from hospital. He managed to return hastily, his name being pencilled onto the bottom of the passenger list. He had mentioned in his letter that he would catch a passage on a liner when the opportunity arose and arrived in Liverpool on 19 November on the America Line's *St Louis*[71]. Susannah was relieved to know that her brother had returned safely.

Jack was brought back to health by his wife in the months ahead but at least he was at home and in Liverpool where his wife, sister, half-siblings and child could dote on him. His daughter, Louisa Elizabeth, his 'sunshine' was now three years old. She was walking and talking when he saw her in November 1915 and he had a chance to strengthen his relationship with her. There are photographs from this period which celebrate this reunion. One shows Jack standing alongside Mary Louisa, with their daughter, Louisa, sitting in a pram. Jack's survival and safe home-coming offered

Susannah hope to sustain her campaign with a sign that the Grace of God was upon her family.

The criticism of Susannah eased. The first signs of support for her proposal of a home for disabled soldiers began to emerge in the edition of the *Chorley Guardian* dated 25 November. A Chorley Pals 'Sister' pointedly reproached 'A Patriot' for his comment that Susannah had 'usurped' the authority of the Mayor: 'I wonder 'A Patriot' does not accuse Miss Knight of usurping someone else's functions by teaching the local soldiers the French language'. There was clearly a wider body of support than the newspaper had implied in its earlier features. The 'Sister' went on to write that 'If Miss Knight has not the support of the 'leading citizens', she has, or ought to have, the loyal support of the Pals' relatives and friends'. Susannah was given comfort:

> Miss Knight can rest assured she will always get a good word from local soldiers who have come in contact with her. If we do not sympathise with Miss Knight's scheme let us give the lady the respect she so worthily deserves.[72]

Though some criticism persisted in the following week's edition, the public storm was subsiding. A letter from 'One of the Workers' called Susannah's scheme a 'noble and worthy one, also an unselfish one, for it includes any soldier, no matter what regiment he belongs to'. At last someone had valued Susannah for what she had said, and not what rumour and prejudice had placed upon her.

The humanitarian core of her project was given fuller expression and the letter writer said: 'It is only when our cripples come home that we shall realise how much the home is needed'. The writer was strongly critical of the government for not providing for invalided veterans and challenged the arguments of Hibbert and Turner that all this should be resolved after the war: 'If we are going to wait until the war is over before we try to raise the money I am afraid our maimed and crippled heroes will have gone to their home above before the money is raised'. In a sharp twist of criticism directed at the town council, 'One of the Workers' concludes:

> If everyone is so anxious for a town's memorial what has the grateful town shown to the heroes of the South African war? ... Let our heroes in the town see that at least one woman in Chorley tried to do them a good turn ... and I hope that there will be a great deal less than 25 men who will need a home.[73]

Susannah, despite the seemingly coordinated efforts of the *Chorley Guardian* and the town council, had allies who had actually listened to and understood her proposal. Her hope for a home to tend the injured remained unfulfilled but her passion to give recognition to the sacrifice the people of Chorley had borne re-emerged in the future.

The Spring of 1917 brought further trials for Susannah. Jack was nursed back to health by Mary Louisa through the winter.[74] While he was safe in Liverpool the sea remained a dangerous place. On 24 March 1917 Jack received a letter which offered a very different type of adventure to the rain forest of South America. An evasively-worded memo from the Admiralty asked Jack to acknowledge the receipt of confidential instructions whilst Master of *SS Francis*.[75] The convoy system was introduced by David Lloyd George in May and Jack was recruited on the basis of his experience and courage. Convoys did much to reduce the loss of merchant shipping, as U-boats continued to prowl for both military and merchant vessels. Jack was bound for Russia like his father, his grandfather, his grandmother and great uncle. His obituary called him the 'Commodore of Convoys' and reported how he protected merchant ships bringing food to and from the port of Liverpool.[76] Jack headed for more bitter climes.

A personal grief touched Susannah at this time. Mary Ainsworth of 4 Wellington Street had already lost two sons, Joseph and Henry, both referred to above, who had been killed in 1915. Another son, Eli, lost his life on 13 May 1917. He had been one of Susannah's most diligent students when the Pals had been learning French in 1914 and since that time, he had served in Egypt, France, and Belgium and had survived the Battle of the Somme which had taken the lives of so many of his friends, escaping with a broken arm and leg. Having been treated in Glasgow, he was sent back to the front. Susannah learned from the 26 May edition of the *Chorley Guardian* that he had been gassed and killed in France after his return to the Front. When she recorded his entry in the *Album* her own voice speaks from the pages, rather that of his family. She gives a very personal epitaph when she records that he was:

> One of the most distinguished of the French scholars of the 'Pals' Company. He devoted all of his spare time to the study of the French language in order that he might be able to render every possible service to his country in her hour of need. He had worked so hard that before leaving England he was able to translate with ease the most difficult passages from French newspapers. He was one of the most gracious and charming of men.[77]

Jack's letters were no different in their sentiment to any of the men who were in uniform in July 1917:

As I sit here thousands of miles away I feel like crying when I think of the trials we have got to go through with the inconstant home comings and the long separations. I shall dear lass gladly welcome the day when I can stay at home and have from you constant company.[78]

The Third Battle of Ypre, or Passchendaele, as it is commonly known, threw lives away through that sodden extended summer and autumn of 1917. One hundred and thirty men of Chorley lost their lives on the Western Front between 30 May and 10 November. The sudden, tragic, brutality of the action faced by East Lancashire Regiment at the Somme was shattering by its brevity. The Third Battle of Ypres was, perhaps, more pernicious in its slow but cumulative and persistent killing. Both these battles took a massive toll on Chorley.

Susannah remained busy with her charitable support for the soldiers and sailors. On 10 November, the last day of the Third Battle of Ypres, the front page of the *Chorley Guardian* featured a notice advertising a 'Tea Party and Concert' in the Shepherds' Hall for men who had already been or were waiting to be discharged from the forces. Susannah took a role in signing up men who were not members of the Chorley and District Disabled Sailors and Soldiers Association.[79] Susannah and her supporters realised that to cast off one's uniform did not strip men of their memories. The war continued to intervene in the daily life at Weld Bank School. Susannah's colleague Elizabeth Porter (née McClelland) had been anxious for news from her husband who was fighting in France. They had been married for just over a year. In November he returned on leave but on 28 November 1917 he had to return to the front line and Elizabeth was given leave of absence on the Wednesday of his return. Such moments of compassion must have been a regular occurrence in many places of work across Chorley.[80]

Susannah regularly visited Mary Louisa in her confinement and Jack appreciated this in the letter he wrote at Christmas. She had to be cautious about her visits at the beginning of January 1918. An epidemic of chickenpox raged through Chorley and on Wednesday 9 January 1918, only 17 pupils attended in the morning. Miss Lilly, the headmistress, sent the children home and when eight pupils attended in the afternoon she decided not to take any registers that day. The town's Medical Officer was so concerned that a list was drawn up of the cases of infection. Susannah, Mrs Porter and Miss Eccles were all absent with illness in the proceeding weeks.[81] The hardships of war were beginning to bite and in January 1918, the *Chorley Guardian* informed of the government's decision to introduce rationing.[82]

Susannah Knight continued to be active in raising funds to support the injured, orphaned and bereaved, despite her mauling by the town's worthies. By January 1918 the Chorley and District Disabled Sailors and Soldiers Association, formed in Blackburn in early 1917, was frequently referred to as 'Miss Knight's Fund' by the *Chorley Guardian*. It reported on a typical social and fund-raising event at Eaves Lane Congregational School in January 1918 which Susannah had organised.[83] Susannah had exhausted herself and it is not surprising that she was off school with sickness from 22 to 25 January.[84] Despite her tireless efforts she seems to have gained little credit from some members of the community. She still faced malicious criticisms after November 1916. Some insinuations were particularly hurtful. In February 1918 she was forced to place a rebuttal to gossip as a notice on the front page of the *Chorley Guardian*:

> Miss Knight, who has been working for the soldiers since August 1914, wishes to state that she is a Catholic and has an utter abhorrence of Spiritualism. It is absolutely forbidden by the laws of the Church and she has never in her life had any connection whatsoever with Spiritualist meetings and the tales in circulation are false.[85]

On 21 March 1918 Ludendorff opened up an offensive along the Western Front at Arras, Lys and Aisne. This was the German Army's last opportunity to take advantage of the withdrawal of Russian troops from the Eastern Front before troops of the United States of America were assembled in sufficient strength in Europe to tip the balance against the Central Powers. The fighting was fierce and the scale of casualties for Chorley approached that of Festubert of June 1915 or the Somme of 1916. In the next 10 days, nineteen men of the town died on the Western Front in the face of this onslaught. Four of these were killed on the very first day of this engagement.

Throughout this period, the men of the Pals maintained a correspondence with Susannah and extracts from these letters were printed in the *Chorley Guardian* in May 1918. They were introduced as coming from different individuals and recorded the experience of the Spring Offensive vividly. One of the extracts recounted the movements of the Pals in the early stages of the German assault, dated 24 March:

> I have been going through it the last couple of days, and it has been dreadful. To begin with, they pulled us out of bed at 1am, and rushed us up to the line in motor wagons. The journey lasted all day, and then with no rest we marched 12 kilometres to our destination. I fell asleep marching and at the end of it I threw

myself down by the roadside and slept for two hours. Then the scrapping came off, which I dare say you read all about in the papers. Even as I write guns are thundering like mad and I have lost many men. I have lost all my belongings and have had no wash or shave for a week. [86]

There was no abatement and on Good Friday, 29 March and another letter illustrates the intensity and the desperation of the battle:

[The] fighting has been fearful and we have had no sleep for a week. Although many a good man has gone west in the Battalion, I thank God I am still alive. Jerry commandeered all my property during the great advance. We fought a rear guard action against overwhelming numbers of the enemy.[87]

The German offensive continued and Chorley lives were claimed in British defensive actions. Eli Heald was in the 2nd/6th Manchester Regiment and he was killed on 31 March. He was 28 years old. Susannah may well have come across him before the war as he had taught at Trinity Wesleyan Market Street School before he worked away from Chorley at Ducie Avenue Junior Boys' School in Manchester. His wife and the son he barely met remained in Chorley. This son, Donald, became the organist for Trinity Methodist Church in Gillibrand Walks. Susannah recorded that 'Whilst in training he was a prize winner in shooting competitions and was more than once offered promotion, but he preferred to remain a Private'. She makes a clear note that he was a schoolmaster and she may well have wanted to make a personal association with his memorial entry. Eli Heald was last seen entering a dugout immediately before it was hit by a shell. There were no survivors.[88]

Far away in Mozambique, Frank Gartside died of dysentery of 11 April. He had been a bank clerk in 1911, living with his parents at 29 Park Road, Chorley. He had only enlisted in April 1916 and most probably as a conscript, but within two years he was a colour-sergeant with the 3rd Monmouthshire Regiment as part of the West African Frontier Force and attached to the Gold Coast Regiment. It was some tragic adventure for a young man to travel such a distance and to die so wastefully at the age of 23.[89]

Meanwhile, in France, the ferocity of battle was sustained. The *Chorley Guardian* printed extracts of letters to Susannah from soldiers on the Western Front. One was dated 16 April 1918 and recorded that 'The scenes you see out here are just awful, and I thank God it is not Lancashire and dear old Chorley. On 23 April 'Fritz' tried to blow us off the Earth, and we are hanging on like grim death'.

In a letter dated from the following day, a correspondent was 'wounded in the head and neck with shrapnel, now in Red Cross Hospital in Boulogne'. The pace of the *Chorley Guardian* article was energetic and concluded with James Johnson Moore recounting to Susannah how he gained the Military Medal. Clearly Susannah had the trust of these men who describe their deepest fears to her in their letters. Her impressions of the war came from a number of sources and there seems to have been a frequent correspondence with a number of the Chorley Pals throughout the war. At the point that these extracts were being published the casualty lists placed outside Chorley Town Hall were be beginning to include men who had not survived the actions described.[90] Another 127 men earned their place in Susannah Knight's *Album* between April 1918 and the Armistice.

Susannah continued to fear for the welfare of her brother. On 23 May 1918 Jack was the captain of the *Hubert* which survived a German submarine attack in the Irish Sea. This was a very different type of adventure from that which he experienced in his Amazon days.

The casualties sustained in the very last weeks of the war are perhaps the most poignant. Herbert Holmes was a member of the 97th Squadron of the newly-formed Royal Air Force and only 19 years old when he was killed on 28 October, yet he had reached the rank of second lieutenant. From being a council clerk he had flown and fallen from the skies above Arras. His captain, F. Ward, wrote that:

> He was a most efficient officer and his charming personality had won him great popularity amongst his fellow officers. His loss is felt greatly by the squadron, both as an observer and a friend. It may be a consolation to you that he died doing his duty, and that his death must have been instantaneous. I cannot say where he is buried, but his grave is in a beautiful locality, and will always be looked after by his squadron.[91]

There was still a fortnight left until hostilities were to cease, and seven more men of Chorley were still to lose their lives.

In Chorley, there were increasingly grave concerns for the health of the children at Weld Bank School. In the summer holidays of 1918, the school had to be fumigated and bleached and indeed, the experience of the poor attendance in the winter of the previous year may have influenced these measures.[92] Measles was the only minor concern at first in the September attendance reports but on 11 October the *Weld Bank School Log Book* begin to note with concern the 'coughs and influenza'. On 14 October the school was closed by the Medical Officer until further notice 'on account of the epidemic'.[93] The school remained closed until the week beginning 11 November 1918.

The *Weld Bank School Log Book* offers a complicated response to peace. The Headteacher wrote: 'Reopened school with 56 pupils. School closed for four weeks. Two unnamed children died from epidemic of influenza. Holiday this afternoon on account of the 'Armistice' being signed. Great rejoicings'. The news of the Armistice seems to demand an exclamation mark but the death of the pupils stripped away the joy.

The church bells rang out in celebration across Chorley for the first time since the Great War had commenced.[94] On the 11 November Ernest Shaw of the 2nd (Garrison) Battalion of The King's Liverpool Regiment died in Salonika. He was 34 years old and left a wife in Geoffrey Street.[95] The war was over but this did not mean that the war stopped taking lives.

5 COMPILING THE MEMORIAL 1918 - 20

THE Armistice was made in November 1918 but the terrible effects of war continued to be experienced by families in Chorley. Twenty-seven men lived beyond the Armistice and yet still gained their place in the *Album*. Albert Whalley died of pneumonia at *HMS Garth Castle* in Rossyth on 12 November. Edmund Hart of the 1st/4th The Loyal North Lancashire Regiment died of wounds in Chorley on 13 November. On 14 November the life of Thomas Balshaw was lost 'accidentally' in Italy with the 2nd Gordon Highlanders and Military Policeman James Smethurst perished of 'pneumonia and malaria' in Salonika. Andrew Magrath died in France on 21 November. Magrath had served in the 11th East Lancashire Regiment as a bandsman, sniper and stretcher bearer in France, taking part in the Battle of the Somme. Magrath's entry in the *Album* tells of some tragic revelry: 'On Armistice Day, the men of his battalion having covered him with flags, marched through the French villages, beating drums etc., and through taking them off, he contracted a chill in the trenches the same evening and died suffering from pneumonia'.[*sic*][1]

'Pneumonia' and 'bronco-pneumonia' often described the stealthy presence of a deadly influenza. The Spanish 'flu was a fatal fellow-traveller for many returning servicemen. John William Alston, Mark Robinson, William Brindle, Peter Nolan, Henry Parker, Herbert Marsden and George Chadwick survived the horrors of war but succumbed to the epidemic between December 1919 and April 1920.[2] Susannah eventually created a memorial that allowed families to record their grief and preserve a presence for their sons within the community, regardless of when and how they met death. Susannah's memorial was not just be a record of men who had died in combat. It was a record of combatants who had died.

As servicemen and refugees of all nations made their way home they unwittingly visited suffering on a vulnerable civilian population. The Spanish 'flu spread quickly. In the *Weld Bank School Log Book* the references to influenza subsided only after April 1919 and there were regular visits from the Medical Officer as well as the school nurse.[3] On a worldwide scale it killed more people than the war itself in 1918 and 1919 – perhaps between 50 and 100 million people, five per cent of the world's population. It may even have caused the death of Susannah's half-brother, Angus, who died in March 1919.[4]

The peace was framed for the defeated nations in Paris at meetings which began in January 1919 and some discussions limped on until 1920. Germany was forced to sign the Treaty of Versailles on 28 June 1919, followed later by separate treaties for Austria, Hungary and Bulgaria. It was required to pay reparations of £6.6 billion and stripped of 10 per cent of its land, its colonies and the pride of its army. Germany was humiliated before the eyes of the world.

German civilians continued to be kept at the point of starvation by an Allied blockade until the Treaty of Versailles had been signed. The victorious nations were not safe from hardship, either. Rationing was introduced in Britain in January 1918 and remained until 1920. The *Chorley Guardian* offered advice on the prudent use of food and textiles and the first winter of victory was long and cold in Chorley. Weld Bank School closed on the 19 March because of a severe snow storm.[5]

During the war Susannah Knight had actively organised collections of money, food and clothing to support ex-servicemen and their families after having tried but failed to create a home for the wounded and incapacitated. Now, even though the war was over, the need for benevolence was just as pressing. Across Europe, regardless of nationality, soldiers returned with mangled bodies and shattered limbs. Susannah sustained her care for the wounded, widows and orphans of Chorley.

How could Chorley create a meaningful memorial to mark the carnage that had just taken place? There was an extended discussion about how the fallen should be commemorated by the town. Editions of the *Chorley Guardian* in April and May of 1919 published the laboured deliberations within the Town Council Chamber. Some of the debate echoed the same terms of reference used in the vicious slating of Susannah in 1916 when she had proposed a memorial hospital, though consideration was given to a both commemorative monuments and community facilities as a legacy to future generations. In April, the Tatton family offered Astley Hall and its parkland as an enduring memorial which resolved both strands of thought.[6] A monument within the grounds was to be a focal point for remembrance. Without inscribed names it could be an eternal space for those held dear, forgotten, or yet to fall for their country in wars still to be conceived. The grounds themselves would offer amenities for future generations to celebrate life.

There continued to be criticism of the planned civic memorial in May 1919, though the council was right to weigh the issue carefully, as the Tatton family was shedding a property which it no longer needed. Chorley did not want to burden itself further on behalf of an absent landlord in the lean years after the war, however well-intentioned the offer.[7] The proposal for the gifting of Astley Hall and its park was much opposed by some members of the Council on the grounds of the cost of its upkeep. It took further negotiations for the plan to be agreed and officially announced in May 1919.[8] The Council then went on to discuss and eventually approve the use of Gillibrand Hall's entrance archway as part of the park memorial. Even then, the plan was not approved until January 1922 and the town's civic memorial was only officially dedicated in April of 1924.[9]

The overwhelming harm wrought by the Great War persuaded Susannah to create an extraordinary and unique memorial for the town. Her attempt to raise support for a memorial hospital in 1916 had been a painful failure, but she had perhaps reflected on the more constructive comments made by a 'Terrier Independent' in December 1916 who had written 'I respectfully ask Miss Knight to propose some other scheme for the Pals'.[10] Her appeal in April 1919 appeared at the very same time that the Town Council was fiercely pondering the nature of a fitting memorial.

The articles and letters in the *Chorley Guardian* throughout the spring of 1919 resonate with recent concerns to recognise the sacrifice made by men and women in more recent conflict zones such as Ireland, the Falkland Islands, Iraq and Afghanistan. The *Album* was part of a popular movement for memorialisation in the years following the Armistice, satisfying the spiritual vacuum created by the loss of so many young lives.[11] Chorley was typical, presenting most types of memorial: in churchyards and chancels, in public places, the town hall, schools, recreation areas and pews as inscriptions, sculptures, monuments and paintings. These memorials were expressions of different communities within the town coming to terms with the empty spaces created by war. De Groot's comment that 'The lost were not those who had died, but those condemned to go on living in horror, grief and guilt' chimes with Susannah's concerns in 1916 and the numerous parallel memorial projects in the town.[12] Susannah's plan for a hospital failed but her *Album* gave a place for remembrance by the living.

The indecision displayed by those men who had been so critical of Susannah in October and November 1916 may well have been her prompt. It was not until 1924 that the town had a formal civic memorial but by this time the raw material of Susannah's project had been compiled and presented to the people of Chorley. She had stolen a march on those who had sought to belittle her 'womanly heart'.

Susannah had a very clear idea about the initial format of the *Album*. When she placed her *Chorley Guardian* notice she had already planned to group the men by the Church they attended. This formed the overarching structure of the memorial entries in the final work. A deadline was set for the end of May. Printed forms were available to be filled in and returned by relatives to The Shepherds' Victoria Hall in Chapel Street, to Mrs Helen Mills' draper's shop at 74 Market Street, or Miss Ellen Balshaw's ladies' underclothing shop on Market Street.[13] Susannah had a small network of supporters who helped her to collect and collate information and she engaged the help of her friend Ethel Leach to format the material. It will be recalled that in November 1916 Susannah insisted that any memorial that she undertook was to be the work of women: 'They should not be discouraged. Their work would reach up to Heaven'.[14] This was a work of mission as well as one of reparation.

Susannah continued to give practical support to ex-servicemen and their dependants. On 22 February she organised a party for discharged soldiers. On 27 September 1919 the *Chorley Guardian* advertised a Cotton Ball organised by Miss Knight. On 8 October 1919 the *Chorley Guardian* reported that the proceeds would be used to support the 'Soldiers' Party' planned for December.[15] The National Association of Discharged Sailors and Soldiers organised a 'Grand Smoking Concert' for 17 March 1920 in aid of 'Miss Knight's Presentation'.[16] Susannah's actions matched the precepts of the Sisters of the Sacred Heart of Mary. No sum of money could repair the physical and psychological damage inflicted by the war and she wanted to heal the lesions it had rent through the community. The compilation of the *Album* did not obscure Susannah's sense of responsibility for the living as well as those who had been killed.

Victory still snatched lives and Susannah ensured that the longer-term consequences of the conflict were reflected in the *Album*. At the end of April 1919 Edward Hardman of the 1st/4th The Loyal North Lancashire

Regiment died in a tragic accident. He had survived action at Festubert, Ypres and the Somme but he suffered a shattered arm and two missing fingers in later front line action. His photograph in the *Album* clearly shows three stripes on his sleeve recording the number of times he was wounded in battle.[17] Despite the crippling injuries he sustained he wanted to carry on with the life he led before the war. He was cycling to his cousin's home in Whittle-le-Woods when he lost control of 'the machine'. He careered into a plate glass window on the corner of Commercial Road and Water Street in Chorley.[18] He was rushed to Chorley Hospital but died as a result of his injuries the following day. His family wanted him to be commemorated as the war, ultimately, had wrenched their son away. His name does not appear on any other civic monument and will not be recorded by the Commonwealth War Graves Commission. Susannah agreed with the family that he deserved a place in the *Album*.

A similar example is the case of John Thorpe, who was Susannah's final inclusion in the *Album* (Plates 17 and 18).[19] He had not only been gassed, but went on to suffer horrendous injuries at Ypres in May 1918, losing his right arm. He lingered, paralysed with a shattered spine, only dying in May 1920. A simple, yet beautifully inscribed silk keepsake still keeps his name in the mind of his family.[20] Many of the memorial plaques in Chorley's churches record those who gave their lives between 1914 and 1919 rather than punctuating at the date of 11 November 1918.[21] Susannah recognised the lasting tragedies of war beyond the Armistice and the Treaty of Versailles. Thorpe was certainly not the last man to die as a consequence of the Great War.[22] The next decades saw many men pass on gradually with persistent and debilitating war wounds.[23]

The initial aim of collating the dead in the *Album* was a challenge in itself, but the project expanded to consume the greater part of Susannah's life. She gradually extended the scope of her project. Six entries refer to men who died after the deadline she set for the collation of material. She composed 776 entries for 763 individuals and included 495 photographs of men lost to Chorley. She spent the next 15 years pursuing hundreds of internationally influential figures to underwrite the sacrifice of the men recorded in the volumes. The *Album* obsessed her and exhausted her. She laboured faithfully to record the sacrifices made by the men of Chorley. It is an inheritance that the people of Chorley and generations to come must be made aware of and cherish.

Ever active, Susannah maintained the momentum for remembrance. On 4 December, 1919, the *Chorley Guardian* placed an announcement on behalf of the National Association of Discharged Sailors and Soldiers appealing for ex-servicemen to join a procession on the Sunday 'as a mark of appreciation and respect for the men killed in the Great War'. There was to be a formal unveiling of 'memorials presented to Chorley by Miss Knight'.[24] This was not a reference to the *Album*, which was not ready for viewing though it was much anticipated. The *Chorley Guardian* was aware that the fuller project was near completion. Susannah had, in fact, a concurrent project in hand.

The *Chorley Guardian* of the following week reported that 'impressive ceremonies were held in the town to commemorate gifts by Miss Knight of paintings and photographs of a number of officers, non-commissioned officers, and men from the district, who took part in the war'. The colours of the 4th Battalion of the Loyal North Lancashire Regiment were brought from Preston, with the procession beginning at 9.45am and comprising the colour party of The Loyal North Lancashire Regiment, ex-servicemen, ex-Terriers, The North Lancashire (Chorley) Band, St Lawrence's Church Lads' Brigade, Girl Guides and Brownies.[25]

They proceeded from the barracks on Devonshire Road, down Pall Mall to the Big Lamp, and then along Market Street to St Lawrence's Church where 'Divine Service' was conducted by Archdeacon Allen and the curate W. Rideal. The stirring hymns were led by the band, 'the effect being fine and impressive'. Allen's sermon focused on the heroic dead and his reference to Abraham and Moses enabled him to make the point that 'they had one and all believed that God had something better in store for the world'. In a statement exhorting sacrifice, he said 'it was sometimes better to die than to live'.[26] It was a jarring and almost contrary echo to the words Susannah had used in November 1916 when she had fought and failed to build the cottage hospital. Following the service, a procession made its way up to the Wesleyan Methodist Chapel on Park Road and then returned to the Town Hall for midday.[27]

Susannah made a lasting gift to the people of Chorley. She commissioned four oil paintings based on monochrome photographs, which were intended to be the initial works of art that would form the basis of a public gallery in the town. The paintings were displayed with a large photograph of the Chorley Pals which had been taken in the Drill Hall on 23 February 1915 as they had been about to entrain to Caernarfon. There were also other photographs of individual soldiers from Chorley which were arranged on a platform in the Town Hall and covered by two large Union Flags so that they could be unveiled by the Earl of Crawford and Balcarres, the town's MP from 1895 to 1913.[28]

One canvas was very familiar to Susannah. A painting of Lieutenant Gidlow-Jackson, Major Milton and Lieutenant William Rigby, set within a leafy setting, was based upon the photograph these officers of the East

Lancashire Regiment had given to Susannah at Christmas in 1914.[29] Rigby had died on the Somme on 7 July 1916.[30]

A second painting 'of the most poignant interest' showed five officers of the 1/4th Battalion The Loyal North Lancashire Regiment who had all lost their lives on the battlefield. A tablet with the portrait was inscribed 'Their path of duty was the way to glory'. They were identified as Lieutenant Colonel Ralph Hindle, standing with Captains Cyril Hibbert, John Whitfield, John Lawrence Brindle and Edward Marmaduke Rennard. Again, the paintings were developed using recomposed photographs as a starting point. The original photograph had been captured on the staircase in the Drill Hall. Beneath their names it continued that they '…gave their lives in the Great War that England might live'.[31]

Two further portraits give an insight into how Susannah tried to give shape and meaning to the sacrifice made by those who fought. She presented a painting of Medical Officers whom she referred to as 'Captain Surgeons' Warburton, Macintosh, Rigby, Rainford and Leighton. It bore an extensive inscription:

> 'Lest we forget. This tablet is placed here as a memorial to the doctors and surgeons of the British Empire; also the doctors and surgeons of France, Belgium, Italy and America, in memory of the magnificent services rendered to the sailors and soldiers of the allied nations in the great war of 1914-18. Owing to the self-sacrifice, devotion, heroism and unparalleled skill of the doctors countless numbers of valuable lives were saved to Great Britain and her allies'.[32]

The Earl of Crawford made pointed reference to the importance of the work of doctors, not only in tackling injuries caused by munitions, but also, in tackling the compass of maladies experienced by men in the trenches and behind the lines.[33] It should be remembered that Susannah's brother had recovered from a serious condition in 1916.

The last of the four paintings depicted Captain the Reverend Carroll, a former assistant priest at St Mary's Roman Catholic Church in Chorley. The tablet beneath his image read:

> In remembering the soldiers and officers of the kings of earth, let us not forget the great captains of our heavenly King. They joined the navies and armies of their countries in order to win souls for God and for Heaven. This tablet is placed here as a memorial to the Bishops and Priests of the Roman Catholic Church who served as chaplains to the sailors and soldiers of their countries during the

great war 1914-18. Undaunted by shot and shell they were ever found where the battle raged fiercest and men fell fastest, encouraging, consoling, comforting and administering sacraments to the wounded and dying Catholic soldiers…[34]

It was a noticeably detailed inscription set on a separate bronze plate rather than a tag tacked to the picture frame. The tablet continued by recalling Carroll's wartime gallantry in East Africa and Egypt.[35] He had been an assistant priest in Chorley between May 1914 and November 1915. He was awarded the Military Cross for his bravery and service to his fellow men. He was selected by Susannah as a local example representing the unstinting service that chaplains gave in the war years. Unknown to all at the time, however, was the fact that Carroll had already been acting as a chaplain on active service with the Irish Republican Army since the end of the war. Carroll's inclusion would certainly have troubled the dignitaries at the presentation and Susannah herself if his full story had been know.[36]

The presence of the Earl of Crawford as the guest of honour is significant for several reasons. As a former MP for the town, he still retained an interest in local events, and maintained a residence at Haigh Hall near Wigan. It might have been equally acceptable for Henry Hibbert to have unveiled the paintings, as a more recent MP serving the town between 1913 and 1918 in the years of sacrifice, but Hibbert was appointed to a lesser role, giving the vote of thanks. It is curious, too that the sitting MP, Sir Douglas Hacking, was not listed in the programme of events or given an official role.[37] There must have been a particular reason for the Earl of Crawford's invitation.

It is true that Crawford was a trustee of the National Gallery and he had an interest in the formation of a new gallery in the town with which he had had such a long association. This was not unusual and in his diary it is noted that on his way up to Haigh Hall between 2 and 6 December he opened a gallery at Stoke-on-Trent.[38]

More pertinently, Crawford had a very personal experience of the Great War, having enlisted as a private in April 1915 and having served in the Royal Army Medical Corps with the 12th Casualty Clearing Station. Retaining his anonymity, he was promoted to lance corporal and corporal within a short period. He saw at first hand the effects of the front line slaughter and the incompetence of some staff officers.[39] The programme for the Chorley presentation drew attention to Crawford's army career by, unusually, placing the initials RAMC after his name.[40] In no other source does this form of address seem to have been used for Crawford.[41] It was in this context that Crawford was invited and accepted.

The Earl of Crawford gave Susannah generous praise during the ceremony, saying that the memorials owed much to her untiring zeal, energy and public spirit. He also made a connection between the national wartime struggle and the representative sacrifice made by, particularly, the men who had joined the East Lancashire and The Loyal North Lancashire regiments. He praised the efforts of chaplains in providing spiritual comfort but had most to say about the role of the Royal Army Medical Corps in tackling not only more apparent injuries caused by the weaponry of war, but also combating infection and disease which was rife in the trenches. Crawford formally accepted Susannah's gift on behalf of the town and said that he hoped the pictures would become the nucleus for a gallery in Chorley.[42]

The composition of the party of official guests recorded in the newspaper and in the programme for the event shows a clear connection with the subject matter of each painting. It gives a glimpse of Susannah's motives. Speakers representing the military, doctors and chaplains were invited to respond at the presentation. The military were represented by Lieutenant-Colonel Parker of The Loyal North Lancashire Regiment. Sir James Barr spoke on behalf of doctors, reinforcing the emphasis on the medical theme associated with Crawford. The Rev. H. Day, a senior Roman Catholic chaplain, gave the reply on behalf of the Army Chaplains and was impressively described as having been awarded the 'Order of the White Eagle of Serbia with Swords' whilst engaged on the Eastern Front.[43]

Susannah asked if 'the portraits could be kept [in the town] forever in memory of those brave fellows who had given their lives' saying her actions were 'trifling' in comparison. She hoped that her gift would become a focus for commemoration, an inspiration for reflection and a remembrance to value veterans as they tackled their future.[44]

Whilst reporting the presentation of the paintings, the *Chorley Guardian* noted that Susannah's *Album* was not quite ready for public viewing.[45] The entries for each fallen soldier were printed by the end of 1920 but were still being prepared for exhibition. The beautiful title page printed by W.J. Sandiford of Chorley is dated for that year. His presence in Belgium in August 1914 gave him a particular connection with the project.[46] It is illuminated in gold ink, headed by a colourful array of the flags of the Allied nations, and is a rousing realisation of Miss Knight's original project outlined in the newspaper in April 1919:

Chorley's Glorious Sons
Her Dead Heroes
The Names and Photographs
Of the Sailors and Soldiers
Of Chorley and District
Who made the Supreme Sacrifice
In the Great War 1914-19 [*sic*][47]

This design chosen by Susannah to begin the memorial represents the reverence she accorded her work.

Susannah continued to compile the printed pages. She collated the information she had received and had had it printed by the beginning of July 1921 at the latest. Her friend Ethel Leach was the daughter of the printer. Sandiford made a room available at his works in Byron Street for Susannah and Ethel to paste the photographs into the *Album*.[48] Ellen Balshaw and Helen Mills were involved in collecting material from April 1919 and may also have been involved in sequencing the pages.[49] The *Album* seems to have been one physical volume at this stage.[50]

Susannah kept to her predetermined structure. The names were, indeed, grouped 'with regard to the churches they attended', as she had planned back in April 1919.[51] This is evident in the layout of the first and second volumes as they are seen today and largely holds the main part of the work together. Within each church grouping precedence is given to seniority of rank with a secondary rule to arrange names alphabetically. There is a common format for the biographies which suggests the original form asked for surname, forenames, number, rank, regiment, date of enlistment, biographical detail, date of death and church. Some of the biographies have been gained directly from newspaper reports in the *Chorley Guardian*. Volumes one and two both begin with pages set aside for autographs but these may well have been bound with the main work at a later date.

In what is now the first volume there are clear sections devoted in sequence to the Anglican, Non-conformist and Roman Catholic churches. Each branch of the Christian family is given a prayerful introduction with a beautifully crafted inscription and each church has titular recognition.

The first volume contains 38 sheets with signatures following the illuminated title page. The Anglican entries are prefaced by two passages, the first of which is very familiar, being taken from John 15:13: 'Greater love hath no man than this, that a man lay down his life for his friends'. The second text is taken from the opening of John Stanhope Arkwright's poem Oh Valiant Hearts which later became a hymn to the fallen of the Great

War:

> O valiant hearts who to your glory came
> Through dust of conflict and through battle flame;
> Tranquil you lie, your knightly virtue proved,
> Your memory hallowed in the land you loved.[52]

The parish churches of St Lawrence, St George, and St Peter are the first to be represented in the volume and are placed in the order of their foundation. The record for St Peter's is fragmented with only two pages in the first volume, the remainder continuing in the second volume. The entries for St James' have been deferred to the second, as have the Roman Catholic churches of Sacred Heart and St Joseph.

There is an array of Non-conformism represented in the *Album* which casts an interesting light on the diverse and perhaps divisive religious composition of the town. These churches are introduced by John 11:25-6 and Revelations 14:13.[53] Susannah tried to group each Non-conformist branch carefully but there are inconsistencies. First are the casualties from the Wesleyan Methodist Churches of Park Road, Trinity, Eaves Lane, Adlington, Brinscall, Coppull, Euxton, Withnell Mill, and Withnell Fold. The Congregational churches of Hollinshead Street, St George's Street, Eaves Lane and Adlington are gathered next. Lyons Lane Independent Methodist Church then lists its fallen. The United Methodist Free Church congregations of Railway Street and Brinscall follow. The entries for Cunliffe Street Primitive Methodist Church are intersected by the United Free Methodist Church at Withnell. The Primitive Methodist Churches at Moor Road, Adlington, and Coppull conclude the Non-conformist roll call.

The Spiritualist National Church has two entries which squeeze in awkwardly before the section for the Roman Catholic Church. Spiritualism gained greater attention during the war as it offered a hope of retaining a connection with loved ones lost.[54] The placing of this section between the Non-conformist and Roman Catholic entries highlights a difficulty Susannah needed to negotiate carefully. Spiritualism faced opposition and derision from the conventional Christianity. Susannah gave the two Spiritualist casualties a distinct place in the Album despite the criticism she had responded to in February 1918 which led to her posting that surprisingly strident public notice on the front page of the *Chorley Guardian*.[55]

The Catholic entries in the first volume are preceded by a series of prayers placed around a setting of Psalm 129 which holds the main focus of the page.[56] 'Out of the depths I have cried to Thee, O Lord; Lord, hear my voice'. Here Susannah made her strongest appeal to God seeking spiritual peace for a broken community. The Roman Catholic churches of St Gregory and St Mary's of Chorley head the sequence, owing to the fact that they were the churches that she had closest association with and were also placed in the order of their foundation.[57]

However, an analysis of the sequencing of the pages reveals a mystery. The title page of the *Album* and the illuminated page introducing the Catholic casualties are almost identical, bar the insertion of the words 'Catholic' and 'RIP'.[58] It seems likely Susannah had two deliberate and different arrangements of the pages which she then tailored to match more than one audience in 1921.

The first volume ends carelessly. There is the remarkable inclusion of the French officer, Paul de Méhérenc de St Pierre. Mark Robinson is recorded in the *Album* in the first of his two entries.[59] Herbert Stables and James Wilson get their names and addresses recorded but no more – neither rank, number not regiment.[60] The final page from St Mary's Church Chorley has had an entry cut out leaving Peter McGuinness a lonely rearguard sentinel.[61]

The second volume begins with 10 pages of signatures. Dramatically, the first page features a photograph, signature and message from Pope Pius XI. The arrangement of the names and photographs of the men in volume two starts in a logical manner but a number of anomalies emerge as the sequence progresses, with the arrangement of subsequent pages seeming quite disorganised.

The Roman Catholic churches of the Sacred Heart and St Joseph's, Chorley, appear to represent a simple continuation from the first volume. The sequence is interrupted by five pages of signatures and a page with pasted memorabilia. Then follow a series of very short sections for outlying churches around Chorley, namely St Oswald's, St Joseph's Withnell, and St Chad's. The logic of the arrangement breaks down with the insertion of the remaining entries from the Anglican churches of St Peter and St James with a section for 'Additional Church of England'. Twelve further Church of England parishes of outlying districts are represented, mustering very few entries between them.

The internal composition of the first two volumes as they are now presented aimed to list Anglican, Non-conformist and Catholic men separately. Most of the men are given short biographies and nearly two-thirds are pictured with photographs submitted by their families. Some biographies are sparse, whilst some contain heart-wrenching detail. There are poignant letters from officers bearing bad news as well as the almost prescient words from the casualties themselves.

There is a mix of material gathered from families and information inserted by Susannah herself. The casualties in the 'Additional' sections often lack detail and tend to come from outlying areas such as Adlington. Some of the entries give little more than a name suggesting that Susannah acted on her own initiative by including hearsay.

There are two problematic entries that Susannah should have been able to resolve easily. For 'Brown' of St Peter's Church, only the surname is recorded. The entry for George Evans bears only a name and a pencilled note by Susannah Knight suggesting he attended St George's Church.[62] These pencil notes become more visible on close inspection of the pages as evidence of Susannah Knight revisiting and qualifying her work, yet not quite bringing it to a conclusion. Despite her careful annotation there are spelling mistakes at significant points which point towards the unsure hand of an inexperienced compositor.

It is understandable that Susannah had difficulty deciding how to include the smaller numbers of casualties who had lived or worked outside the boundaries of Chorley. The *Album* is not a strictly geographical record and there are men who perhaps more properly belong to French, Canadian or Australian memorials. Some men had been born in Chorley but had moved elsewhere or emigrated, retaining some familial footprint in Chorley. Some, like Leon Moreau and Count Paul de Méhérenc de St Pierre, were men who were known to Susannah personally.[63] All the individuals in the *Album* were included because they were valued and missed by someone in the community of Chorley.

There is no guarantee that the present sequence of pages is exactly as Susannah envisaged. There was at least one revision of the *Album* and there are traces of oversights in editing, careless re-ordering and inconsistencies that do not seem to match her obsession for detail. It has already been noted that there are irregularities in the ordering of Catholic churches that were dedicated to St Mary in Chorley, Euxton and Leyland and that an unfamiliar hand may have tried to make sense of Susannah's cataloguing. St Peter's Church is incongruously split across two volumes, while the entries for Cunliffe Street Primitive Methodist Church are disrupted by Withnell United Free Methodist Church.

Thirteen individuals appear more than once. This is sometimes because they moved between different regiments, sometimes because they had an affiliation with more than one church, and sometimes simply out of carelessness. Some Non-conformists appear in the listings of their local parish church as well as with their own congregation and this might reflect a tension between the place of church and chapel in society. Thomas Warburton is recorded with St Lawrence's and St Peter's Churches, pictured first as a cadet and then when he re-enlisted in 1918 (Plates 14, 15 and 16). One man was born out of wedlock and is listed under his mother's maiden and married names.[64]

The fact that the alphabetical structure used within church groupings is not sustained suggests at least two periods when pages were printed, with some distortions also having taken place at the printing rather than binding stage of the compilation. Multiple spelling mistakes on the entries throughout and especially for both of the French casualties are indeed a surprising oversight on the part of the printer and Susannah herself. It seems that the compositor was inexperienced or careless. If Susannah was a diligent proof-reader, she may not have had the means to have the pages corrected.

The pencil notes throughout the *Album* reveal much about Susannah's editing process. There is even tantalising evidence of a penciled dedication on the reverse of the reused sheet in the third volume: 'Dedicated to [the name has been removed] in memory of all the Boys who fought in the Great War 1914-1918. By S.M.C. Knight Compiler'. [*sic*][65] Susannah consigned the page for scrap only for it to be reused in 1924 when she met members of the American Bar Association. Significantly, it is the only place in the *Album* where Susannah can be seen to claim any degree of authorship and indeed by 1949 it was widely believed that it had been compiled anonymously.[66]

Susannah remained modest about her achievements throughout her life, only anxious that a remembrance of the men themselves should be kept. The books were subjected to a significant reorganisation in the late 1940s, re-structured and re-bound to be presented as they currently appear.

6 UNDERWRITING THE LOSSES 1921

THE *Chorley Memorial Album* is more than a record of the town's war dead, though this is what may have been initially intended. It became important for Susannah to include the autographs of distinguished figures of her age in the *Album* and she wrote in a later letter to Eleanor Roosevelt that she wanted to strengthen the 'allied friendships' that had been forged during the Great War.[1] The artwork on the *Album's* title page brings together the flags of the nations that stood together against the Central Powers and she was able to include signatures from every one of these allies.[2] The *Album* eventually became a means to draw the attention of people of influence to the sacrifice that had been paid by the people of Chorley. It also became an attempt to secure the peace that had come with victory.

The *Album* contains over 2000 signatures. They tend to be inscribed by politically powerful men, those with spiritual authority, those who held military command, those who tended the injured, and those who worked to rebuild a world broken by the war. Despite Susannah's complicated relationship with local politicians, she had a deferential respect for people with genuine power and influence. The short entries for each of the men who had served and died for their country are moving and worthy of lasting remembrance. It is Susannah's astonishing endeavour in collecting numerous signatures of world leaders which make the *Album* both compelling and unique.

In the first two volumes, Susannah actively sought out signnatures from distinct categories of people matching the groups represented in the four portraits which she presented to the town in December 1920. The wider themes that these portraits represented formed the basic structure to which all diversions are connected. There are those responsible for the victory, doctors who tended the injured and clergy who nourished spiritual needs. The selection of signatures acts as a guide to the purpose of Susannah's travels and can be used to understand the underlying meaning of the memorial and what Susannah wanted it to signify to the community of Chorley.

In 1919 and 1920 the biographical entries had been compiled through the labour of women. In the *Album* itself, women are to be found only occasionally. Female doctors were allocated their own page, Nancy Astor and Margaret Wintringham were sought out as the first female Conservative and Liberal Party MPs.[3] Women as lawyers and members of the US Congress were highlighted in pencil. By the 1930s, women were also represented in the *Album* as academics and cultural leaders. Individual pages were given over to individual women to share their literary work. The representation of women amongst the signatures reflects the changing expectations and opportunities of the period as well as Susannah's own process of selection.[4]

The extension of the *Album* was an exceptionally ambitious undertaking. Dedicated pages were printed for the King and Queen of Great Britain, the President of France, the King and Queen of Italy, the King and Queen of the Belgians, Pope Benedict XV and the President of the United States.[5] The pages for these heads of state are colourfully illustrated with their national flags. They were probably produced at the same time as the title pages and biographies of the casualties before the end of 1920. Susannah had taken a calculated risk in preparing the pages beforehand. Benedict XV viewed the *Album* in August 1921 but, unfortunately, he did not give his signature.[6] The fact that she was to acquire neither the signatures of the King and Queen of Great Britain, nor the Queen of Italy reinforces the conclusion that this element of Susannah's project was premeditated and only partially achieved.[7]

The earliest dated signature in the *Album* is that of Field Marshal Douglas Haig on Tuesday, 5 July 1921.[8] He referred to himself as 'Haig of Bemersyde' and though he had experimented with this signature during the war, the confidence of his hand betrays a real pride in the fact that his ancestral home had been purchased through public subscription and gifted a fortnight earlier.[9] On 5 July Haig and his wife attended a banquet at Buckingham Palace held in honour of the King and Queen of the Belgians who were on a state visit which was widely promoted beforehand.[10] This event was one of a series demonstrating Belgium's gratitude for the support given to their refugees in the war years.[11] This would have caught the attention of Susannah because of the small role she had taken in this relief, and the interest she had in supporting wounded Belgian soldiers whilst they were recovering in Chorley Hospital.

One surprising factor is the date of Haig's signature. On 5 July 1921, Susannah still had another day to work at school before the summer holiday and there is no evidence in the *Weld Bank School Log Book* that she was absent. It seems unlikely Susannah received Haig's autograph personally and it us a curious date to resolve. The implication must be that Susannah had the help of at least one other individual to acquire some of the autographs. Though it might be assumed that Susannah obtained the signatures of King Albert and Queen Elisabeth of Belgium on this same occasion, it is more likely that she had a more direct opportunity in August 1921.

Haig's devotion to his men during the war and his consuming concern for their welfare in the peace offers an explanation for Susannah seeking his assent to the *Album* from the very beginning. Haig was instrumental in setting up the British Legion, biding his time while various factions of ex-servicemen's welfare groups moved towards collaboration and cooperation. Susannah was closely involved with the local branch of the National Association of Discharged Sailors and Soldiers.[12] It is surprising that none of the leading figures of the Legion's early years appear within the list of autographs.[13] Susannah's interest in the welfare of the wounded, widows and orphans was sustained into the 1930s and she formed strong attachment to the Legion's branch in Chorley.[14] Despite later criticism and sustained antipathy from Lloyd George, Haig was held in great esteem by the British public.

Field Marshals Henry Wilson and Thomas Albert Blamey added their names to the page that Haig began with 34 other names ranged around them.[15] Byng of Vimy, Commander of the Canadian forces, appears on the previous page and has the distinction of appearing a second time on a later page.[16] There are several other military personnel on this page including Captain Robert Gee, VC, and two Lieutenant Colonels. There are also a number of politicians: Frederick Guest, Secretary of State for Air; Samuel Hoare, the Conservative MP with an earlier career in espionage who became Foreign Secretary in the 1930s and Sir Henry Craik, a member of the Privy Council. There is no firm evidence of the timescale during which these signatures were gathered, though some areas of the page show a similarity in the tone and thickness of ink. Another significant signature on this page is that of Philip Sassoon, Haig's Private Secretary from 1915-18. His cousin, Siegfried is one of the most celebrated poets of the Great War. When Sassoon placed his signature in the *Album* he was probably Parliamentary Private Secretary to Haig's nemesis, Lloyd George. Chorley's

Member of Parliament, Sir Douglas Hacking, is squeezed vertically amongst earlier contributors.[17]

Although the autograph of Edward, Prince of Wales, holds pride of place at the head of the very first page of signatures in the first volume and is its centerpiece, Susannah failed to obtain the signatures of the King and Queen and this was her only British royal endorsement.[18] Though this was not the first of her signatures it was certainly a coup.

The Prince of Wales made an official visit to Chorley and Euxton on Friday 8 July 1921. He had spent the whole week in Lancashire and ended his progress by travelling from Preston towards Wigan via Leyland, Euxton, Chorley and Adlington. He had expressed a strong interest in engaging with people who had been affected by the war during these visits and he opened the War Memorial Club in Euxton. Chorley made arrangements for ex-servicemen to assemble in the Town Hall Square and then march from the Drill Hall on Devonshire Road.[19]

The schedule gave the Prince 20 minutes within the town boundaries. Edward made his way through Chorley to the Coronation Pleasure Ground on Devonshire Road where his father had opened the park in 1913.[20] In the previous week's edition the *Chorley Guardian* had estimated that 5,000 children were to be present.[21] The pupils of Weld Bank School marched there as a body at 3.15pm and there were 300 ex-servicemen present. The children and veterans were given the best positions in front of the podium.[22]

There were 25 people in the official greeting party, largely made up of town council dignitaries with representatives of the Anglican, Catholic and Non-conformist churches. Sir Douglas Hacking was there as MP, accompanied by his predecessor, Sir Henry Hibbert. Dr James Harris and Dr John Rigby were included and were followed by Miss Ethel Whittle, the honorary secretary of the Chorley Branch of the Red Cross Society. Susannah was the last of the favoured guests presented to the Prince of Wales. The *Chorley Guardian* credited her as 'a prominent worker for the soldiers during the war'.[23]

The Prince was keen to move on from the formalities and meet some of the people of Chorley and spent the next 10 minutes of the event amongst the crowd. As the *Chorley Guardian* reported:

> [He] went at once to the disabled soldiers who were seated just below the stand to the right. There were fifteen or sixteen men here, some of whom had lost limbs, and the Prince made kindly

enquiries of every one of them, as to how and where they had obtained their wounds, what was the nature of them and in most cases whether they were receiving their pensions all right.[24]

One of those disabled soldiers was Michael Dolan, a local character who was now in a wheelchair. Prince Edward met and shook hands with the father of James Miller, who had won a VC and had been killed in action. Mr Miller had lost two other sons in the war. The Prince talked to children who had lost their fathers and who wore the medals their fathers had won. One boy was Albert Clarkson, who had been born eight days after his father was killed at Le Touquet.[25] Albert stood with his father's two South African medals and the Mons Star. Edward was a little gauche in his conversation and the *Chorley Guardian* wrote: 'The Prince told him he was a 'bonny little chap' and that it was a pity his father had died'. Edward also met Nurse Holmes, a regular visitor to Weld Bank School, who stood with the disabled soldiers and children. These were the very people at the heart of Susannah's own faithful calling to educate and to give comfort.

As the Prince stepped towards his car, Mr Jackman presented 'the Mayor's autograph book' to be signed and this he did 'on a page which also contained the name of his father. It was difficult, however, to write it while standing, but 'Edward P' was entered firmly'. This was certainly an early format of Susannah's *Album*. The phrasing of the signature in the *Album* is as described in the newspaper. It has been written unsteadily and he had to extend the line beneath the 'P' in a separate action, rather than in his more accustomed single flourish (Plate 5). This unsteadiness may, of course, lend some credibility to the local story that dates back to the time, that Edward had become a little inebriated already when he visited the War Memorial Club in Euxton earlier that afternoon.[26] The journalist's reference to the name of the Prince's father being on the previous page is a truth, though the King never signed the pre-printed page.[27]

With Hacking present as a friendly supporter, the Catholic Mayor, and Susannah's parish priest, Father Crank as the Mayor's Chaplain, Susannah had been given a golden opportunity to gain recognition for the sacrifice made by Chorley. The appropriately named Major Blow called for 'three cheers' and the Prince departed standing and waving from his motor vehicle. A girl in the procession was noted to say 'let's hurry up and have another look, he's a grand fellow'.[28]

Susannah need to do some hurrying too. She had planned an ambitious journey to Europe and had probably packed her bags to depart as soon as the summer term ended on the previous day. She did not to go directly to the channel ports. There was a purpose in her continental journey but she had reason to tarry and she went to London with the intention of obtaining a number of very significant signatures.

Below Prince Edward's signature is that of David Lloyd George. The context of the occasion when the signature of the Prince was obtained and its placing both suggest that his was the first to grace this page. Indeed, it would have been an embarrassing moment for the Mayor of Chorley to ask the Prince to squeeze his signature on a page if it had already been marked. Interestingly, considering his Liberal opposition to Lloyd George's coalition in the latter part of the war, the signature of a former premier, Herbert Asquith 1908-1916, steers a jaunty angle to Lloyd George's left. Stanley Baldwin and Winston Churchill are positioned to Lloyd George's right, neatly reflecting the hue of their politics. There are 40 signatures altogether, with the cabinet and wider ministerial roles represented. Susannah must have looked over these signatures many times with disbelief as they comprise a virtual catalogue of Britain's leading politicians in the 1920s. She even annotated the signature of John Henry Whitley, the Speaker of the House of Commons, to remind herself of his office. A more familiar figure to Susannah amongst the names is the Earl of Crawford; Chorley's former MP and the presenter of Susannah's commissioned portraits in 1920 (Plate 5).[29]

The individuals on this page were the key members of Lloyd George's government of 1918-22. It was the government that had overseen the conclusion of the Great War and its settlement through the Paris Peace Conference. They were men who had been chosen, for the first time in Britain, by an electorate of both men and women. Political rivals and allies in the post-war government are set side-by-side. This page offers a fascinating array of signatures for the government that controlled an empire that was at its greatest in terms of power and scale.[30]

The earliest possible occasion for these dignatures to have been gathered was the day of Lloyd George's cabinet reshuffle on 2 April 1921. The Earl of Crawford had entered the cabinet on this date as Commissioner of Works and it is in this context that his signature is found just below Birkenhead's, just left of centre. The Prince's signature must date the siginatures after 8 July. Most of the men that signed this page were all in London within a short time frame from this date. The resignation of Christopher Addison as Minster of Health on 14 July 1921 offers the terminal point for the majority of signatures on this page.[31] Susannah needed to have gained Addison's signature by 14 July for the connections on the page to make sense. Using the *Weld Bank School Log Book* and other dated signatures in the *Album* it is probable that Susannah acquired the signatures between 9 and 18 July.[32] It seems likely that the signatures of

Lloyd George, Asquith, Byng of Vimy, Emmott, Sutherland and Addison were made at the same time, as their inks match and they are laid out at a similar angle.[33] To collect all or most of the names on this page within nine days might seem improbable, but Susannah was clearly an exceptional woman and most of the signatures on this first page do seem to have been made in the same, narrow period.

It is possible that Susannah gained access to these individuals by her own efforts. Given her previous success in gaining the Earl of Crawford's attention when she wanted the portraits presented in December 1920, it seems more likely that Crawford approached the cabinet on Susannah's behalf. He had been a senior Member of Parliament and his elevation to the upper house had not prevented him from sustaining his active public life. As the only member of the cabinet to have served in the front line in the Great War, the Earl was the obvious person to approach for support.

Some parts of this page have certainly been added at a later stage. John Simon, whose signature is edged into the bottom and well below that of Prince Edward, was re-elected as an MP in November 1922. He had been absent from the House since he lost his parliamentary seat in 1918 but to Susannah the inclusion of his signature was important in 1922 when he became deputy leader of the Liberal Party. It is likely that Susannah made small additions to this page over time and there are faintly pencilled lined sections indicating where later signatures could be added.[34]

Another signature that has been added at a later date to this first page casts light on the way in which some of the signatures may have been obtained. There is only one dated signature, level with and to the right of Prince Edward's. It belongs to Sir Laming Worthington-Evans and is for 24 February 1922, outside the time frame in which the other autographs were placed. The date itself is significant as he had taken office as Secretary of War only nine days previously. As in the case of Haig's signature, it was acquired during term-time and there is no record of Susannah being absent from Weld Bank School. The only event of note in the *Weld Bank School Log Book* is that school was closed on the 28 February, Shrove Tuesday, on the occasion of Princess Mary's Wedding.[35] Susannah is unlikely to have received Worthing-Evans' autograph personally. However, there is a coincidence which might well offer a solution. Sir Laming Worthington-Evans' Parliamentary Private Secretary was Sir Douglas Hacking, the MP for Chorley in this period. Moreover, Hacking had been an officer in the East Lancashire Regiment and had served two years in France with the regiment during the war. He had a motive for collaborating with Susannah to honour the men who had served under him.[36]

The strength of Hacking's acquaintance with Susannah cannot be ascertained but he was well aware of her loyal service to the Pals and his support of Susannah's charitable work later in 1921 suggests that there was a certain coordination of their efforts.[37] Though Hacking was a junior member of the minister's staff it seems entirely reasonable to suggest that he may have had a hand in gaining his superior's signature. He did not have the degree of influence necessary to have acted on Susannah's behalf in collecting the signatures on the rest of the page.[38]

Further conclusions can be drawn from the dating and distribution of signatures in the *Album*. The signatures have sometimes been acquired cumulatively in connection with a particular theme, but more often one date or event defines a single page. Almost all the signatures are gathered within a context that marks their association. Some pages can be connected by chronology but are displaced across the volumes and this gives warning that careful analysis is necessary. It can never be assumed that Susannah or later compliers retained the context or chronology of every page.

Susannah's mission in London had to have been concluded by 17 July at the very latest. The *Album*, probably as a set of loose sheets, was with her when she left for Rome. Susannah's greater mission had begun.

7 THE EUROPEAN ADVENTURE 1921

S USANNAH had a great affection for Europe. The Sisters of the
Sacred Heart of Mary in Bootle from Béziers had made her an eager
linguist. Both Susannah and Jack inherited an instinct for travel,
something which had driven Jack throughout his maritime career. Susannah
pored over the adventurous tales narrated in his letters. She had already
travelled to Ireland and the USA, and had been caught in France on her
return from Switzerland in August of 1914.[1] It was time for her to pursue
the first of her greater adventures.

It is probable that she made a voyage from Southampton to St Malo by
boat train. Susannah had previously embarked from Southampton when
she went to the United States in 1913 but there was more to her choice of
route into France than familiarity. An illegible signature of a Roman
Catholic priest connects Susannah to St Malo in the second volume.[2] There
are further Breton connections which have been touched upon already.
Susannah had been governess to Paul de Méhérenc de St Pierre in Paris in
1895 before the family moved to their chateau at Bois de Salle, close to
Lanvallon in northern Brittany. The chateau is not too distant from St Malo
and a branch of the family still resides there today. De Méhérenc was the
earliest casualty to be recorded in the *Album* in 1914 (Plates 6, 7, 8 and 9).
The photograph in the *Album* was a relatively recent one of him in his
military uniform.[3] Susannah had good reason to include the family in her
visit, to pay her respects personally.

It was not a difficult matter for Susannah to travel to Rennes and make her
first extensive collection of French signatures. On the afternoon of 17 July
she was in the city when Marshal Foch, the Supreme Commander of the
Allied forces on the Western Front in the last year of the Great War, just

happened to arrive for an official visit. A formal photograph captured the welcome of the general outside the railway station with seven other dignitaries (Plate 12). Somehow, Susannah was aware of Foch's itinerary. Careful observation reveals her in the far right of the picture, white hat, firm eyebrows and a mouth held straight with determination (Plate 13).[4]

Foch was there partly to celebrate the sixth centenary of Bertrand De Guesclin, a Breton hero in the Hundred Years War. He was also there to give his support to the town as it recovered from the Great War. He had a strong connection with Rennes as it had been his first posting as a captain of the 10th Regiment of Artillery in 1878. He spent seven years based in the city and clearly held it in fond regard. He is unlikely to have shared the opinion of one of his biographers who described Rennes as 'not a particularly interesting city …'.[5] He was revisiting an old haunt to show his affinity with the ex-servicemen of the city and the families of the fallen, perhaps he was reminded that he had not always served at the very highest level of command. Rennes was, as he recalled in a speech later on his visit, where his military career began.

Foch walked to the Hotel de Ville from the railway station, flanked by veterans from the Franco-Prussian war of 1870, medal winners and the wounded of the *Hospitaliers Sauveteurs Bretons*. These men suffered in the same way as those men whom Susannah held so dear in Chorley. The Marshal was among men who shared with him an understanding of what war meant. By 5pm he had reached the Hotel de Ville, where he stepped from the office onto the balcony to a long acclamation of cheering.[6]

On the morning of 18 July, Foch was engaged in a number of functions. At 9.45am he was met on the threshold of the church of Saint-Germain by Bishop Charost and Canon Jordan. The *L'Ouest-Éclair* describes it as a poignant scene which brought tears to even the most indifferent, for 'one was a prelate who was unshakeable for four long years under the threat of a conqueror, the other was a soldier who had delivered him from this nightmare'.[7] He again met ex-servicemen who had been injured in the war and gave his attention to war widows. He spent time in the Eastern Cemetery, where he paused amongst the ranks of wooden crosses that marked Rennes' war dead.[8] He also visited the city's war memorial, at which another surviving formal photograph was taken.[9] There are three unidentified British officers alongside Foch and Janvier and the legacy of war was resonant throughout his visit.

Foch's public duties ended with a banquet held at the Cadet School. Susannah's audacity is quite apparent, in that she somehow managed to get the *Album* into the hall, though it is not clear if she was present herself.

Foch's dated flourish was placed at the top of a new page (Plate 11).[10] On the following day *L' Ouest Éclair* stated that 'The Marshal then affixed his vigorous signature in its place in a list of names, beside the other famous people'.[11] As a Commander of the Allied Armies, but also as a Roman Catholic in a position to direct both war and peace, Foch was an important figure to include in the *Album*. Four other men gave their signatures, three of whom had already been photographed with Foch on his arrival at Rennes railway station. These were Jean Janvier, the Mayor of Rennes, M Maupoil, Préfet of the Ille et Vilaine region, and General Passaga of the 10th Army Corps.[12] It is likely that the Archbishop of Rennes, Auguste Dubourg was at the banquet when he signed his name, though the newspaper makes a point of cutting short the list of guests to emphasise how many were invited.[13]

On the same page of signatures, just below that of Dubourg, there is evidence of an intriguing acquaintance with someone named Hauchert. He wrote in French 'In memory of our friends seriously injured English Camp Bautzen 1918'. While none of the casualties recorded in Chorley's *Album* were at the prisoner of war camp in Bautzen, Germany, it appears that Susannah established a connection.[14]

By 22 July, Susannah was in Reims, over 270 miles away from Rennes. De Méhérenc had completed his schooling in Reims and his name is recorded on a memorial in St Joseph's School in the city. He had also been killed in this area, close to the Marne, in September 1914. Once she arrived, she searched out the civic and spiritual leaders, following the same pattern as she had in Rennes.

On that day, Susannah met the former mayor, Jean Baptiste Langlet and his wife. Langlet had a gripping wartime story to share with Susannah. As mayor or Reims he had been taken hostage by the Germans whilst they occupied the city in Great War. He had been a surgeon and the director of the School of Medicine, but also a deputy for the Marne region. At the time that Susannah met Jean Baptiste he was the director of the Museum of Fine Arts and had been awarded the Légion d'honneur.[15] As a political leader, a doctor and a victim of war, he combined many of the themes which Susannah looked for when seeking individuals to underwrite the sacrifices recorded in the *Album*. Of course, she met religious figures too. Ernest Neveaux was the auxiliary bishop of Reims with the titular see of Arsinoe.[16] Unsurprisingly, Susannah also met the Archbishop of Reims, Cardinal Lucon, who offered a whole page of the *Album* to express his thoughts on 24 July. He wrote:

England and France became allies to defend grand principles of

Rights, Humanity and loyalty to treaties which form the basis of protection and peace for all peoples: they will remain united to secure for the world, with the help of God, the benefits of peace in justice. Gratitude and honour to the valiant soldiers in both nations' Army and Navy who spilled their blood on the battlefields for the cause of civilization![17]

Susannah also secured the autograph of the French President, Alexandre Millerand at an early stage of this European journey.[18] He had served as Minister of War for 14 months of the war. It is impossible to be sure when she gained his signature as it is undated, but if she had a direct hand in its acquisition then it was after 18 July when Susannah was in Rennes but before the end of the month.[19] Susannah was in Reims by 22 July and she remained there until at least 24 July. Millerand visited Le Havre on 25 June as he began a tour of the Lower Seine region, well out of the way of Susannah. On 26 and 27 July he visited Rouen and Dieppe but by this time Susannah was already deep in the South of France. Somehow Susannah, if she did indeed meet Millerand directly, had managed to engineer a meeting with a pre-printed page in hand between 18 July and 22 July when he was in Paris. If the signature was gained through a proxy, the trail is cold. Whether by design, determination or the most incredible hand of fortune, she had brought the *Album* to the attention of the President of France.[20]

On 26 July Susannah was in Béziers in the south of France. Her connection to this city has already been established. It was the town in which Leon Moreau had lived before he joined the 11th/139 Regiment d'Infanterie. She had probably continued a correspondence with the Moreau family over a number of years. Extracts of letters from the Moreau family appeared on two occasions in St Mary's *The Messenger* in 1916[21]. It seems likely that she had been to Béziers on a previous occasion, even on her European visit in the summer of 1914. Susannah recorded Moreau's death in the *Album* after he laid down his life for France.[22] Now Susannah returned to Béziers to carry her condolences. She must have met members of the Moreau family. It is most likely that she visited Sacré Coeur and recalled the Sisters of the Sacred Heart of Mary who had educated her.

Just as she had done in Rennes and Reims, she met the foremost civic and religious leaders of Béziers. She met the city's mayor and Constant Blaquière, who was the Archpriest as well as being a local historian, author and poet.[23] Blaquière had published a range of historical works on Catholic subjects, most recently on the Brothers of Charity of Béziers (Plate 11). More significantly, perhaps, he had just published a book called *Sur le seuil d'un monde nouveau* – [*On the Threshold of New World*].[24] The recovery and rehabilitation of the world in the years after the Great War became an emerging theme of Susannah's quest for autographs. She also visited the regional hub of Montpellier and gained the signature of Joseph Raffit, the Cardinal's secretary.[25] Béziers was her last stopping point before she made her way along the south coast of France towards Italy, no doubt enjoying expansive views of the Mediterranean Sea as she travelled by train through the Languedoc to Rome. Her pilgrimage was not complete.

By the beginning of August, Susannah had arrived in Rome. Her head teacher at Weld Bank noted the fact that she had written to the school: 'Miss Knight absent all week from school. Received letter written in Rome on 1st August on Aug 8th'. The *Weld Bank School Log Book* betrays an inconsistency in Susannah's itinerary, for Miss Lilly continues the entry: '… she says she will start on homeward journey the following day. She was suffering from exhaustion owing for excessive heat'. [*sic*][26]

Circumstances changed, however, for Susannah was certainly not on her way home the next day. Perhaps she had been genuinely tired but there was an unforeseen delay. She was being a little dishonest in her letter to the head teacher. She was still in the eternal city nine days later, and she did not seem to be fatigued.

Susannah took short-term residence at the Hôtel Pension Terminus on the Piazza Esedra. This impressive semi-circular range of buildings still exists and has not lost its splendor. It now faces onto the renamed Piazza della Republica. As its name suggests, the hotel was adjacent to the railway station, meaning Susannah was well-placed to catch a train when she finally decided to make her way home. It was to this address that the Secretary of State to the Vatican, Cardinal Gasparri, sent a letter dated Wednesday 10 August, written in response to a request by Susannah.[27]

The main focus of her journey had been to present the *Album* to Pope Benedict XV. In terms of her faith, this was a means to heal the physical and emotional wounds wrought upon the community of Chorley. She had planned her journey meticulously and had only to extend her itinerary as a consequence of circumstance. Susannah may well have been exhausted and had need of time to recuperate, but the redirection of her plans overnight on 1 August argues against this. The *Album* – and a single volume is referred to – was retained at the Vatican for a longer period than she had expected. There was little she could do if her precious pages were clasped behind the doors of the holy enclave. Her desire for a blessing for the *Album*, and the slowness of the Papal bureaucracy left Susannah with little option but to delay her homeward journey.[28]

It remains unclear if Susannah had courted any particular connections at the

Vatican. One weak line of enquiry has been that the son of Susannah's half-sister Mary, Angus 'Bubbles' Dickinson, was in close contact with the family of Mary de Navarro and her husband, the Papal Privy Chamberlain, Antonio Fernando de Navarro. A sensitive and endearing reply to a letter of condolence in 1932 from the then ten-year-old 'Bubbles' suggests more than an appreciative acknowledgement but his tenuous line of enquiry linking Susannah's nephew indeed seems strange and any evidence of a connection between the families has now been lost, if indeed it ever existed.[29]

Another thread is that Susannah Knight's half-sister Lizzie (Sister Mary Clement), who was a Sister in the Society of the Holy Child Jesus, may have provided the necessary influence. A more conservative argument might be that a letter of introduction was given by Susannah's Parish Priest, Father Crank. It may, of course, have been a matter of Susannah's own persistence. It can be inferred from the letter that the Pope had been made aware of Susannah's activities during the war on behalf of the servicemen of Chorley. His own wartime diplomatic and humanitarian activities were very much in tune with Susannah's interests. It cannot however, be determined whether this introduction was supplied by Susannah herself or rather through one of these intermediaries.

We do not know the contents of Susannah's letter of request. Gasparri's response on 10 August makes it clear that Susannah did not meet Benedict XV in person. The reply was in Italian, which supports an assumption that Susannah had made the initial request in the language and read it well:

> The Holy Father has received the volume containing the photos of the Catholic soldiers and sailors of the town of Chorley (Lancashire) who died in the war and has noted with pleasure the considerate expression of Christian Faith and veneration for the Vicar of Jesus Christ which has moved you to offer to him that devout and pious knowledge.
>
> In fact you, who feel such deep gratitude to the Father of the Faithful for always having strived in every way at His disposal for His sons during the whole course of the terrible war and who at the same time harbour such deep pity for the wounded, wanted to associate the two considerate feelings and to testify to them with this volume before the throne of the August Pontiff.
>
> I am pleased therefore to inform you of the thanks of the Holy Father for this evidence of devotion and at the same time to share with you the Apostolic Blessing which His Holiness has been

pleased to bestow on you in anticipation of the greater thanks of heaven.[30]

The context of the reply suggests that she had sent the *Album* as a single volume with a request for the book to be viewed by the Pope. The volume was subsequently blessed and Susannah was granted an Apostolic Blessing. She must have been heartened by the reply, as she made her arrangements to return home.

The single volume that was presented to the Pope was the product of a little chicanery. Susannah was either deceiving the Pope or she was not truly representing the people of Chorley as Benedict XV believed that he was being given a collection of the Catholic casualties of the town, an impression which can only have been given by Susannah herself. This was either by word of mouth through a papal representative or by a written petition which accompanied what the Pope saw. The persuasive indicator in this ruse is that curious twin to the title page of the first volume. The illuminated page that precedes the entries for St Gregory's Roman Catholic Church may well have been the title to the compilation of biographies Benedict XV viewed in the summer of 1921.[31] Susannah was able to select what was made public at any one time when she carried the *Album* to Europe. She may well have taken all the material she had gathered but there is some suggestion that she deliberately filtered the pages to create the 'Catholic' volume. The pages with biographies and photographs of the men were in a loosely bound format which allowed her the flexibility to re-order the entries. Blank pages destined to be used for the autographs were kept as separate sheets, as a pencil note in the third volume notes that: 'This page fell in the mud as I was getting off a bus in Rome'.[32] In effect, Susannah performed a sleight of hand to ensure the sacrifice of the Catholic men of Chorley received a papal blessing.

Susannah's concealed mission was dislocated, however. She had prepared a pre-printed page with Pope Benedict XV's name and title printed beforehand and it must have been her intention to gain a papal signature.[33] She was thwarted. Separated from the *Album* in Rome, she could not ensure that the page was given directly to the Pope. He did not sign. At a later stage she added the half-comic epitaph 'Dead' in light pencil where his name should have been placed. Benedict XV passed on to the care of St Peter on 22 January 1922 and Susannah's first European pilgrimage with the *Album* was a mission only partially complete.

The schedule of travel and arranging meetings with 'the great and the good' had been punishing. The exhaustion, even if exaggerated in her letter of 1 August, must have been genuine by the time she returned home. The combination of travel, tension and the suspense and the heat of the Mediterranean climate as she waited in Rome for the return of the *Album* must have stretched her nerves to the limit. Despite the pressures of time and the onset of the new school term, Susannah made an indirect and deliberate deviation via Brussels on her journey home. It is possible that this was in order to obtain the signatures of the King and Queen of the Belgians though, equally, these signatures may have been gained by proxy around 5 August 1921 at the time Haig penned his name.[34] Susannah arrived from Brussels on the night of Monday, 15 August and was at school on the following afternoon.[35]

When Susannah returned from her trip to Europe one might think her project was at an end. This was not so. Susannah organised an 'animated and happy gathering' of 800 widows and orphans at the Town Hall in Chorley, on 5 October 1921. The *Chorley Guardian* noted the 'smiling rows of faces' as refreshments were distributed beneath flags and streamers hung as decoration. Susannah's long-standing reputation as one who had 'distinguished herself by the work she has already done and continues to carry out on behalf of ex-servicemen and their dependants' was referred to and she was praised for her continued service to the community. This was indeed quite a different manner of reporting compared to that of November and December 1916.[36]

Her acquaintances and supporters, Father Crank, Mayor Fearnhead and Captain Hacking MP were there to give their support. The speakers on the platform at the Town Hall gave their thanks for the sacrifice of those who had not returned from the war, but drew attention to those who were maimed or crippled as a consequence. Twenty-five of the children who had lost their fathers in the war were now also motherless. Inevitably obedience, patriotism and loyalty were instilled in the minds of the children through the speeches, but more poignantly, Father Crank urged that they should 'imitate their fathers and help their mothers to enjoy the life that was before them'. The mayor took his opportunity to make it clear to the relatives of the deceased servicemen that 'what had been done by those they had lost was not forgotten'. Hacking spoke with great sympathy, urged pride and noted with some disgust the difficulties ex-servicemen were having in the search for employment. The *Chorley Guardian* then unhelpfully tells us simply that 'Miss Knight responded'.

The *Chorley Guardian* only occasionally gives us a snatch of Susannah's voice in diluted paraphrase, however in this case the newspaper's concluding paragraph gave significant news of the *Album*. It was given its first public viewing at the event. As on her visit to Rome, the evidence suggests there was a single volume. It was exhibited in the Mayor's Parlour at the Town

Hall. If Susannah had compiled a Catholic sequence for the Pope then she would have had to re-bind her material to include Anglican and Non-conformist entries. What went to Rome might not have been what was shown in the Town Hall. [37]

The *Chorley Guardian*'s description in October 1921 of 'a handsome volume' deserves a full quotation, not only because it gives a positive account of the book but because it also outlines Susannah's further plans:

THE WAR ALBUM

The book containing the photographs of men killed in the war, and with which Miss Knight has visited the Continent and secured the signatures of many prominent personalities in the Allied countries, including that of the Prince of Wales and the King and Queen of the Belgians, was shown to many visitors in the Mayor's parlour. It is a handsome volume, the front being inlaid in 18ct gold plate of the coat of arms of the Borough of Chorley. Miss Knight intends paying another visit to the Continent to secure further signatures and also to visit America for the same purpose. [*sic*][38]

8 THE WASHINGTON CONFERENCE 1921

SUSANNAH was audacious. Her plans to visit the USA and revisit Europe when the *Album* was displayed in the Mayor's Parlour at the beginning of October 1921 were expressed almost casually to the *Chorley Guardian*. She had not yet gained a leave of absence from the Local Education Committee.[1] Despite Susannah going to the Education Office in Chorley on Thursday, 27 October, Miss Lilly, her head teacher, recorded in the *Weld Bank School Log Book* that no definite answer to the request was to be given until a meeting that evening. It was only then that the Schools' Management Sub-Committee, which met on the last Thursday of every month, considered her letter requesting paid leave from 29 October 'in order to gain certain signatures for her War Book'. Susannah's timing was very specific, and the request to be absent in term-time most exceptional.

She was permitted a full salary for one month whilst on her travels and the matter was to be reviewed at the end of that period.[2] This was an highly unusual concession and it is not clear how Susannah persuaded them, as the content of her letter, which has since been lost, was not expanded upon in the minutes. One wonders how much goodwill, how much dogged determination and how much sheer brass neck won her this dispensation.

It was only when she returned to school on the morning of Friday, 28 October, that she learned that her request had been approved.[3] She was confident that she would be successful. She had already booked her transatlantic ticket. Dutifully, she went in to school briefly that morning and left at 9.50am to catch the train for Liverpool.[4]

Susannah left the port of Liverpool on *RMS Scythia* on Saturday, 29 October 1921.[5] It was an excursion which, at the best part of two months, far exceeded the time allowed by the Education Committee.

Jack Knight was listed as next of kin which suggest he had already retired from Booth Shipping Steam Shipping Company. He was living at Litherland Road but soon moved to Merton Road now that he had settled for life on dry land. Perhaps Jack contributed some of Susannah's costs, though several sources note that Susannah made her travels at her own expense. It is possible, of course, that Jack's connections with Booth Steam Shipping allowed Susannah the opportunity to purchase her ticket at a favourable rate. She had one major donor who remains elusive. A millionaire cousin makes a fleeting appearance in Susannah's own account of the journey to Eleanor Roosevelt in 1936. Though the name of this cousin is not known, he or she was almost certainly connected to her mother's relatives in New York.[6]

Miss Knight stepped aboard *Scythia* on its second westward voyage. It was a fine ship that had completed its maiden voyage in August of that year. Susannah was committing her trust to over 19,500 tons of the finest maritime engineering, able to thrust through Atlantic sprays at 15.5 knots. After a brief pause at Queenstown on the south coast of Ireland, the liner made its way towards New York. Susannah travelled as one of the 381 second class passengers, accompanied by 87 in first class and 1,017 in steerage.

The liner was a marvel of design and its fittings were luxurious. The *New York Times* provided a fantastic pen-portrait of the liner on its first voyage, describing how there were three garden lounges with sliding windows for the comfort of first class passengers in storm or shine. These lucky passengers dined in a room that spanned the ship and was encompassed by a domed ceiling, while second class passengers such as Susannah could enjoy the veranda café. One can imagine Susannah settling her books or sheets of loose paper in the drawing and writing room, or perhaps in one of the alcoves on each side of the elliptical dome that arched above. Perhaps the great fireplace flickered its warmth to combat the chill of November while she perched herself on the Adam furniture picked out in purple and yellow.[7]

Despite the luxurious surroundings Susannah kept her focus on the *Album*. On the day she departed from Liverpool she secured the autograph of the commanding officer, William Alfred Prothero, who was offered a clean page and placed his crisp lines in the centre. Lieutenant Commander Alexander Greig gave his autograph alongside that of his superior on 7 November as they met the coast of the United States, just off the Nantucket Light Vessel.[8] At that same point in time she had engaged the ship's surgeon, Douglas Elder, to place his signature on a blank page that was eventually devoted to other men of medicine, echoing the status Susannah gave to the Captain Surgeons in December 1920.[9]

One fellow second class passenger who made a big impression on the voyage was James Eads How. On *Scythia's* arrival, the *New York Times* picked up the story of the 'Millionaire Hobo' who had returned from Europe having organised a 'hobo hike' from London to Brighton to draw attention to the poor and unemployed. He had done much for the homeless of the United States already and persisted in drawing attention to the plight of the vulnerable, applying his inherited wealth and his deep-seated Christian Socialist principles to resolve social ills. By all accounts he had made a positive impression. His customary down-at-heel garb and shaggy beard perhaps caused initial social awkwardness but his engaging charm and kindness won the affection of the passengers.[10] His signature is not in the *Album*, but it is probable that Susannah was aware that he was on board. His sympathy for the poor and unemployed might have attracted her interest.

Susannah arrived at the port of New York on Tuesday 8 November. It had been eight years since she had last been in North America. A war had been fought and peace established in that time and on a more personal level, her cousin, Annie, had settled into married life. The passenger records suggest Susannah initially stayed with a cousin, identified as Mrs O'Brian at 516 East 83rd Street in New York. They state her intention to remain in the America for one month, concurring with the information Susannah had given to the Education Office and Miss Lilly. She was creative in interpreting her employers' limit as she had not taken into account the time required for the Atlantic crossing.

It is unlikely that Susannah tarried in New York, though she had much catching-up to do with members of her mother's family who had emigrated. Annie was certainly one relative that both Susannah and her brother held in affection. Jack had been disappointed when he narrowly missed Annie's marriage to a Mr O'Connell in late November 1915.[11] But family reunions would have to be delayed.

The city would have offered plenty of excitement and distraction. A report in *New York Times* report of 10 November 1921 noted an exceptional influx of celebrities. Despite prohibition, the city was as vibrant as ever – perhaps even more so with the wash of bootleg alcohol which flowed freely in the speakeasies of the prohibition era. Richard Strauss, Mary Garden and Charlie Chaplin may have appealed to Susannah and indeed, the 'cowboy' film stars of the 1930s will be revealed as an interest in her later travels.[12]

But, again, such diversions would have to wait.

There were significant public events which drew Susannah's fullest attention.[13] The remains of an American soldier killed in France were to be laid to rest in the Tomb of the Unknown Soldier at Arlington Cemetery. America marked its first formal Armistice Day on 11 November 1921.[14] On 14 November, President Harding lay the cornerstone of the George Washington Building and Victory Memorial in Washington.[15] The particular resonance of the burial of the Unknown Soldier provided a compelling attraction for Susannah and it is worth noting that she had already acquired the autograph of Walter Keeble of the Royal Navy who had been part of the guard at the burial of Great Britain's Unknown Soldier at Westminster Abbey.[16]

An even more incredible opportunity can be confirmed by analyzing the signatures in the *Album*. On 12 November, President Harding convened an international conference at the Memorial Continental Hall in Washington to negotiate the limitation of armaments. It was a far cry from the hopes of disarmament his predecessor Woodrow Wilson expressed at the Paris Peace Conference in 1919. Its aim was to balance the relative naval strengths of the victorious allies and to relieve tensions in the Far East. This was not only an occasion impossible for Susannah to resist, but the deliberate objective of her visit to America. It was the basis for the preparation, timing and duration of her visit. The conference had been delayed by one day so that the delegates could attend the commemoration at Arlington Cemetery and representatives from the United States, Britain, France, Portugal, Belgium, the Netherlands, Japan, Italy and China had been invited.[17]

Charles Evans Hughes, the United States Secretary of State, chaired what eventually became known as the Washington Conference. Not only did Susannah have his signature in the *Album*, but also two of the three other leading American delegates: Senators Henry Cabot Lodge and Oscar W. Underwood.[18] Susannah homed in on the diplomatic contingent, having already gained the autograph of Sir Auckland Geddes, the British Ambassador to the United States, whilst he was still in England. [19]

Many of the distinguished diplomats and military leaders of the Allied nations who attended the conference signed Susannah's *Album*. She met the members of the Belgian delegation, including the Ambassador Baron Cartier de Marchienne, who added his signature on Wednesday, 16 November.[20] Her interest in Belgium stemmed from her association with the wounded Belgian troops who had convalesced in Chorley and the Belgian refugees who had been billeted at the convent at Gillibrand Hall during the Great War. Of course, she gained the signatures of the King and

Queen of the Belgians earlier in August of 1921 and this could well have been a talking point which helped her to add the signatures of the Belgian diplomats.[21] On the same day, she also presented the *Album* to two French delegates, recording a third French diplomat on the 19 November. Frustratingly, the French signatures are indecipherable, though one may be that of Albert Sarraut, the French Minister of the Colonies who was the leading French negotiator.[22] Marshal Foch was there of course, though he had placed his name in the *Album* at Rennes in July.

General Diaz, Commander of the Italian Army, added his name to the *Album*, as did his secretary. Diaz was a key adviser to Victor Emmanuel and later steered his king towards appointing Benito Mussolini as Prime Minister in 1922. Susannah Knight noted in pencil that he was 'Commander in Chief of the Italian Army' and he was a member of the Italian Senate. He was Chief of General Staff from 1917 and went on to become a Field Marshal and Minister of War under Mussolini.[23] Admiral of the Fleet David Beatty of the Royal Navy was present but probably signed his name on an earlier occasion alongside Haig, Blamey and Wilson.[24] General Pershing, Commander of the American Expeditionary Force in Europe during the Great War, took a page for himself before Susannah approached many leading officers of the Quarter Master Corps to form ranks around his name.[25] Admiral Coontz of the United States Navy also made his signature the centrepiece of a page before other American Naval and Marine personnel scribed their names.[26]

In a hectic period of just over a week, Susannah succeeded in outrageous feats to promote the *Album*. A crowning achievement might seem to have been to receive the autograph of President Warren Harding and his Vice President, Calvin Coolidge.[27] On one page alone she recorded 11 of Harding's cabinet. On 20 November, she obtained the autograph of the Secretary of the Interior, Albert B. Fall. Three days later the dated signature of James J. Davies, US Secretary of Labour, was also recorded. The other cabinet members are: Charles E. Hughes, Secretary of State; John W. Weeks, Secretary of War; Edwin Danby, Secretary of the Navy; Andrew W. Mellon, Secretary of the Treasury; and William H. Hays, Post Master General. Their signatures are accompanied by those of John F. Hylan, the Mayor of New York City.[28]

Herbert Hoover, as Secretary of Commerce, was the only man in the cabinet to have had direct experience of the war in Europe, having been closely involved in the relief of Belgian refugees. Of course, Susannah shared his interest in their plight. Hoover was a useful point of reference for Hughes in his role as chair for the Limitation of Armaments Conference, adding to the USA's credibility in hosting the event.

Persistence, determination and an element of brazenness might go some way to explain Susannah's success. The name of the Secretary of State's Private Secretary, William H. Beck, appears twice in the *Album* and perhaps he had a role in Susannah gaining access to the US cabinet, too.[29] Unfortunately, this cabinet was only months away from a financial scandal which unravelled from April 1922 until 1929. The men who brought down cabinet members Edwin Danby and Albert B. Fall are in the preceding pages of the *Album*. Senators Thomas J. Walsh, John B. Kendrick and Robert M. La Follette destroyed the careers of Danby and Fall in what became known as the Teapot Dome Scandal, underlining the weakness of Warren Harding's presidency.[30]

Had Susannah known what would transpire, she might have been less inclined to include these men.[31] By the time Fall was convicted, Harding had been succeeded by Coolidge, and Coolidge had been succeeded by Hoover. Susannah had gathered the signatures of a triplet of present and future presidents in 1921 that history did not entirely garner with praise.

Alongside the signatures of the US Cabinet are those of Howard Davidson, an Army Air Attaché, and Kenyon A. Joyce, a Military Attaché. It could be assumed that their association with the cabinet signatures connected them with the Limitation of Armaments Conference.[32] There is a quirk of coincidence which adds a little ambiguity to this conclusion. Whilst Joyce was probably present in Washington in 1921, he and Davidson were both at Croydon Aerodrome on 17 July 1924 when the signatures on the right hand side of this same page were added. The circumstances of this later event will be examined below.[33]

The positioning of the signatures makes it hard to determine an absolute chronology of all of Susannah's activities in the USA. However, there is strong evidence that 23 November was a key day on which to gain access to Congress. The Senate was in session and several bills were debated. Within this period, Susannah managed to seek out 71 of a possible 96 Senators, all of whom were present in the Capitol.[34] Susannah also managed to bring the *Album* to the attention 72 members of the House of Representatives including its Speaker. These august men, as well as Congresswoman Alice Mary Robertson, added gravitas to Susannah's testament to the men Chorley had lost in the Great War. In 1936 Susannah identified Senator Boies Penrose as 'my friend' and it is likely that he had a role in helping her gain these signatures, though he has to be considered as no more than a useful acquaintance in that Susannah refers to him as 'Boris' in error by this later date.[35]

There are some intriguing individuals in the record of signatures that remind the reader that Susannah had, at her heart, the experiences of the ordinary soldiers who faced hardship both at the front line and at home. She did not just search out political and military celebrities of the time. Susannah also sought to repair the physical and social damage wreaked by the war. One signature from Washington was Regimental Sergeant Major George D. Powell of the 24th United States Infantry which appeared beneath William H. Beck's second autograph just before the casualty biographies of the first volume of the *Album*.[36] Powell was featured in a short article in a 1916 edition of *The Crisis* published by W.E.B. Dubois representing the National Association for the Advancement of Colored People. As one of the magazine's 'Men of the Month', Powell was celebrated for his long military career stretching back to the Indian Wars and the Spanish American War in the late 19th Century, and his service in the brutal action in the Philippines from 1898. The 24th Infantry was one of the 'Buffalo Soldier' units made up of African-American soldiers with white officers.[37]

The policy of segregated regiments in the United States Army, of course, was controversial. Powell is likely to have experienced racial discrimination whilst both in and out of uniform and risen above this to seek recognition through promotion. Susannah sought him out in his retirement.[38] The signature of General John Pershing, Commander of the United States Army in the Great War, adds a further dimension to Powell's signature.[39] Pershing had been an officer in the 10th Cavalry, another 'Buffalo Soldier' unit, and had served in Cuba and the Spanish American War. George Powell certainly knew of Pershing by the time both men put their names to Susannah's pages. Pershing had tried to combat the institutional racism of the Army from his early career and had even earned derision from his fellow officers because of the respect he showed to African-American troops. George Powell's experience represents a wider battle that was being fought beyond the confines of the battlefield and Susannah appreciated this, perhaps, from the perspective that the disabled soldiers, widows and orphans continued to bear the burdens of decisions made by politicians. Both of these men saw service in the 'Fighting Sixty-Ninth' Regiment, which becomes relevant at a later point in this narrative.

Susannah did not slow the pace of her activities. Her capacity to persist in her efforts is a constant surprise. Her progress after Washington is unclear but she passed through New York again, gaining a series of signatures representing the American military and the Medical Corps. Many of the 36 names associated with the Quarter Master Corps accompanying Pershing went on to have the very highest roles in the United States Army in the 1930s through his patronage.[40] There are also connections to New York and the Air Service.[41] Susannah managed to represent every service of the United States armed forces.

The full chronology of her route is elusive but by 5 December, Susannah had made her way to Toronto and contacted the commanding officers of the No2 Military District.[42] Whilst in Canada, so briefly, she was able to gain the signatures of both a previous and the current Governor General of Canada. Sir John Campbell Hamilton Gordon, 7th Earl and 1st Marquess of Aberdeen and Temair and his wife, Isabella signed the *Album* together. They were joined by Byng of Vimy, Commander of the Canadian forces on the Western Front in the Great War, who was making his second appearance in Chorley's memorial.[43]

Susannah was pressed to return to New York by 13 December so she could board *RMS Aquitania* for her homeward voyage. In all probability she gave herself time to bid farewell to her extended family although there is no record of this. Before she left New York she made one more significant encounter.

Father Patrick Duffy was three years younger than Susannah. He had served, briefly, as a chaplain during the Spanish-American War. In 1914 he became chaplain to the men of New York's 'Fighting Sixty-Ninth' and served on the Mexican border in 1916 under Pershing's command.[44] The 69th Infantry Regiment was mainly composed of men with an Irish-American heritage. Duffy remained chaplain to the regiment when it was renumbered as 165th Infantry and embarked with them to France. By the end of the war he was the senior chaplain of the 42nd 'Rainbow' Division and served in Luneville in the Lorraine sector of the Western Front. The regiment experienced heavy casualties in 1918 and faced the horrors of mustard gas. Like Britain's own Woodbine Willy, Duffy was loved by the men for his compassion and courage and earned the Distinguished Service Medal, the Conspicuous Service Cross from New York State, and the Légion d'honneur of France. He had been devoted to his men throughout the conflict and would have looked upon the faces in Susannah's *Album* with the heavy sadness of one who knew what it meant to face death with one's comrades.[45]

It is possible that Susannah's family was acquainted with Duffy. Scions of the O'Brian and O'Connell families in New York may have known him in 1921 as the parish priest at Holy Cross on 42nd Street in Broadway. He had previously been the parish priest at Our Savior in the Bronx between 1912 and 1914 which was also close to where Susannah's relatives were living. Whatever the context of her meeting with Duffy was in 1921, the presence of his name in the *Album* was significant to Susannah. After his death in

1932 his reputation was such that in 1937 his statue was erected in a square named after him adjoining the more famous Times Square. Susannah had been struck by him and attended a memorial service held by his comrades in 1936.[46]

Chorley's *Album* was a symbol of the sacrifice undertaken by all the allies and the illuminated front page of the 'Golden Books' is emblazoned with the flags of the victorious nations. By being present at the Washington Conference and presenting the *Album*, Susannah was pursuing her hope, reflected upon in 1936, to create a 'gift to the British nation in memory of the Allied Friendships' (Plate 22).[47]

On 20 December it was time to take her gift home.[48] The departure of *RMS Aquitania* was briefly delayed by an incident in which an almost literal '11th hour' reprieve was secured for a passenger, Bertah Frohlinger, who was facing deportation. After a 15 minute pause in embarkation, the hawsers were cast off at a quarter past noon.[49] *Aquitania* gradually built up steam towards the Nantucket Light Vessel and cut through the waves into the Atlantic. There was an air of excitement amongst the passengers who were going home or abroad for Christmas. The ship was carrying 403 first class passengers, 338 second class passengers and 606 steerage passengers. The *New York Times* noted that there were 2000 sacks of letters and 3,000 sacks of parcels stowed in the hold taking Christmas greetings to Europe.[50]

Naturally, Susannah approached the Commanding officer, James J.W. Charles, who helpfully added a script to his autograph: 'Commanding *RMS Aquitania* Dec 17th … Miss Knight being present on board. Also on *Lusitania* 1913'. This added sentence implies that Susannah engaged the Captain in conversation and Charles' signature appears above that of Prothero of *Scythia*. There are also signatures from several of his crew, including the Purser, the two 2nd Pursers, three Assistant Pursers, and a Lounge Steward.[51]

There is a curious inscription which was made on this page sometime before this voyage and it adds further context to the exchange between Susannah and Commander James Charles. On that very same page can be found the signature of Commander Daniel Dow, which seems to have been made before that of Commander Charles. Dow had been the Commanding officer of *Lusitania* when Susannah returned from the United States in September 1913. A note of this fact is made on the page of the *Album* in Susannah's own hand. He had been lucky during the intervening war years, or perhaps not. Whilst the German submarine sank *Lusitania* in 1915 with the loss of 1,153 souls, he had his own encounter with a torpedo in the same year on *Mauritania* which, in Susannah's comment alongside the autograph, missed his ship 'by six inches'.[52] Susannah had taken passage on *Mauritania* when she went to the United States in 1913. *Lusitania* played a part in Susannah's tangled relationship with the sea and it is this network of brushes with fortune which likely drew both of them into conversation. It is no accident that Susannah referred to *Mauretania* and *Lusitania* in the comment alongside his autograph.

The explicit connection clearly interested Susannah greatly but the association does not end here, as several crew members on *Aquitania* had been on board *Lusitania* when it was torpedoed. Assistant Purser William Harkness was accompanied by Fred Jones (Chief Steward), Henry Matthews, Elizabeth Dewhurst, Samuel Caldercott, Jonathan Denton (barber), William Fletcher, Fullerton Boyd (bar keeper), Frank Sutton (chief bar keeper), Vernon Livermore, Hubert Newbold and James C Clarke had all escaped the tragedy of May 1915 and were on *Mauretania* in 1921.[53] These humble crewmen had gained their place in the *Album* alongside monarchs and presidents, pontiffs and archbishops. The men of the Merchant Navy had as many adjustments to make in peacetime as the men who returned to civilian life in Chorley.

Susannah knew the fear of submarines had sapped her brother's emotional and physical strength over those last harsh years of his career. Commander Dow's spirits were broken by his wartime experience, too, and he never went to sea again. Dow was most definitely on land when he signed the *Album*.[54] The conversations that accompanied each signature were so often about recovering the peace.

There had been good weather across the Atlantic despite some heavy seas. *The Times* reported that *Aquitania* had made good time with speeds of around 22.6 knots. Susannah seems to have exuded a greater confidence on her return journey, for there are many signatures from this period, indicating that she interacted with her fellow passengers more readily than on her outward voyage. There was a general lightness of atmosphere as Christmas approached, and these passengers were more inclined to strike up conversation as they reflected on meeting family and friends over the holiday season.[55]

As Susannah neared the end of her voyage, entering the Channel and putting in at Cherbourg, she made the acquaintance of a number of guests on the ship. There was a good sense of camaraderie aboard the liner, and *The Times* gave a heart-warming report of the atmosphere on board:

> High revel was held between decks in every part of the great ship during the voyage. On Saturday Santa Claus (impersonated by Mr

Edwards, the boatswain), accompanied by King Rat and other satellites, came aboard. After being presented to Sir James Charles, the captain, and the other officers of the ship, Santa Claus and his suite were piloted round the decks by the officers, gathering up the children as they went. The procession finally made its way into the saloon, where stood a giant Christmas tree, with its branches weighed down with gifts. The tree itself was provided by the Cunard Company, and the first-class passengers subscribed a sum of £240 for the presents.

In the evening came the turn of the 'grown-ups' for whom a Christmas dinner was served in picturesque medieval fashion. Two of the sturdiest men in the ship, dressed as baronial retainers, carried in the boar's head and the baron of beef, escorted by the chefs and preceded by trumpeters. After dinner there were concerts and dances.[56]

The boundaries between first and second class passengers remained fluid on the following day and Susannah met the Horlick brothers, sons of the inventor of the celebrated malted milk drink. Ernest and James were on their way 'home' for Christmas, though they had been brought up in Racine, Wisconsin. The additional information the brothers chose to add to their signatures suggests that the conversation Susannah struck up with them revolved around the Great War. When they signed their names, James noted he was still a Lieutenant Colonel in the Coldstream Guards, and Ernest added he had been a captain in the Royal Flying Corps.[57] Given the nature of the *Album*, it is likely that they remarked that their youngest brother, Gerald, had been killed in action in Egypt in July 1918. Ernest had just taken up a baronetcy upon the death of his father but the background of their wartime experiences seem to have been more important.[58] Ernest was of sufficient note to be named by the *New York Times* in advance of embarkation.[59]

At this same point in her journey Susannah met Colonel Thomas Ogilvie of the 4th Gordon Highlanders who was another of the passengers distinguished enough to be named by the *New York Times*.[60] He made a note of his service in France and Belgium 1915-19 alongside his signature in the *Album*.[61] One fellow passenger was a rather unlikely individual for Susannah to approach, yet his name appears on the page recording the Prince of Wales and the British cabinet. Prince Rene de Bourbon-Parma made his mark whilst aboard *Aquitania* and as the brother of the exiled Empress of Austria.[62] He had an incongruous association with those who had pursued war in 1914.

There are some omissions in Susannah's signature record of the voyage on *Aquitania* and some distinguished first class passengers are notably missing. The presence of a 21 Japanese delegates from the Washington Conference led by Baron Nakashima is a surprising omission, while Lord Arlington and the Marchioness of Crewe were also guests who might well have caught Susannah's attention. Other conspicuously absent passengers include Commander D.G. Patrazzino of the Italian Navy and Count A.D. Falcon. In fact, of the 35 'celebrity' names listed by the *New York Times*, Susannah secured the signatures of only Bourbon-Parma, the Horlick brothers and Colonel Thomas Ogilvie.[63]

Aquitania put into Southampton dock at 11am on 21 December 1921 and with charming precision, both the *Weld Bank School Log Book* and *The Times* confirm the date and time of Susannah's landfall.[64] Her school's term ended the following day and it is not clear whether or not she was able to make it home in order to wish her pupils and colleagues good cheer. No trace of her experiences is recorded.

Plate 1. Susannah Knight, undated.
(Walmsley Collection)

Plate 2. Jack Knight, post 1916.
(Walmsley Collection)

Plate 3. Weld Bank school, pre 1914. *(Westmorland School Archive)*

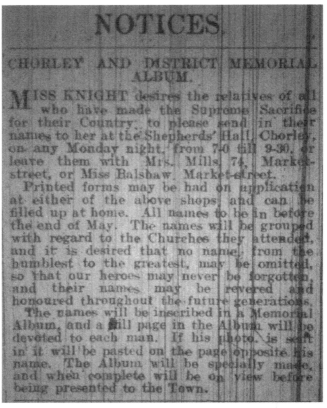

Plate 4. Advertisement announcing the compilation of the Chorley Memorial Album, 5 April, 1919. *(Chorley Guardian, Chorley Library)*

Plate 5. First page of signatures, July 1921, including Prince Edward, Lloyd George, Herbert Asquith, Byng of Vimy, Lord Birkenhead, Lord Derby, Stanley Baldwin and Winston Churchill, amongst others. *(Astley Hall Museum and Art Gallery)*

COUNT PAUL de MEHERENE de St. PIERRE,
Lieutenant in the Armée Française.

Killed in Action, September, 1914.
Address: Chateau du Bois de la Salle, par
Llan vollon.

Plates 6 and 7. Lieutenant Paul de Méhérenc de St Pierre: his photograph and misspelt entry in the Chorley Memorial Album. *(Astley Hall Museum and Art Gallery)*

Plate 9. Lieutenant Paul de Méhérenc de St Pierre's *fiche.* *(Mémoire des Hommes)*

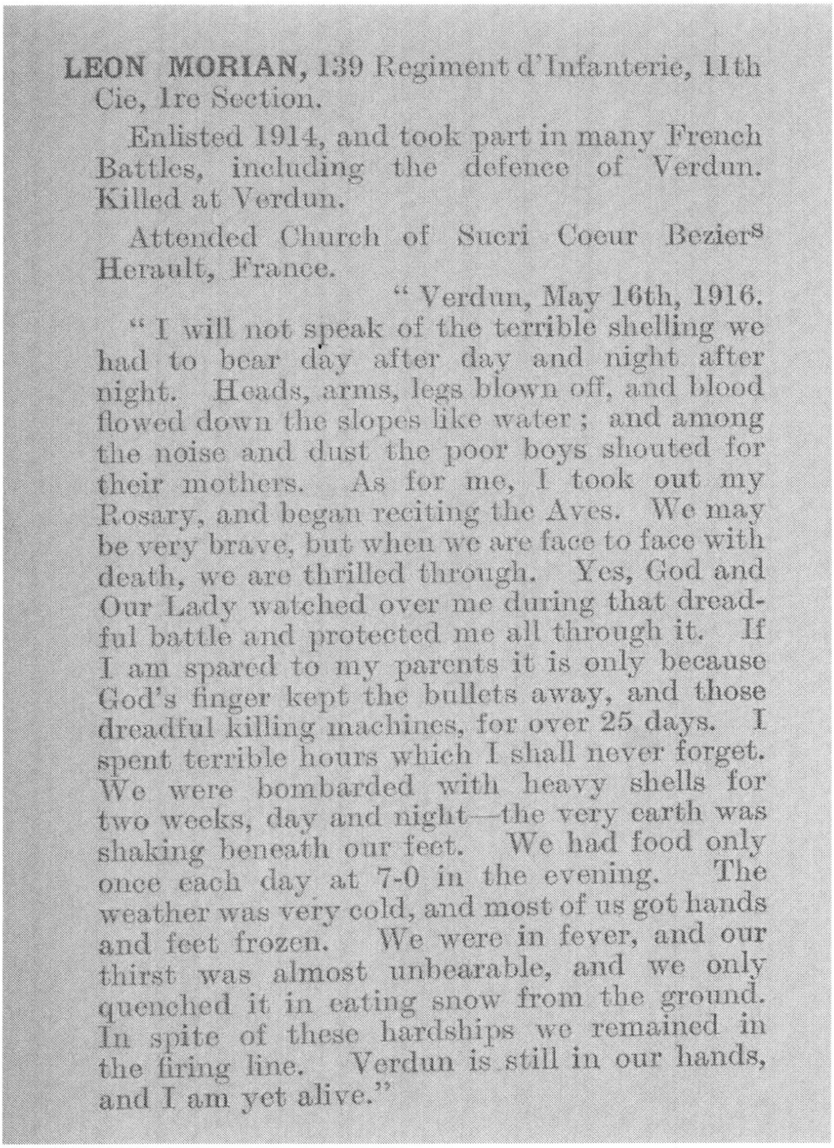

LEON MORIAN, 139 Regiment d'Infanterie, 11th Cie, 1re Section.

Enlisted 1914, and took part in many French Battles, including the defence of Verdun. Killed at Verdun.

Attended Church of Sucri Coeur Beziers Herault, France.

"Verdun, May 16th, 1916.

"I will not speak of the terrible shelling we had to bear day after day and night after night. Heads, arms, legs blown off, and blood flowed down the slopes like water; and among the noise and dust the poor boys shouted for their mothers. As for me, I took out my Rosary, and began reciting the Aves. We may be very brave, but when we are face to face with death, we are thrilled through. Yes, God and Our Lady watched over me during that dreadful battle and protected me all through it. If I am spared to my parents it is only because God's finger kept the bullets away, and those dreadful killing machines, for over 25 days. I spent terrible hours which I shall never forget. We were bombarded with heavy shells for two weeks, day and night—the very earth was shaking beneath our feet. We had food only once each day at 7-0 in the evening. The weather was very cold, and most of us got hands and feet frozen. We were in fever, and our thirst was almost unbearable, and we only quenched it in eating snow from the ground. In spite of these hardships we remained in the firing line. Verdun is still in our hands, and I am yet alive."

Plate 10. Leon Moreau's misspelt entry in the Chorley Memorial Album. (*Astley Hall Museum and Art Gallery*)

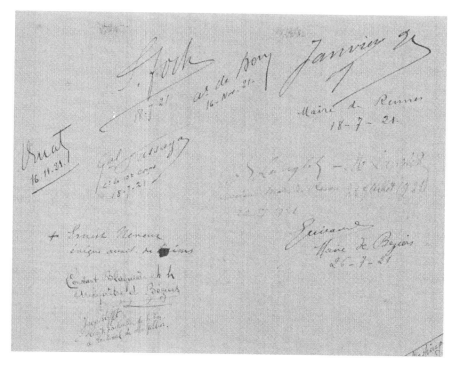

Plate 11. Ferdinand Foch's signature in the Chorley Memorial Album, 18 July, 1921, alongside signatures from Béziers and the Washington Conference in December *(Astley Hall Museum and Art Gallery)*

Plate 12. Ferdinand Foch's arrival at Rennes railways station, 17 July, 1921. *(Rennes Archive)*

Plate 13. inset with Susannah Knight at the back right of the main picture. *(Rennes Archives)*

95

Plates 14, 15 and 16. *Left, above and below:* Thomas Warburton's photographs and one entry in the Chorley Memorial Album *(Astley Hall Museum and Art Gallery)*

THOMAS WARBURTON, 96075, Private, 2/6th Sherwood Forresters.

Served in France and Belgium. Killed 1st December, 1917, in Belgium.

Attended the Parish Church of St. Lawrence.

Plates 17 and 18. *Below and right:* John Thorpe's photograph and entry in the Chorley Memorial Album *(Astley Hall Museum and Art Gallery)*

JOHN THORPE, 243466, Lance-Corporal, Loyal North Lancashire Regiment.

Enlisted March, 1915, and served in France. Took part in the French Front Battles. He was gassed once, and on May 29th 1918 was wounded. Spent two years in hospital, a complete wreck as a result of frightful wounds, his right arm was gone, and he was paralized, owing to a wound in the spine.

Attended St. George's Church.

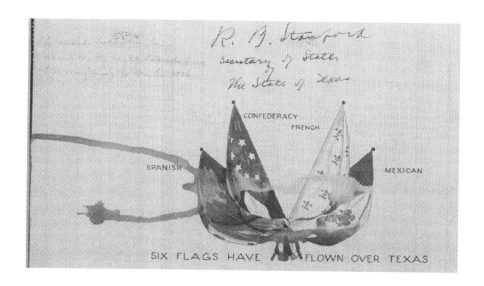

Plate 19. The signature of R.B. Stamford, Secretary of State, The State of Texas. One of the Chorley Memorial Album pages deliberately dampened by water from the Colorado River in 1936. *(Astley Hall Museum and Art Gallery)*

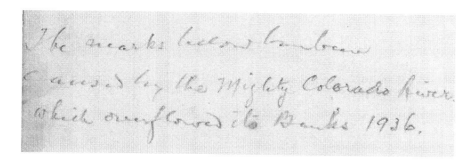

Plate 20. Detail of Plate 19 with a penciled comment by Susannah 'The marks below were caused by the Mighty Colorado River which overflowed its Banks 1936.' [*sic*] *(Astley Hall Museum and Art Gallery)*

Plate 21. Susannah Knight on the far left with one of her later classes at Weld Bank (St Gregory's) School, undated. *(Astley Hall Museum and Art Gallery)*

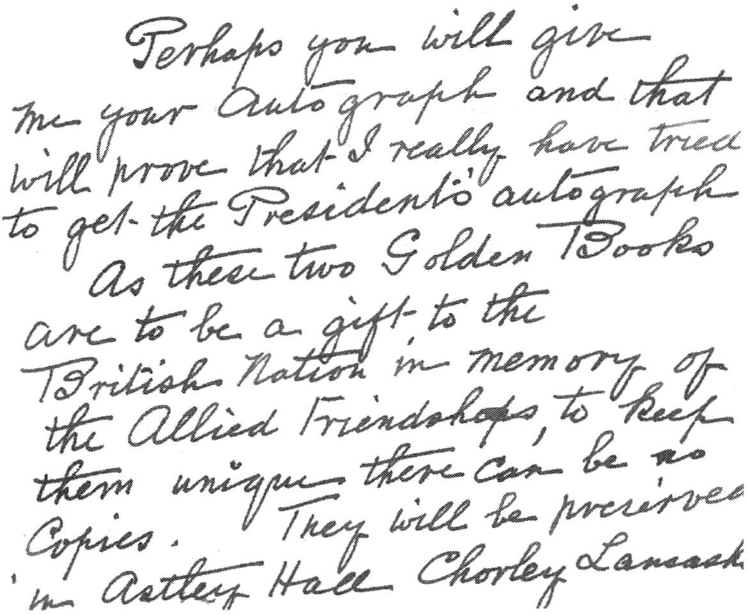

Perhaps you will give me your autograph and that will prove that I really have tried to get the President's autograph. As these two Golden Books are to be a gift to the British Nation in memory of the Allied Friendships, to keep them unique there can be no copies. They will be preserved in Astley Hall Chorley Lancash.

Plate 22. Part of Susannah's correspondence with Eleanor Roosevelt, outlining her purpose in compiling the Chorley Memorial Album 4 July, 1936. *(Astley Hall Museum and Art Gallery)*

9 THE RECOVERY 1922 - 33

PEACE brought economic hardship for many families in Chorley. There were the widows and orphans, but also families that needed to support the men who returned physically or mentally broken. Susannah attended to the needs of many families with practical care.[1]

The *Album* slowly evolved over the next decade. Susannah began to represent a wider breadth of society in her collection of signatures. These still fitted broadly into the categories of 1921 but became more inclusive. It is clear that she travelled, but her movements are more difficult to discern. Her work was methodically but the chronology becomes fragmented. Slowly, though, the *Album* was becoming her obsession.

Susannah's spiritual outlook remained at the heart of all she did. Those responsible for the later re-sequencing of the volumes were sensitive to the depth of her faith. The second volume opens with the photograph and signature of Pope Pius XI.[2] Susannah was impelled to renew her efforts. The *Chorley Guardian* had already reported in October 1921 that she intended to return to Europe.[3]

Susannah returned to Europe in 1922. The papal blessing for the *Album* and her own Apostolic Blessing were not enough. Susannah sought out Benedict's recently-consecrated successor in April at the most sacred time of the Christian calendar. It is impossible to determine exactly when Pius XI signed the page but some inferences can be made. Weld Bank School's Easter holiday began at the close of lessons on 12 April, on Holy Wednesday. With careful planning, it was perfectly feasible for her to travel by sea and rail to arrive in Rome by Easter Sunday, four days later.[4] Her attendance at a Mass in Rome at the Church's highest festival held immeasurable significance for Susannah.

From the composition of the page it appears that the signature of the Pope was obtained by proxy. A loose sheet has been folded with the message on the right hand side as if it were a large greetings card. It has not been signed *in situ* within the volume, but carefully pasted in. A photograph of Pius XI on the left hand side, clearly cut from a magazine, is likely to have been added by Susannah herself, distracting the viewer from the fact that she did not have a pre-printed page to hand.[5]

Susannah remained in Rome during Easter week and had to wait for some time for a reply from the Vatican, as had been the case in the previous year. On 18 April she received the signature of Cardinal Francis Aidan Gasquet, an English Benedictine Librarian in the Vatican Library who became Archivist of the Secret Vatican Archive in 1929. She was still in Rome on 20 April when Raphael Cardinal Merry del Val, Pius XI's British-born Secretary of State, also added his signature on the same page. So, too, did Francesco Cardinal Ragonesi. This final signatory had the coincidental connection that he eventually died in the mother-house of those Sisters of the Sacred Heart of Mary at Poggio a Caiano, Pistoia.[6]

Susannah was able to get the signature of King of Italy. She had prepared a pre-printed page with the clear intention of gaining the signatures of Victor Emmanuel III and his wife, Margherita. Given that he is not mentioned in the *Chorley Guardian* in October 1921, Susannah must have engineered an opportunity on her travels in 1922 to complete this page. In the event, disappointingly, Susannah was not able to acquire the signature of the Italian queen despite preparing a space for her in the *Album*.[7]

Weld Bank School began the new term on 24 April 1922. Susannah did not return home until 4pm on Friday 28 April and returned to work on the 1 May.[8] Thus, Susannah had absented herself from her teaching just as she had in August, 1921. The comment in the *Weld Bank School Log Book* seems to suggest that an extension of her vacation had been expected and there is no further comment about the nature of her travels. The *Weld Bank School Log Book* is frustratingly silent on Susannah's activities out of school. She must surely have shared some of her adventures with colleagues, pupils and parishioners but there is no evidence to be found and it may well be a mark of her modesty that there is so little comment.

Susannah valued the work of medical professionals during and after the Great War. She methodically collected the signatures of doctors in the mid-1920s. The principles that had guided her to propose the cottage hospital in 1916 and to invite Lord Crawford to present the painting of the Captain

Surgeons remained a primary force in Susannah's continued work. This portrait commended the contribution of the Captain Surgeons Warburton, Macintosh, Rigby, Rainford and Leighton to signify that local men had played a part in caring for the wounded. Susannah's close association with returning soldiers gave her an intimate understanding of the physical and psychological consequences of battle. The doctors who signed the *Album* helped ex-servicemen fight the battles that continued to afflict bodies and minds beyond the Paris Peace Conference of 1919.

Many of the male doctors featured in Susannah's pages had served with the Royal Army Medical Corps, as indeed had seven of the men whose deaths were recorded as casualties in the *Album*. At least nine pages of the *Album* are given over to civilian doctors across the three volumes, with six pages devoted to British doctors and surgeons. One bears a pencil annotation commending seven female doctors.[9] Another of these pages focuses on 'specialists in tropical medicine' heading a list of a further seven doctors, recalling the correspondence from Susannah's brother that discussed Yellow Fever in South America at the turn of the century.[10] Some of the signatures Susannah gained in America in 1921 were from senior officers of the United States Army Medical Corps.[11] She retained this interest when she visited America in 1935 and 1936 and three of the four pages she collated on this theme had a clear interest in men who were serving or had served in the Corps.[12] As Susannah pursued her autographs through this decade many doctors appeared in the pages of the *Album*. She specifically sought out men who had given medical service in the forces of the allied armies. While on *Aquitania* in 1921 Susannah gained the signatures of surgeons on board who had a previous military role.[13] On her arrival she managed to get 14 surgeons from the United States Army, Navy and Marines to sign the *Album*.[14]

Occasional signatures of crew or passengers with medical training appear whilst Susannah was in transit across the Atlantic. One of the pages in the third volume has an eclectic selection of doctors but also has the pencil heading 'Indians'.[15] One of the more curious inclusions on this page is that of Sir Shanti Swaroop Bhatnagar, later knighted in 1941 for his services to research in chemistry. Curious, because he was one of the select few to appear more than once in the autographs.[16] Susannah certainly ensured that those who brought healing to the sick were recognised for their contributions in war and peace.

The portraits presented in 1920 had also commended the contributions of military chaplains in the Great War. Several such men are found in the record of signatures. Susannah makes no obvious distinction between the Catholic and Protestant chaplains, though, unsurprisingly, Roman Catholic clergy feature more frequently in the signatures. Of the few local signatures to appear are the priests of St Gregory's and St Mary's churches in Chorley, namely Canons Crank and Banks. The Roman Catholic bishops of Liverpool, Lancaster and Shrewsbury can also be found on this page, as can Bishop Robert Dowson, Titular Bishop of Cynopolis and Arcadia. Indeed, it is this signature that probably dates this collection to 1928 or later.[17] Clergy lower down the Roman Catholic hierarchy from London, Scotland and Ireland all added their signatures at points during this period of the *Album*.

Susannah maintained her connections with Ireland in the mid-1920s. Thomas Perrott was a young Jesuit priest teaching mathematics at Clongowes Wood College, Naas, between 1923 and 1927. He made a point of mentioning his teaching post when he signed the *Album*.[18] Regardless of where the encounter took place, Perrott must have had a great deal of charisma even in these early years of his training. He went on to be the first Jesuit to serve in Western Australia and became instrumental in helping to found a number of schools and colleges in the territory.[19] Clongowes Wood College was, and remains, a prestigious academic institution offering a firm Catholic education for Ireland's gifted and elite.[20] James Joyce, writing not too long before Susannah's connection with the school, recalled his time there as a pupil through the character of Stephen Dedalus in *A Portrait of the Artist as a Young Man*.[21] It is intriguing that Susannah chose Perrott, a priest yet to distinguish himself, from the number of other notable staff there.

The chaplain perhaps most well-known to the British audience was Geoffrey Studdart Kennedy, more commonly referred to as 'Woodbine Willie'. He was a courageous individual, winning the Military Cross for entering no-man's-land at Messines Ridge to give comfort to the wounded. Susannah added the following annotation below his autograph: 'He was dearly loved and honoured by all men on the battlefield. As a person he was one of the most popular of the Padres'.[22] Kennedy was renowned for distributing Woodbine cigarettes as he toured the trenches on the Western Front, winning both his nickname and the hearts of the troops. Most of the men returning from the front line had heard of him by reputation and some may even have met him.

Susannah sought out the signature of another chaplain, James Ogden Coop, in the early 1920s. He had been a Senior Chaplain to the Forces, 1st class (equivalent to a Colonel), and had been attached to the 55th (West Lancashire) Division of the Army. As an Anglican chaplain, his focus had been on his own flock, though his inclusion indicates Susannah's encompassing appreciation of the role of all chaplains. Coop's account of the Great War reads as an exhaustive statistical report that lacks a real spiritual element, though he is said to have been attentive to his pastoral duties at the front line and showed great valour. It cannot be by chance oversight that his narrative ignores the casualties of the 1st/8th King's Liverpool (Irish), a predominantly Roman Catholic battalion.[23] Susannah seems to have risen above denominational divisions in her work. Another chaplain to the forces included by Susannah was H.S. Broadbent, serving between December 1914 and December 1917. Susannah had always engaged with clergymen on her travels. Alfred Barry, a former chaplain of the Royal Navy, had met Susannah on *Scythia* off Halifax, Nova Scotia on 6 November 1921, while Rev. Charles Oliver of the Royal Army Medical Corps was on *Aquitania* in the English Channel on 19 December 1921. Susannah made his acquaintance and asked him to place his name on the same page as Coop, Broadbent and Barry.[24] She also managed to include a chaplain representing the Canadian forces, Charles Dobson Lute of the Newfoundland Division. He was a British Chaplain-Surgeon, giving the final signature in the first volume of the *Album* in 1922.[25]

The padres who had tended the souls of ex-servicemen in the war and the clerics of the subsequent peace have a prominent place in the *Album* and clergymen with connections to the armed forces or education appear frequently throughout the volumes. There is even one page entirely devoted to 24 men of the cloth from various corners of the British Isles and even Europe.[26] Susannah may even have regarded Ferdinand Foch for his spiritual conviction as well as his military role for he was noted for being at odds with his colleagues in his open and ardent Catholicism.[27]

There is just one final cleric to note at this point, though he probably signed the *Album* in the summer of 1921, namely W.H. Carnegie, the chaplain to the Speaker of the House of Commons.[28] The military chaplains had straddled the worlds of the spirit and the battlefield and had often given both spiritual and physical healing. Later, in 1936, Susannah determined that she wanted to 'get the autographs of those who have piloted their nations safely through the most terrible Period the world has known'. [*sic*][29] Who better to sign the *Album* in its early stages than a man providing spiritual counsel to John Henry Whitley, the Speaker himself, who also signed his name.[30] Susannah made a point of gaining the signatures of two Deputy Speakers, Edwin Cornwall and James F. Hope, recognising the role that the speaker had in the sober conduct of democracy.[31] The Speaker of the United States House of Representatives, Frederick H. Gillett, also took a prominent place in Susannah's pages.[32]

Susannah continued to seek out political figures throughout the 1920s following the phenomenal tally of signatures gathered in the summer of 1921. There are many undated signatures of members of Parliament including the future Prime Minister Neville Chamberlain and, more ominously, Oswald Mosley.[33] Both The Earl of Crawford and Balcarres and Douglas Hacking, former and contemporary MPs for Chorley, penned their names for Susannah, though one signature conspicuous by its absence is that of Sir Henry Hibbert who held the seat of Chorley during the war years.[34] It is unlikely that any ill-feeling on the part of the abrasive baronet remained after the spat surrounding the cottage hospital proposal of 1916 as he was invited to give the vote of thanks when Susannah's portraits were presented at the town hall in December 1920. One of the paintings she donated to Astley Hall in 1920 even featured his son, Cyril Hibbert, who had been killed at the Battle of Festubert on 15 June, 1915.[35] Susannah's entry in the *Album* for Hibbert's son, Cyril, was both graceful and fitting.

Opportunities for women to engage in politics were limited but Susannah gained the signatures of the first femal MPs, Nancy Astor and Margaret Wintringham, in support of the *Album*.[36] When Susannah was in the United States in 1921 Alice Mary Robertson, the second woman to sit in the House of Representatives, added her signature.[37] Susannah also managed to include the signature of the newly-appointed Senator Thaddeus H. Caraway in 1921, whose wife Hattie became the first woman elected to the Senate in 1931.[38] With these connections in mind, it is a curious thing that Susannah, as a woman of great determination and independence, who wanted to shake and challenge those who held the power to move nations, does not appear on the electoral roll of Chorley at any point in the 1920s and 1930s.[39]

Susannah had the opportunity to seek out signatures from the world of commerce. She secured a signature record of the captains of industry of Liverpool. A series of pages in the first volume relate to the city and its leading men. The first signature in this phase of Susannah's collection is that of Frank Campbell Wilson, the Lord Mayor of Liverpool between 1922 and 1923.[40] He seems to have been one of the earlier signatures on the page with Oswald Mosley and Neville Chamberlain added later and in a different context. A heading for Alfred Holt and Company lies inconspicuously to the right of this page and yet, squeezed onto the edge of the page, there is a list of the management and directors of the Blue Funnel Line.[41] Richard Durning Holt heads this marginal list. He was the nephew of Blue Funnel's founder and played a considerable role in the complex and overlapping controlling interests active on Liverpool's docks.[42] Holt's father, Robert, had been the first Lord Mayor of the City of Liverpool in 1893 and his brother, Lawrence, became Lord Mayor in 1929-30. On the reverse of this page are the signatures of directors together with commercial stamps of the Pacific Steam Navigation Company, Cayzer Irvine & Co Limited and the Clan Line.[43]

Susannah gained access to the shipping magnates based in the city through the influence of her brother. Jack retired from service after 1921 but he had gained a reputation for courage, skill and loyalty in the war years. He was well-placed to introduce her to his employers. Charles and George Booth, sons of the founders of the company, were now directors. Alfred Booth's son, taking his father's name, was not only a director of Booth Steam Shipping Company at the time, but also on the board of directors for Cunard. Alongside these directors of Booth Shipping is a list of the company's management.[44] On the following page of the *Album* are Cunard's directors: Thomas Royden, Delos W. Cook, Percy E. Bates, and Aubrey Brocklebank. At some point in the early 1920s Susannah was able to acquire the signatures of all of the management of Booth Steam Shipping Company.[45] The systematic layout of signatures suggests that Susannah was still dictating how they should be set out. Shipping was of prime importance to Liverpool and Bootle in driving the economy in the hardest years of the post-war depression, so Susannah surely wished to secure the signatures of these men who were crucial in creating work. Susannah may also have wanted to recognize the risks and sacrifices made by shipping during the war, her brother had personal experience of these risks, but many from Liverpool and beyond took these very same risks and did not return to their home port.

Susannah was fascinated by travel and technology. Modernity excited her. She had sailed on *Scythia* on its second Westward voyage, she kept abreast of medical developments and we have seen that Jack kept her informed of interesting accounts that he came across when he was travelling around the coast of South America. Susannah pursued (or made a lucky association with) that pioneer of radio, Guglielmo Marconi, who appears under a helpful pencil note made by Susannah, 'Italy Marconi', giving the year 1924 in his own hand.[46]

With these interests in mind, it is not surprising that she was at Croydon Aerodrome on 17 July 1924.[47] In fact, she was probably there the previous day when she met a Captain J.W. Wood and gained his signature. Alongside Wood is the name of the flamboyant Robert H. 'All-Weather Mac' McIntosh, one of the 16 original pilots of Imperial Airways which had made its fledgling flights from Croydon in the previous month.[48] The signatures of Wood and McIntosh were squeezed into a page used in 1921 below Field Marshals Haig, Wilson and Blamey, but they were not random acquisitions.[49]

On 18 July an American flight of three American Douglas World Cruisers arrived at the aerodrome. Lowell H. Smith, Leslie P. Arnold, John Harding, Henry H. Ogden, Erik H. Nelson and Leigh Wade were attempting to make the first circumnavigation of the world by air. Having left Paris they landed to refuel and recuperate before proceeding to Iceland. McIntosh, with the flair for which he had become famous, piloted an Imperial Airways Handley Page aircraft to escort the American aircraft from Paris to London. With a patriotism typical of the period, *The Times* made the point that McIntosh flew 20 mph faster and, as a measure of courtesy, pulled back on the throttle to try and keep the Americans in formation and allow them the pleasure of landing first.[50] Susannah snatched the signatures of all the crew members of this record-breaking flight and put them, in honour, next to the signatures of the cabinet of the United States government that she had gained in November 1921.[51]

Susannah mingled with the melee of spectators and guests and managed to meet members of the American diplomatic corps who had come to greet their compatriots and she did make the acquaintance of two interesting American guests. Colonel Kenyon A. Joyce was there as a Military Attaché and Major Howard Davidson was an Army Air Attaché. Curiously, the page selected to record the 'American World Flight' was the page she had previously used for the signatures of the United States cabinet in November 1921. It is conceivable that both men were at the Washington Conference and could have already been aware of the *Album* by 1924. [52]

Unfortunately Susannah did not manage to cross the path of the American Ambassador, Kellogg, who was unable to attend. His apologies were noted in *The Times*. From 16 July he was engaged in discussions in London led by Prime Minister Ramsay MacDonald to confirm the Dawes Plan, an attempt to reconcile reparations with just punishment by lending Germany money to resolve the post-war economic slump. Kellogg later shared a role in trying to establish peaceful relations between nations in the Kellogg-Briand Pact of 1928. Whilst the air crews were promoting their own brand of global optimism through the adventure of flight, Kellogg, with others was applying diplomatic solutions to the international problems of the 1920s.[53]

It cannot have been a coincidence that Susannah's next subjects of interest were reported to be arriving at Southampton in the very edition of *The Times* that celebrated the arrival of the American airmen. Within a week of her exploits at Croydon aerodrome Susannah had transferred her attention to an extraordinary meeting in London, where 3,000 visiting lawyers of the American and Canadian Bar Associations were officially welcomed to Britain at a ceremony in Westminster Hall on 21 July. The newspaper had a photograph of lawyers from North America disembarking *Aquitania* at Southampton.[54] In the following days RMS *Berengaria* brought more lawyers to Southampton, and *RMS Laconia* landed a further batch at Liverpool.[55] The event was judged by *The Times* as 'a valuable opportunity for professional men from all parts of the United States to appreciate at first hand and cement the fundamental unity of the English-speaking peoples'.[56] The delegates shared their thoughts on British common law, evaluated the benefits of a constitution, strengthened professional ties and also had an opportunity to see the sights and culture of Britain. The medieval setting of Westminster Hall was impressive. Excursions to Oxford and Cambridge were partly focused on professional matters but were clearly jaunts to see the historical sights. Westminster Abbey and St Paul's Cathedral were inspiring locations for the delegates who attended specially arranged services on 20 July.[57]

The Bishop of Norwich's sermon at St Paul's gave much pause for reflection:

> 'In days long gone by every man defended himself by personal contest. Victory went to the violent; but now law has replaced certain of the old ways of testing disputes. It was also – thank God – by a wonderful achievement in our own time, beginning to take part in settling international affairs. Law meant liberty, and in this way made us free to set forward peace and happiness, truth and justice, religion and piety, and to prepare the way for the coming among men of the Kingdom of God, whose service was perfect freedom.'[58]

There could be no clearer message for the members of the American and Canadian Bar Associations. After four years of pitiless war, the work of lawyers could now resolve conflict without the need for men to bear arms. For Susannah, this was an example of how the friendships she sought to foster between the allied nations could conquer war and achieve an enduring peace. Susannah's determination to record this event is barely credible and yet she collected around 425 signatures from both Bar Associations. There appear to be 189 Canadian signatures and 268 signatures of delegates from the United States in the *Album*, with several members of the Canadian contingent hailing from Prince Edward Island.[59] It is probable that more of the signatures elsewhere in the *Album* were given by delegates from Britain and the colonies. There are at least four lawyers from Punjab represented which are closely associated with a signature from a South African, though the provenance of their signatures cannot be established with certainty.[60]

The American Bar Association published a souvenir *Memorial Volume* for the 1924 convention as a 'permanent record of the great event in the relations of the lawyers of America with their brethren in England, Scotland and Ireland' and Susannah's collection of signatures matches perfectly with the names in this brochure.[61] Susannah made her way sequentially through her own copy of this document. She collected the signatures of 17 per cent of the 1376 American delegates listed, meeting men and women from all but three of the 48 states. Only one significant name on the pages devoted to the American delegates does not appear in their *Memorial Volume*. There was no need to gain the autograph of American Secretary of State Charles E. Hughes, present in his capacity as the President of the Association and the Vice Chair for the committee that put together the programme of events. Susannah had already gained his signature three years previously at the Washington Conference.[62] Hughes, though not in London on official state business, still had more than a passing interest in the progress of the Dawes Plan.[63] Susannah did however get the signature of the Chairman, Grenville Clarke.[64]

The Bar Associations, conference was an example of cooperation between the allied nations. In August, in the diplomatic and economic sphere, the terms of the Dawes Plan were confirmed. It aimed to ease the burden of the reparations that had been forced upon Germany by the Treaty of Versailles, a peace with justice after the 'war to end all wars'.

Susannah made the most of her time in London. In the summer of 1924 she approached the management of *The Times* newspaper, which resulted in eight signatures of men who commanded one of the most powerful organs of the media of the age. The men put their names beneath a special print of their paper's masthead impressed on one of Susannah's own sheets of paper. This suggests a level of preparation and planning rather than a grasped opportunity. Though the face of the page is undated, it is the reverse which provides the most enlightening evidence. This was the page that fell in the mud as she was getting off a bus in Rome.[65] It is unlikely that Susannah offered a soiled page to John Jacob Astor and it would initially seem fair to conclude that this page was completed in the short window of opportunity presented to Susannah in London before she made her way to Europe in 1921 or 1922.[66] However, the page must be dated between 1 January 1923 and 15 September 1927. Geoffrey Dawson became editor in January 1923 but had been in this role in an unofficial capacity since December, with Ralph Walter becoming a director in 1923. Thus the page must have been signed after Susannah's European adventures in 1921 and 1922. Robert Grant, the third signature on the page, left his post as a Director of *The Times* on 15 September 1927, so this provides a latest possible date for the signatures to have been recorded. Though Susannah may well have been to Rome on an unknown occasion and she certainly had the means and opportunity to visit London in any of her vacations, the spate of action in the summer of 1924 does give a strong argument to place the signatures of the management of *The Times* within this period.[67]

The post-war German Republic had stabilised under Gustav Stresemann's brief chancellorship and steady influence in other government roles. He had been involved in the Dawes Plan discussions whilst the Bar Associations were meeting in July 1924. The fledgling nation had steered its way through the previous year's disasters of the French invasion of the Ruhr, hyperinflation and a failed putsch in Munich by a small group of radicals called the National Socialist German Workers' Party. Europe was still insecure both politically and economically, but the year of 1924 was a hopeful awakening for many and Susannah was not alone in yearning for peace and recovery.

Whilst diplomats, lawyers and judges tried to weave a web of optimism, the American Douglas World Cruisers flown around the globe by Lowell H. Smith and his crews were drawing the world as a community itself more closely together. One man she met at the London conference of the American Bar Association who made his own lasting impact on the world politics was Henry L. Stimson.[68] As a former US Secretary of War, he was a worthy name to add to the signatories of the *Album*. He shone in office again in the Second World War when he was in his 70s but his name was tarnished in the second half of the 20th century for he was responsible for setting up the Manhattan Project which led to the detonation of the first atomic weapon in New Mexico.

There is some evidence to suggest that Susannah made a further visit to Canada, though not to the USA. If this did take place, then she is likely to have visited Prince Edward Island between September 1924 and October 1925. She had already shown an interest in Canada when she had made a brief excursion across the border from the United States in early December 1921.[69] There is also the possibility of a connection with a permitted absence before the close of the summer holiday of 1926, raising suspicions of another visit abroad.[70] A list of signatures representing Prince Edward Island could have been familiar to her, for some of the men she met had been in London at the meetings of the American and Canadian Bar Associations. Susannah included a headed page with a printed crest for the government of Prince Edward Island and secured the key officials including the Lieutenant Governor Frank R. Heartz and Premier James Davis Stewart.[71] The majority of the 35 names gathered represent men at various levels of the judiciary across the province,[72] underlining the fact that justice and law certainly became stronger themes in the later stages of the *Album*.

Meanwhile, Susannah remained committed to those in Chorley whose lives had been scarred by war. Disabled ex-servicemen, widows and orphans were her priority on a day-to-day basis. She saw the lasting effects of the war on families as fathers tried, and often failed, to adjust to civilian life. Susannah made generous and perhaps rather random gifts to support the physical and spiritual well-being of her pupils. On February 16 1923, Weld Bank School received 80 boxes of biscuits from Jacobs, the cracker manufacturer, and two large pictures through the efforts of Miss Knight.[73] Exactly a month later it was reported that 'Miss Knight brought four pictures (not new) three religious subjects'. [*sic*][74] She was clearly anxious to satisfy both the material and spiritual needs of the children.

Nothing in the *Weld Bank School Log Book* hints at the great enterprise Susannah had undertaken. The pattern of work and play for Class 1 was only occasionally broken, such as on 26 April 1923 when Weld Bank School was closed for the marriage of the Duke of York and Lady Elizabeth Bowes-Lyon.[75] On 17 May Susannah's class visited the corn fields 'for observation' on Burgh Lane between 2pm to 3pm.[76] It was not unusual for Susannah to lead her pupils into the rural margin of Chorley and she often took pupils out of the classroom to experience the contrasting worlds of work and nature.

Jack had retired from seafaring by 1921. The thread of letters which has been used to trace the interactions between the members of the family untwines from this point. The bond between sister and brother which had been so close over thousands of miles began to unravel – perhaps dramatically. There is a fleeting phrase later in the 1920s suggesting that some sort of mistrust arose. In an undated fragment of a letter Jack wrote to his wife, Mary Louisa, he noted:

> [My] sister [Susannah] arrived & that with Louie [Louisa Elizabeth] & yourself had spent an enjoyable day in town, Evidently your daughter and her auntie are rapidly becoming great friends, Now mind she is your daughter and do not let anyone get any hold over her in any form whatever. You will know in what direction I mean. [*sic*][77]

There is no further evidence of the nature of this fracture, though it is possible that religion was a cause. Jack was as fervent in his Protestantism as Susannah was in her Catholicism but they had had a lifetime to grow to appreciate their different outlooks on faith, such as when they both supported Lizzie through convent school. Mary Louisa was a firm and abrasive character, but Susannah had known her for two decades. Her interest in Father Carroll, the former assistant priest of Chorley and Irish nationalist whose portrait hung in Astley Hall, may have led to disagreements over the independence of the new Irish state in the 1920s, but there is no other evidence to take this further. Perhaps it was simply Susannah's obsession for the *Album* which troubled Jack. The full explanation for any rift will never be discovered.

Jack Knight was active in his retirement, pursuing a real ethic for work. He purchased a string of shops on Litherland Road in Bootle, one of which he ran himself as a sweet shop. He collected rent from the other premises, making a good income as a landlord. He quickly became a well-respected businessman, associating with civic officials and town councillors, perhaps making use of his masonic connections.[78]

Susannah's vigour, meanwhile, began to be impeded by age and declining health.[79] Early in 1920 she had had a fall which left her lame for life.[80] In December 1920 she had a period of illness which was probably caused by the Spanish 'flu.[81] It is a credit to her constitution that influenza did not claim her, for so many had died as a result of this epidemic in the months that straddled the end of the war. The year of 1925 saw two absences for Susannah, in February and October.[82] She was also absent through illness in April 1928.[83] By the end of the decade she was beginning to struggle but she still had a burning desire to travel.

Susannah was determined to witness the ceremony at the newly-dedicated Menin Gate in Ypres on 8 August 1928. She was one of 60,000 who joined a 'pilgrimage' organized by the British Legion. Susannah was footsore and blistered from marching to 'Pack Up Your Troubles', 'It's a Long Way to Tipperary', and the hymn 'All Hail the Power of Jesu's Name'. Her letter to the *Chorley Guardian* sharing the experience was published on 18 August:

> We marched in procession through the city and finally took up our stand directly in front of the Menin Gate. We had a splendid view of the proceedings and heard every word that was spoken. It was a most wonderful stay, and every moment of it was of intense interest.

> Men came from the Colonies and, I should think, from every part of the Empire. I felt that I could not have our town left out in that glorious ceremony of homage and remembrance to our dead, so I bought a large wreath of roses, for Lancashire, interwoven with beautiful palm, ivy and vine leaves. The inscription reads: 'This wreath is placed here to the memory of all the officers, non-commissioned officers and men of Chorley and district as a tribute of the love and affection of Miss Knight'.

Susannah was conscious that she was in a privileged position. With no dependants, she could afford to make the journey. She felt that she was representing the people of Chorley as a whole.

> So many people among our workers will never get to the Menin Gate to place a wreath for their beloved dead, and I wanted the townspeople to know that my wreath has been placed on the memorial in memory of all, both rich and poor.

She emphasised the blurring of division between class and rank, echoing the principles of Fabian Ware, the man behind the creation of the memorials and graveyards that are seen today across every corner of the globe where servicemen of the British Empire lost their lives.[84]

> There were many distinguished officers present, amongst them being the Prince of Wales, who sat amongst the men amid the ruins to eat his lunch.

She had visited Flanders in April 1922 and had witnessed the devastation of the towns and cities of the region. She expressed her wonder at how the region had been transformed by reconstruction programmes over the intervening six years.[85]

Susannah continued to commit her life and work to the people of Chorley. In the *Chorley Standard* of 28 June of 1930 there was a report of a 'British Legion Treat' at Yarrow Bridge beyond the southern edge of the town. The event was for 250 children of ex-servicemen, and Susannah was the guest of honour, making the presentations. Ever shy of the camera, she can be seen in the right-hand edge of a photograph of all the participants. The Chorley Guardian's report concurs with that of the *Standard* but gives a little more emphasis to Susannah's appeal to support the work of the British Legion. It is clear that she was closely involved with the activities of its Relief Committee.[86]

Foul weather, coupled with her exertions in charitable works, had a direct effect on her health in the following weeks. She was absent from the school through illness on 10 July almost immediately after the return from the Whit holiday. There had been previous occasions when activities in the school holidays had brought exhaustion upon Susannah. Several late returns to school can be linked with her travels. It is certainly possible that Susannah was also recovering from a hectic sortie in search of some final autographs for the *Album*.

The injury to her leg continued to trouble her and on 9 January 1931 Susannah even absented herself from school because the roads were too slippery. [87] Her limp had become increasingly pronounced by the 1930s.[88]

After giving three decades of her service to the school, Susannah must have sensed the changes taking place around her. In October 1931 she lost her responsibility for Class 1, which was taken in hand by the head teacher. Susannah was charged with Class 2, occasional supporting the youngest pupils. In the following year there was an even heavier blow. Miss Lilly had been head teacher of the 'Mixed Section' until her retirement in September 1927. Susannah maintained a close friendship.[89] When Miss Lilly died on 22 June 1932, the school allowed Susannah three days absence to mourn.[90] Miss Lilly was unmarried and her brother called into the school on 28 June to thank the children for prayers and sympathy.[91]

Susannah looked back upon her life, her career, and the mission of the *Album*. There were two volumes at that point and they had become her 'Golden Books'. They were a personal possession now that the civic authorities were no longer interested in her achievements. Tellingly, Susannah started to record the number of signatures in pencil at the foot of some of the pages. Her health had started to hinder her ambition at a time when her mission had become an obsession. She retired without having given her head teacher any clear warning or time to prepare. One final bout of 'flu in February of 1933 was perhaps the final reminder that retirement beckoned, for she has just reached 65 years of age.[92] On 1 March the *Weld Bank School Log Book* punctuates Susannah's career in the briefest of terms:

> Miss Knight – uncertificated assistant mistress retired on pension – yesterday – never giving any notice. She saw Rev. Manager on Tuesday evening – then visited Education office.[93]

Miss A Grime, the supply teacher, had a hard act to follow.[94]

10 RETIREMENT 1933 - 35

AS Susannah ended her career, the world was edging towards a second global conflict. Hitler had succeeded in grasping the chancellorship in Germany a month previously and the embers of the Reichstag building were still smouldering following the destructive fire two days before Susannah's retirement. Despite the dismantling of liberal democracy that propelled Germany towards extremism, the world economy was slowly recovering.

Susannah knew that her work was unfinished and she felt that her infirmity had hampered her efforts.[1] She saw the harm wreaked by the Depression following the Wall Street Crash of October 1929 at a local level and it has been shown that even in the 1930s, she continued to support struggling ex-servicemen and their families. Some of those men, of course, would always carry the physical and psychological wounds sustained in the war. There was an economic cost for their families too. For the maimed and damaged, their Great War never came to an end.

In the two months following her retirement, Susannah was certainly not idle and the first identifiable signature of this stage of her life is that of Cardinal Bourne, the Archbishop of Westminster. This was probably around 15 May 1933, as on the following page is the dated signature of his auxiliary, Edward Myers, Bishop of Lamus. In a wonderfully direct pencil note to the cardinal, Susannah had helpfully pencilled the instruction 'Line for autograph'. Determination, perhaps to the point of abrasiveness, helped Susannah to bring the sacrifice of the men of Chorley to the attention of so many leading figures of the allied nations.[2] Bourne was significant to Susannah because, as the leader of Roman Catholic Church in England and Wales, he certainly deserved the entire page to himself, leaving lesser individuals before and after May 1933 to be squeezed on to previously used sheets. Despite this, there are pencilled lines for printed borders which she never developed.

On Saturday, 24 November 1934, death separated Jack from his sister more surely than the ocean had when he was a mariner. Susannah's brother had never fully recovered after his period of illness in 1916. The vestiges of tropical fevers picked up in the Amazon and the cumulative effects of his diabetes had been exacerbated by his service on the Russian convoys. His health was subsequently broken and he died at the age of 65. Jack had been well-regarded throughout his retirement, retaining the respect that he had earned during his career. His civilian and war time feats were noted by the *Bootle Times* and his bravery was commended. The gold medal he was given from the Mayor of Sydney for saving two mariners from a shark was recalled and his command of food convoys maintaining supplies to a beleaguered Britain during the Great War was celebrated.

A Representative from Booth Shipping Company was there to acknowledge his loyal service when he was buried in Bootle Cemetery on the following Tuesday. The chief mourners were listed by the *Bootle Times* and his wife and daughters were there at the graveside, as were several members of the Johnsons from Mary Louisa's side of the family. Mary Louisa's sisters and nephews were there to pay their respects. Significantly, despite a fulsome account of those who were clearly close friends and relatives, there are some surprising absences. There is no mention of Jack's half-sisters Lizzie, Ada or Mary and there is certainly no mention of Susannah. They are not included as mourners and they do not seem to have made a floral tribute.[3] It is possible that the tension of the 1920s remained but it is more likely that the Catholic branch of the family felt bound by the '*communicatio in sacris*' clause of canon law which discouraged Catholics from attending services outside the faith.

This seems a harsh way for Jack and Susannah to part, as their paths of conviction had to a large extent been chosen by their parents. It is possible that religion had been an occasional point of contention in their lives. But Susannah had been sufficiently open-minded to organise events for ex-servicemen at Catholic, Anglican and Non-conformist venues. She included a Church of England service to dedicate the portraits in 1920. This real and divisive chasm between Catholics and Protestants blighted the lives of many Lancashire families.

A large sum of money was made over to Mary Louisa Knight on Jack's passing and he had left a comfortable estate to his wife to the tune of £2,442 12s 12d. This was a great sum for the time, approaching £100,000 today.[4] The commercial properties on Litherland Road continued to provide an income and it is probable that there were residential properties aside from 79 Merton Road. Jack's granddaughter, Janice Walmsley, believes that some of these properties remained in the family until the 1950s. She recalls: 'I remember as a child calling at several [properties] with [Mary Louisa] to collect the rent'. Jack's family was still relatively young when he died and the younger daughter, Jean, was only 16 years old. Louisa Elizabeth was a little older at 21 and at a point in her life where she craved independence. She married Harold Walmsley and left home. Mary Louisa had already earned herself the nickname 'The Duchess' by the time that Jack died, but as widow she projected an even greater aura of dignity. Later photographs of her show an immaculately attired woman with a confident and animated smile.[5] At some point Mary Louisa moved into the home of her younger daughter, Jean, as *Huascar* (the house, not the ship) must have felt empty without her husband – a vessel adrift without its captain.

A significant event in Susannah's life's work took place on 6 February 1935 when she was invited to attend the Chorley and District Overseas Ex-Servicemen's Reunion at the Arcade Café. It was the third occasion that a reunion had been arranged and over a period of three years the attendance had risen to just under 220 men. The comrades hoped to meet annually and Susannah declared that she longed for a time when the size of the room would not be sufficient to accommodate everyone. The mayor recalled how the organisation had arranged a visit to Belgium in the previous September to give veterans the opportunity to honour the friends they had left in the battlefields of Belgium two decades before. Susannah's role in helping to form the organisation was commended and Major Baines, who had commanded the 4th The Loyal North Lancashire Regiment, underlined the part Susannah had played in the work of care and support for ex-servicemen. He described Susannah as the soldiers' second mother. He said he did not know why she had not been honoured by the town, which was greeted with applause. He reiterated that she had devoted the past 20 years of her life to the welfare of the ex-servicemen and their families. He said he was sure that:

> ... the King, did he but know of her wonderful services, would be only too pleased to honour her in a manner befitting a lady with such qualifications. He declared that he would do his best in his role as President of the association to get some recognition for Miss Knight.[6]

The origins of Susannah's project lay in her attachment to the Chorley Pals battalion in the first months of the Great War. On 22 February the remnants of 'Y' Company of the 11th East Lancashire Regiment met to commemorate the 20th anniversary of their departure from Chorley, an event which Susannah attended. Miss Sumner of West Cottage organised the first reunion with a concert and dinner for the Pals at the Ambulance Hall and the event had been preceded by an extensive publicity campaign through adverts in the *Chorley Guardian* as well as slides in the local cinemas. The newspaper declared that of the 210 men who had been at the original dinner, more than 80 had lost their lives in the war. Invitations had been sent to 110 for the anniversary of the farewell dinner but despite the publicity, it had been difficult to contact all the surviving ex-servicemen and only one of the commanding officers, Lieutenant Bartwistle, had been traced. There were a number of familiar faces at the meal. Dr Rigby, whose brother had been an officer in the Company and whom Susannah had captured in one of her commissioned portraits, was one of the guests. So, too, was the son of James Sumner, a mere four years old when he had been taken to the original dinner. Major Baines of The Loyal North Lancashire Regiment was also present.

The purpose of the reunion was to honour a promise made by Miss Sumner's father, James, who at the 'farewell dinner' of February 1915 had pledged to the Chorley Pals that there would be another meal waiting for them when they returned home. For many absent friends this had been their last footfall in the town, waved off by the children who had been given time off school to bid farewell. The Pals' Association gave credit to Susannah for her sustained support of former soldiers. They granted the title of 'Honorary Dame President' to honour her commitment to the Company.[7] She recalled the young men to whom she had taught French two decades before. The conjunction of reunions and remembrances compelled Susannah to make one last journey to broadcast the story of Chorley's sacrifice.

Susannah was very much aware of the hardships the survivors of the trenches continued to face, as physical and mental scars disadvantaged ex-servicemen in the workplace. As Europe struggled out of the post-war Recession from 1919, the spectre of poverty still hung over the British working man – through the General Strike of 1926 and the economic collapse of 1929. It is possible to see 1935 as a point where the world was emerging from the Great Depression, but at the same time it was careering towards conflict.

The British Union of Fascists was active in Chorley and rallies were hosted by the Black Shirts in the town, with Oswald Mosley's right-wing movement having offices in Gordon House, 14a Chapel Street, above Burton's shop. Mosley's signature in the *Album* likely belongs to the 1920s when he was a Labour MP with more mainstream views.[8] Mosley's trappings of fascism were a frightening reflection of Hitler's own methods of propaganda and when the uniformed Mosley spoke at Chorley Town Hall on 11 December 1934, he stood alone on the stage in front of a huge Union Flag. All eyes were focused on the man who demanded the support of Chorley's working men, as he urged 'a national revival, a new flame of faith to revive the flagging spirit of the nation'.[9] The *Chorley Guardian* report at the time suggested that 'other towns had greeted Sir Oswald with broken bottles and knuckle dusters and made enthusiastic efforts to break up his meetings, but not so in Chorley'. In fact, it seems that the most vocal support came from the 60 black-shirted bodyguards who chanted 'Two, four, six, eight, who do we appreciate, M-O-S-E-L-E-Y, Mosley' at the end of the speech. This was hardly a rousing display, though the presence of the Black Shirts did raise some attention. It was reported that there were serious and challenging questions about education, religion and anti-Semitism, though it is not clear whether they were posed by supporters or critics of the British Union of Fascists. [10]

Chorley's Rotary Club also had a guest speaker, a German called Walther Kurchenmeister who peddled a dangerous mix of anti-Communism and anti-Semitism, exhorting the people of Chorley to observe the miracle of Germany's economic revival under Hitler. The same edition of the *Chorley Guardian* reported a verdict of 'suicide whilst of unsound mind' for a 52-year-old man of Highfield Road North. The wife and daughter had returned from a concert at Trinity Methodist Church Hall to find a mat wedged against the front door and a strong smell of gas. The man, who was already under medical guidance, had been restless, suffering from 'nerve troubles' and the headline read 'Victim of Depression'. In 1911 he had been a cotton spinner but by 1935 he was unemployed. Like so many men who had lived through the terror of the trenches, he struggled with civilian life in the 1920s and 1930s and the psychological consequences of war. Depression was as real a mental state as an economic one.[11]

Susannah had done her best to support former soldiers and their dependants in the years of Depression. Some of the men she looked after may have been swayed by the politics of the extreme right, though whatever else was happening in Europe, Susannah felt that recovery was underway. There is not enough evidence to guess at Susannah's political persuasions and the diversity of signatures she collected indicate no particular prejudice. What Susannah did want to do, however, was to give her Second Book the title 'Recovery Period', and seek the autographs of those she described as 'those who piloted their nations safely through the most terrible Period the world has ever known'. [*sic*][12] She was about to commence a third volume and though recovery had taken a time to emerge, Susannah was an optimist. Susannah cast her mind back to the faces of the men she had taught French to in 1914 and 1915. She recalled the cohorts of students that had passed through her classes. Susannah had spent so much of her time in the 1920s trying to make 'the great and the good' take notice of Chorley's sacrifice. She decided to return to the United States.

Within nine months of the reunion meals of February 1935, Susannah obtained a visa for a final voyage to America. It was issued in Manchester on 22 October.[13] The unnamed cousin who had paid for her 1921 visit to America had died, as had Senator Boies Penrose whom she later claimed had supported her.[14] A tenser relationship between Susannah and Mary Louisa suggests that she did not rely on a significant portion of Jack's estate. The improved conditions of service enacted by Lloyd George in 1917 may well have allowed her pension to cover her expenses. [15] She paid for the ticket herself and stated on the passenger records that she intended to be abroad for six months. It turned out to be a year-long adventure.[16]

11 THE LAST AMERICAN ADVENTURE 1935 - 36

S USANNAH boarded *Laconia* at Liverpool on 26 October 1935.[1] This had been the ship that brought members of the American Bar Association to Britain in 1924. The Cunard liner docked in New York on 4 November.[2] She reacquainted herself with the members of her family that were still living in the city. Annie O'Connell, her now widowed cousin, was still at 2374 Amsterdam Avenue.

Susannah didn't stay long in New York and the blast of noise and activity of the city was a jarring contrast to life in Chorley. She had an intriguing friend who provided a base for the next 12 months. Her New York family vouched that she had an address and a purpose on the paperwork that accompanied her previous visits. On this occasion a man called Bob Barker was named as her host on the passenger list of *Laconia*.[3] This is the first time that Barker's name appears in the evidence that remains of Susannah's life, and yet she seems to have already had a very strong connection with him and his family. Within a fortnight of her arrival in America she was with his family at 2249 Sixth Avenue in Fort Worth, Texas. The city is relatively close to Dallas located in the centre of the state and seems to have been the place to which she periodically returned over the next year.

Bob Barker was the Secretary to the Senate of Texas, the clerk who made sure that the documents prepared for the state's Senate were in order. He was seven years younger than Susannah and his wife, Nora Jones Barker, was nine years his junior. Neither the Barkers nor Texas had ever featured in Susannah's life up to this point.[4] He was really too old to have been a veteran of the Great War, and yet he registered for service in September 1918, four days after he reached the age of 44. He was unlikely to have seen action.[5] He seems to have been independent of mind, and the fact that he was a self-employed farmer in 1918 was a surprising preparation for a career in state government. Somehow, Susannah had struck up a friendship with Barker and made his home state the focal point of her visit. Barker, respected but not necessarily celebrated by his contemporaries, had influential connections that put Susannah at the heart of Texas political, civic and cultural life. Naturally, Barker and his wife are recorded with their signatures in the third volume.[6] Susannah's interest in including civic, political, spiritual and medical representatives in the *Album* remained at the core of this later work. She continued to record the names of the key figures, the great and the good who held communities together in the difficult years after the Great War.

Texas appears to have gripped Susannah, and if she had a little knowledge of the state before she arrived, she certainly gained a deeper understanding of its essence by the time she returned home. There are more than 70 pages in the *Album* devoted to the people of Texas and there is strong evidence to suggest that she had been drawn by the dream of America when she saw Buffalo Bill Cody's performance in Liverpool in 1891. Buffalo Bill's show even passed though Chorley in September 1904, and though there is no direct evidence, it is almost certain that she made the effort to see the parade through the town.[7] The figure of the cowboy continued to fascinate her on this final journey and may have represented the adventurous spirit of the West that she had tried to recapture throughout her life.

The significant event that spanned the full period of Susannah's visit was the Texas Centennial, celebrating a century of the state's independence from Mexico. A carefully choreographed series of events had been the germ of an idea in a speech presented by former Texas Governor James Stephen Hogg in 1900. This idea became an active venture as early as 1923. A permanent Centennial Commission was formed in July 1934 and Dallas was chosen as the venue for a spectacular exposition – a world fair in all but name. Susannah gave her full attention to these events and the Centennial can be associated with many of the signatures that form the third volume of the *Album*.[8] The celebrations dominated her movements, but did not hold her attention exclusively. Susannah did not lose sight of her underlying mission and she shared many encounters with American veterans of not only the Great War, but other conflicts in which America had engaged.

It is possible to track most of her adventures by following the chronology of the signatures. It is a trail that throws her into the company of a fascinating array of people who are representative of many different walks of life. On 20 November 1935, Susannah recorded her first dated signature of the American adventure. She had not stayed in Fort Worth for long and was in the city of Austin in the south of the state. Charles Lockhart, the

Treasurer to the State of Texas, at 45 inches in height, had the notoriety of being the smallest treasurer to have held office for an American state.[9] His photograph appears with his scratched signature. The autograph of Claude D. Teer was made on the same day, just beneath that of Lockhart. Teer worked closely with the State Treasurer as he was the Chairman of the Board of Control, purchasing supplies for state departments, maintaining its properties and preparing the budget.[10] The official stamps of Teer's office were embossed upon the page and three other officials from the state administration signed the *Album*.[11] Susannah also added the management and staff of the *Austin Dispatch* and the *Tyler Daily Courier-Times* on one of the occasions that she was in Austin.[12]

Susannah established herself in Austin. She took a keen interest in meeting members of the University of Texas from 11 December onwards, perhaps through connections Bob Barker had opened up. Harry Yandell Benedict was a surprisingly remarkable individual and already had a long career to look back upon when Susannah met him, having led the development of mathematical astronomy at the university. He oversaw an extensive building programme in his long presidency of the university and was responsible for the McDonald Observatory.[13] On that same day she met: Edward Jackson Mathews, the Registrar and Dean of Admissions; Hanson Tufts Parlin, Professor of English and Dean of the College of Arts and Sciences; and Benjamin Floyd Pittenger, Dean of the School of Education. They are all recorded together, with gold seals of the University of Texas alongside their names.[14] The following page of the *Album* confirms that Susannah continued her tour of the University later that day. She recorded the names of: John William Calhoun from the Mathematics department; Albert P. Brogan, the Dean of the Graduate School; Victor Ivan Moore, Dean of Student Life; and J. Anderson Fitzgerald, the Dean of the School of Business Administration.[15]

The connection between business and academic studies was no accident, as one of the aims of the Centennial Committee was to promote the state's canny commercial acumen. The remaining six signatures on this page were connected to engineering, geology and petroleum. The University of Texas was providing the academic credentials for a post-depression revival for the state. Susannah visited the Physics department, which also played a part in the economic transformation of Texas. She met key individuals who had been instrumental in forming this department and driving its research. Though they are undated, the signatures must come from this period of Susannah's journey – either in December or January. She met Lucien LaCoste who invented the gravity meter – perhaps not the most widely-known innovation to most people, but a fundamentally important piece of equipment which is still used today to in surveying for oil. She also met physicists John Jaimison 'J Squared' Miller, Olan Harvey Hamilton and Renna Bonner Walker.[16] Walker went on to see service in the Second World War in the Women's Army Corps.[17]

Susannah made a point of acquainting herself within the Physics and Mathematics departments. The work of these departments was intrinsically connected with the activities of the department of Petroleum Engineering. Physics and Mathematics made the link between theory and practical reality to power the development of the industry. In mid-December and mid-January Susannah met a number of academics whose work blurred into the commercial world of the oil industry. These men and women gave their autographs as well as adding their achievements and publications. The names of Frederick Byron Plummer, E.C. Sargent, Helen Jeanne Plummer, George H. Fancher and Thomas Ulvan Taylor are placed together in the *Album*, representing an essential source of expertise on which the oil industry depended.[18] Mel Oakes, a former member of the department acting as its historian and archivist, described Taylor as 'a very special faculty member at the University of Texas' stating that 'he founded the engineering program here'.[19]

Susannah had arrived in Texas at an exciting time when science had the opportunity to drive the recovery. The physicists, geologists, engineers and mathematicians led the way in providing the science and technology behind the revival of the economy and the Centennial Exposition was as much a celebration of the spirit and culture of Texas as it was a driving force to attract commerce. Though Henry Ford's automotive company occupied one of the most dominant of the Art Deco structures in the Fair Park in Dallas it was the oil industry of Texas that was enabling Ford's vehicles to become metaphors for freedom through capitalist endeavour. Oil was, quite literally, fuelling the future of the state.

There are also academics of the University of Texas in the *Album* who represented the cultural and historical character of the state. Caleb Perry Patterson was a particularly distinguished figure on the staff and placed his name at the head of a representative group of staff drawn from the History faculty.[20] He had an influential background in history and political science, something he emphasised by including a list of his publications and editorships beneath his autograph. Susannah was thus given a very personal summary of his career and an appreciation of a time spent in London. This personal element suggests a strength of the connection that Susannah made with Patterson when she met him. It is impossible to reconstruct what passed between Susannah and the people that she met, though the fact that many contributors gave more than their name suggests an underlying conversation which Susan had refined over time. The fact that Patterson was a firm believer that the USA should become a member of the League of Nations does add a certain interest that links him to other names that can be found in the *Album*.[21] Susannah recorded the signatures of several senators and congressmen on her journey who had similar desires and it is likely that she sympathised with the aims of the League. Men such as Thaddeus H. Caraway, also a cheerleader for the League, had been sought out in 1921.[22] The United States, of course, had never pursued President Woodrow Wilson's desire for America to be a keystone in the promotion of world peace following the Great War. The profile of the signatures collected by Susannah suggests she had a strong sympathy with the efforts of individuals who sought to secure a post-war recovery.

Susannah wanted to absorb the culture of Texas and was keen to include representative figures in the *Album*. Milton Rietow Gutsch was a specialist in Medieval British history and had occupied senior roles in the department and faculty at the University of Texas from 1916. He placed his name on the same page as Patterson and annotated his entry in the *Album* with a reference to his book on the Crusades. He had a strong interest in British history and had previously been an editor of the *Texas History Teachers' Bulletin*. He made a note of this, too, beneath his name, though this referred to work that had kept him busy between 1912 and 1920. Above all, however, Susannah was drawn to Gutsch because he was responsible for compiling the Texas War Records Collection. This included enlistment, casualty and personnel records of the men of Texas who had enlisted between 1916-19, an archive that expanded throughout the 20th century.[23] Gutsch and Susannah had a shared interest in recording those who had served and suffered in the Great War.[24] Frank Burr Marsh was another History professor at the University of Texas to add his name to the *Album*, noting his specialism in Roman history and drawing attention to this with a summary of his main publications.[25] Charles William Ramsdell is the final historian to be included on this page, regarded as the 'Dean' of Southern historians as someone who specialised in the Old South.[26] He was about to take up the presidency of the Southern Historical Association when he met Susannah.[27]

Susannah continued to engage with the history of Texas, a state which has a unique history of which it remains proud. A significant cultural connection that Susannah made was with Rev. Paul Foik, a Roman Catholic priest with a deep academic grounding.[28] He had helped shape the development of librarianship in the USA and began the collation of material that became the Catholic Archives of Texas. More pertinently, he was also a key member of the Texas Centennial Committee and, together with J. Frank Dobie and

Louis Wiltz Kemp, selected the historical sites to be featured in the celebrations of 1935-6.[29] Dobie, an artillery veteran of the Great War, contributed a full page expression of his thoughts about Texas history to the *Album*.[30] He was the leading spokesperson for the state on cultural and literary matters during the Centennial.[31] His wife, Bertha, recorded a moving piece of historical prose in the *Album*, quoting from her 'Women of the Salt Marshes'.[32] They were both folklorists and gave a context to the sense of the depth of faith and feeling Texans had invested in the Centennial. Susannah also met Theresa M. Hunter, who was an active poet in the 1920s and 1930s. Hunter filled a full page of the *Album* with her poem entitled 'At Dusk' from her collection *Panorama*, which told the story of three women kneeling as the sun dipped into twilight: 'Like radiant stars, three virtues shone, Faith, Hope, and Charity!' Faith, Hope and Charity have a great resonance, as these might well be virtues one could ascribe to Susannah. It seems that Hunter had a good measure of Susannah's interests and activities and she chose the poem well.[33] Foik, Dobie and Kemp were the architects of the spirit of the Centennial and Susannah had got to the very heart of the event. It seems that Texas had got to the very heart of Susannah, too.

Susannah was a linguist and so it is no surprise that she acquainted herself with academics who studied languages. She included the signature of Professor Robert Adger Law of the English department who had edited several editions of Shakespeare. Members of the Classics department were also represented. Professor William James Battle added to his signature, describing himself as 'an apostle of Greek and Roman culture for more than 40 years'. Harry J. Leon, Professor of Classical Language and also President of the Texas Classical Association gave his autograph.[34] Aaron Schaffer, Professor of Romance Languages, went so far as to give his signature twice. Schaffer had written and signed a half-page account of his published work with his other achievements and wrote his name again on the reverse of the page.[35] The state's history represented a meeting point of cultures and languages which Susannah might well have recognised in connection with her own project. Texas was a meld of Native American, Spanish, French, and American cultures, now unified under a single star.

Susannah pursued an historian called Carlo E. Castenada who was given the liberty of a whole page of the *Album* with what was effectively a bibliography of Texan history. Castenada was known to Foik, who had edited his *Our Catholic Heritage in Texas, 1519–1936* which he had begun in 1936.[36] The Catholic bias within the choice of texts listed suggests that Susannah had shared her interests and purpose with Castenada, and that he had time to make a considered response. There is no personal touch or a message of greeting in his entry and it may be that this was one of those entries gained through a written request. There is just his signature, followed by a list of publications.[37] He clearly felt that he was giving the detailed guidance that Susannah had sought. What Castenada did, however, was to provide Susannah with a bibliography which could help her to understand the course of Texan history between the 16th and the end of the 19th centuries from a Catholic perspective. It cannot be shown whether or not she read more deeply into the history of Texas but she returned to the subject of the state's past on several occasions during her visit.

These custodians of the essence of Texas were joined in the *Album* by Mary Jourdan Atkinson, who included a passage from her recently published *The Texas Indians*.[38] Alongside an extended quotation summarising an invasive process of discovery, colonisation, conflict and nation-building, Atkinson sketched the roughest of maps of Texas. It gives the locations of the Native American tribes of the region and her text records the brave but futile resistance of the Comanche and the guileless hospitality of the Tiguas. She saw the tide of European migration as an historical inevitability.

Mary Jourdan Atkinson's unsettling account may have influenced Susannah to learn a little more about the experience of Native Americans and about the adventure of frontier life in the 19th century. European settlement had excluded Native Americans from the lands they had been accustomed to roam and hunt upon and one of Susannah's encounters casts the status of Native Americans into sharp relief. Several 'exhibition' features of the Centennial reflected on the life of Native Americans as defeated enemies or cultural curiosities. A Sioux man, Two Eagles, a descendant of Sitting Bull of the Battle of Little Big Horn seems to have been a participant in a display at the Dallas Centennial. There is even an ambiguity of punctuation that could place Two Eagles at the great battle himself. Susannah met him and must have made enough of an impression for him to present her with a signed photograph and a full page recounting his history. To Susannah, Two Eagles was as much a victim of war as any veteran, stripped of his pride and nationhood and left to make his way living out a parody of the proud Sioux way.

Susannah was given an extensive monograph in this period by Rev. John M. Riach, the Chaplain of the Newman Club at the University of Texas. He was also a member of the Missionary Society of Saint Paul the Apostle which was a Catholic society originating in New York which focused on evangelising young men. More importantly to Susannah, he was a veteran who understood something of the restorative nature of the *Album*. He had served as an Ordinary Seaman in the Royal Naval Division on HMS Tiger at the Battle of Jutland in 1916. He wrote:

As a survivor of the Battle of Jutland, living overseas, I have been asked to give a short message to the English people. What shall I say? To my mind the only thing now in order must be something about the maintenance of peace, and so I urge that a strong friendship come to maturity between the American and British nation. Without their help, no major war can be fought; with their help, a favourable balance in fighting for peace will deter any militaristic activity. This unofficial and tacit alliance, at least under the present unsettled conditions, should be sought now, for to-morrow may be too late. At any moment, the spark may come which will set the world alight. God grant that saner counsels prevail. [*sic*] [39]

Despite the excitement of her American adventure Susannah still recalled the suffering war had inflicted on society and shared Riach's hope for the future. As a Catholic Priest, a veteran, and associated with an academic institution, Riach embodied many of the qualities that Susannah believed were needed for the rebuilding society in the recovery years.

It was also at this time that Susannah was in contact with Charles C. Betts, the State Service Officer for Texas, based in Austin. This is almost certainly one of those contributions which was sought by letter as he typed his extended contribution directly onto one of Susannah's sheets. It also confirms that she carried loose sheets to bind later. The role of the State Service Officer, in Betts' words, was to 'work for the rehabilitation of the disabled veterans, their widows, orphans, mothers and fathers ... 198, 238 men and nurses from Texas served during the World War in the Army, Navy and Marine Corps'. Betts included a summary of his own active service in France between October 1917 and January 1919 and he had seen action at Toulon, Aisne, and Chateau-Thierry. He had qualified as a sharpshooter and had been awarded a Good Conduct Medal. He was clearly a soldier of ability and courage whose experience of war was typical of many men approaching middle age in the mid-1930s.[40] John W. Brown of the State Health Office and Herbert N. Barnett of the State Health Department were both veterans of the Army Medical Corps and ensured that veterans were given the attention and care that they deserved.[41] Susannah's interest must have triggered so many memories for men who were active, like Susannah herself, in making sure that the plight of ex-servicemen was not forgotten.

Just as in the earlier pages of the *Album*, Susannah wanted to include those with authority in government. With the assistance of Bob Barker, she was able to gain the signature of the Governor of Texas, James V. Allred, and other key individuals. Allred's signature is featured on two occasions, on consecutive pages. R.B. Stanford, his Secretary of State appears beneath his second entry.[42] These men were probably introduced to Susannah's project, personally or by proxy, at the turn of the year. Wilbourne B. Collie, the Acting Governor of Texas gave signatures on both 31 December and 1 January. These help to give a context of time and place to the signatures of this part of the *Album*.[43] Walter F. Woodul, the Acting Governor of Texas, gave his signature on 28 April.[44] This collection of pages has been magnificently illustrated with arrays of flags and gold seals, making these the most vibrant pages to be found in the whole *Album*. The flags of the United States and the Lone Star of Texas feature in brilliant watercolour. There are also the four other flags which had flown over Texas: those of Mexico, Spain, the Confederacy and France.[45] To complete her reckoning of those who had directed Texas through to the years of the recovery, Susannah secured the signatures of all 30 members of the Texas Senate of the 44th Legislature and over 100 members of the state's Legislative Assembly.[46]

There is the barest evidence of a fleeting visit back to New York in February 1936, through the inclusion of the signature of Alonzo F. Whyert of New York University, his name edged towards the centre fold of the volume as if an afterthought.[47] New York offered a cold contrast to Texas at this time of year and she might have struggled with her weakened leg. If she did travel she did not linger, for by 26 February the dated signature of Earnest O. Thompson, the Chairman of the Railroad Commission of Texas, appeared, two days after Susannah's 68th birthday. He was listed with other men of influence in the state. The page was headed by William C. McCraw, the Attorney General of Texas. The page included two other members of Thompson's Railroad Commission: Charles Vernon Terrell and the Secretary, C.F. Petet. The growing dominance of motor transport was represented in the *Album* by Mark Marshal, the Director of Motor Transportation.[48] To emphasise the growing dominance of the automobile, in which the oil-producing state took a role, Petet can be rediscovered in August 1942 presiding over a hearing in Austin Texas to discontinue a passenger railroad service. [49] It is clear from his testimony that the age of rail had given way to roads soon after Susannah met these men, and the Centennial Exposition had played its part in this by extolling a state economy based on the new black gold and the automobile.

Susannah was intensely active in the late spring on 1936. On 2 April Susannah was back in Austin and asked Guiton Morgan, the City Manager, to sign the *Album*. She must have held this signature in high regard, as she kept it clear of any other autographs until 31 August when she offered the page to George D. Fairtrace, the City Manager of Fort Worth.[50] Morgan's office was in the same building as that of the mayor and other representatives of the Austin civic infrastructure. It is no surprise that Susannah moved around the building, presenting the story of the *Album* to all she met and of course Mayor Tom Miller placed his name alongside two City of Austin seals.[51] Accompanying pages include the signatures of George Sheppard, the State Comptroller, as well as representatives from the Industrial Accident Board and the Commissions of Life Insurance, Casualty Insurance, and Fire Insurance.[52] Susannah even managed to convince John J. Buchan, Executive Secretary of the Game, Fish and Oyster Commission, to include two gold seals with his signature.[53] The wonderfully named Zeta Gossett, the Banking Commissioner of Texas, was also allocated a page to himself with a gold Texas seal next to his signature.[54]

The Police Department was also housed in Austin's City Hall and the city's Chief of Police, R.D. Thorpe, shares two pages of the *Album* with 11 of the officers and men of his department. The names and ranks given range from Roy L. Smith, Captain of Police, to J.B. Taylor, the desk clerk. Susannah even asked a traffic engineer and the police photographer to sign the pages.[55] The two crews of the Austin Fire Department fill two pages of the *Album*, too, and an image of the State Capitol Building has been pasted alongside. Even in these conversations with men who were giving service to their city, Susannah was able to ask them about their service to their country, and Captain Platt of the Fire Department added details of his time in the 42nd 'Rainbow' Division.[56] This, of course, had been the division in which Father Patrick Duffy had been so prominent. Susannah gained signatures of law enforcement officers from around the state including Lee O. Allen, Sheriff of Travis County, with his assisting officer.[57]

May 1936 is a period where Susanna's activity is difficult to trace. It is, perhaps, worth considering that she had originally planned to stay in the United States for six months. This was something which the passenger records for November 1935 had made clear. However this was not to be the case, as for whatever reasons, Susannah decided to remain in America.

An extended entry in the *Album* around this time is from the State Reclamation Engineer, Ralph J. McMahon, who offers his signature in Austin on two consecutive pages on 11 April. Susannah had a rather more serious conversation than might be imagined on this occasion. McMahon gave a good deal of detail to his two pages, including a typed outline of his responsibility for the management of the vast waterways of Texas and the importance drainage had for its agriculture. It reads as a statement prepared for all enquirers and the four-paragraph account gives a great deal of technical and legal detail which seems out of place. What is surprising, however, is that it was typed directly onto one of Susannah's blank leaves. A degree of purpose and effort had gone into this contribution when a simple signature might have sufficed.

The second of his sheets displays two photographs. The first is of the Trinity River at Dallas before the reclamation and improvement of the margin at its banks. The second photograph was taken during the deluge of May 1935, demonstrating the effectiveness of the improvements that he had made to the flood defences. This page is punctuated with one of the most colourful of the Texas seals and striking gothic script above McMahon's name to describe his post.[58] The Texas Board of Water Engineers takes up the entire following page, listing C.S. Clark (Chair), A.N.W. McDonald (Secretary), A.H. Dunlap and John W. Prichard as members. There is a rather incongruous collection of inserted material – a model of an 'Engineers Transit', an etching entitled 'stream measurement' and a map of Texas river watersheds.[59]

These men were succeeding against natural forces, moulding the world for the benefit of communities along the Trinity, Brazos and [Texas] Colorado Rivers. Susannah recognized the importance of their work. Later in the year she witnessed floods like no other she had seen.

Susannah travelled northwards in June 1936 and was in Washington DC by the beginning at the month. Of all the correspondence that Susannah made in her lifetime, she was about to send her most audacious letter. On 4 June she sent a letter on headed paper from the Astor Hotel to the President's wife, Eleanor Roosevelt. Susannah was in a strident mood, having been told that she could not seek the President's signature as she had done successfully in 1921. She begged: 'surely, if one man stands high above all others that man is President Roosevelt it grieves me to think that I shall have to go back to England without his'. [sic][60] She outlined the course of her project to underscore her plea, giving examples of the prestigious signatures she had previously secured:

> [In] 1921 I got President Harding's, the cabinet, Senators and Congressmen. In addition I had the officers of the land, sea and air forces … I have the autographs of the King and Queen of the Belgians, the King and Queen of Italy and hosts of Allied officers … The first book is for the War Period and contains distinguished people of that period … I thought I would call the second book the 'Recovery Period' and get the autographs of those who piloted their nations safely through the most terrible Period the world has ever known … As these books are to be a gift to the British nation in memory of the Allied friendships to keep them unique there can be no copies. [sic] (Plate 22)[61]

As a form of consolation she asked that she might have the signature of the President's wife: 'Perhaps you will give me your autograph and that will prove that I really have tried to get the President's'. She implored: 'I hope Mrs Roosevelt you will not refuse the request I make. And in anticipation I thank you most sincerely'. [sic][62]

Unsurprisingly, Eleanor Roosevelt did not reply personally and it was her secretary, Malvina T. Schreider, who returned her compliments on 6 June on behalf of the First Lady. There is, perhaps, a touch of irritation from Eleanor Roosevelt's staff as there is a pencil note added saying 'I think this was done'.

Susannah acknowledged Schreider's reply on 10 June, this time writing from New York, to where she had suddenly removed to tend a sick cousin, Annie O'Connell. Susannah informed Schreider that she intended to return to Washington DC by 1 July. Eleanor Roosevelt's signature was to be sent on to the Astor Hotel.

Susannah was determined to add a Roosevelt signature to the volumes and she succeeded with a signature dated 26 June 1936.[63] In the absence of the President's signature, Susannah resorted to pasting in a photograph offcut from Cunard's *Ocean Times* of 5 November 1936 on her homeward voyage aboard *RMS Samaria*.[64] She ended her correspondence by promising that to Eleanor Roosevelt when the books were to be handed over to the nation.

The Roosevelt correspondence is revealing for it tells, obliquely, that Susannah's 1921 visit to the United States was apparently funded by a wealthy but unnamed cousin. Susannah also claims that she gained contacts at government level through the influence of Senator Boies Penrose. She gives an outline of the structure behind the volumes, now to be in two parts to represent the 'War Period' and the 'Recovery Period'. Most importantly, the letter gives a sense of Susannah's own strength of purpose. The 'Golden Books were to be a gift to the British Nation in memory of the Allied Friendships to keep them unique there can be no Copies. They will be preserved in Astley Hall Chorley Lancashire'. [sic][65] Susannah even goes as far as to tell Eleanor Roosevelt of her lamed leg and how it had limited the pursuit of her project. The letters to the President's wife also reveal parts of Susannah's itinerary as in them, she wrote that she intended to go on to Houston and Galveston in Texas.

Nevertheless, Susannah lingered in New York, where there was a particular event which may have been one of the anchor points for her tour of America later that month. On 28 June 1936, Susannah was at a memorial service for Father Francis P. Duffy, the 42nd Rainbow Division's celebrated senior chaplain, held at St Raymond's Cemetery in the Bronx. Susannah recorded signatures of men who attended this memorial on the very last page of the third volume.[66] At least three earlier signatures in the *Album* also note a connection with the division.[67] Duffy had signed the *Album* when Susannah visited the USA in 1921.[68] Susannah stood shoulder-to-shoulder with more than 100 veterans of the 69th Regiment of New York.[69]

The *New York Times* reported on the memorial service and indicated that there was a veterans' association for Roman Catholics of the Rainbow Division. While in New York, Susannah also secured the signature of a Rev. Bernard Walston, who had served with the British Army throughout the Great War in the Artist's Rifle Corps of London, converting to Catholicism after the war and eventually becoming ordained. Susannah had met Father Duffy on her visit to New York in 1921. Walston had known Duffy during the war years and it is possible that the latter may have had a hand in prompting his conversion. Walston succeeded Duffy at Holy Cross Church in New York on his death in 1932 and in the context of the memorial service on June 1936, he was the chaplain of 'Fr Duffy, Post 54, Catholic War Veterans'.[70] Susannah deliberately attended the memorial service at which Walston was present, taking the time and trouble to return to New York when the focus of her visit had been Texas.

Susannah returned to Texas and was in Dallas by 28 July. It is possible that she travelled to and from Fort Worth within the day, as the distance is just over 30 miles, but there was much to see and every reason to stay over a longer period to take in the full programme of events. She gained the stamp and signature of the city's Postmaster, Walter B. Lunar, on that day. The Assistant Postmaster, George C. Young also gave his signature.[71] The visit to Dallas must have been one of the most memorable parts of Susannah's year of travel, with the city's Centennial celebrations well in hand after opening on 6 June.[72] Bob Barker had probably helped Susannah grasp a sense of the excitement at Fort Worth's rival Frontier Centennial which had opened in at the beginning of July.[73] On 29 July, Susannah met Read Johnson, the manager of the Veterans' Association in Dallas and he subsequently added his stamp and signature.[74] Even in the clamour and bustle of the Centennial's main attractions, she was attentive to the main purpose of her project and in all probability they spoke of Father Duffy's memorial service. It may have been at this time that Susannah was introduced to Fort Worth's Chief of Police, Henry B. Lewis.[75] She also made sure that George Sergeant, the Mayor of the city, gave his civic assent to the *Album*.[76]

Whilst Fort Worth's exhibition focused on the 'Old West' of the 19th century, it has been seen that the Fair Park Exposition in Dallas also promoted opportunities for economic progress. The presentations were based at a site already used for the regular State Fair and it was lavishly re-modelled for the occasion at vast expense, with Dallas committing $10 million at the outset – twice the total expenditure at the Frontier Centennial. Susannah took the autographs of two representatives of the Centennial Commission of Control that released finance for many of the structures created for the celebrations. John A. Hulen was the representative from Fort Worth and Henry Hutchings was the Commission's secretary.[77] The full sum of the Exposition at Fair Park amounted to a phenomenal $25 million and in a recovering economy this was either a great expression of confidence or an incautious gamble.[78]

The exhibition halls, many of which still stand today, reflected the state's brazen spirit, pushing boundaries of 'classic modern'. Susannah is sure to have strolled across the Grand Plaza and along the Esplanade of State, seeing her reflection on the waters which mirrored, as the Texas State Almanac has it, the 'multitude of beauties of the surrounding structures'.[79] The Hall of Transportation and the Hall of Varied Industries, Communications and Electricity faced each other across a 700-foot reach of water which stretched to the Texas Hall of State. The Poultry, Agriculture and Livestock Buildings were given the same aesthetic consideration as the Hall of Natural History, Hall of Horticulture, Hall of Domestic Arts, Aquarium, and Hall of Fine Arts.[80] The Art Deco architecture defined the Centennial as 'Texanic in ideals, continental in proportions and international in scope'.[81] George Dahl, the Centennial Exposition's architect, balanced beauty and function in every aspect of the associated buildings.[82] Paul Foik, J. Frank Dobie and Louis Wiltz Kemp, already mentioned above, gave the historical perspective that allowed the modern architecture to contrast the historical narrative of the Centennial.

Dallas had spared no expense on creating an exhibition and park to thrill. The Fair Park was extended to give a superb venue for many of the exhibits and entertainments. Having been held under the flags of United States, Mexico, Spain, the Confederacy and France, the Lone Star was the one banner that the state was devoted to. A parade of flags gave an opportunity for spectacle and a display of devotion. The pageant featured a staged 'Cavalcade of Texas', with standing ovation from the vast audience on each occasion that the Lone Star of Texas appeared. This was not just about the past and Texan nationhood, but also an opportunity to display to the world the material worth of the state. Gaining a foothold in the international market place was an underlying purpose of the Centennial. It is no coincidence that Susannah sought the signatures of the leaders of the Chambers of Commerce of Houston and Dallas and these men may even have been manning official stands at the Fair Park.[83]

One of the more extensive collections of autographs in this period is composed of members and veterans of the Texas Rangers, the force responsible for preserving law and order throughout the state. The Texas Rangers had a significant impact on Susannah and account for nearly a tenth of the tally of names in the final volume. Perhaps it was her association with Read Johnson at the Veterans Association on 29 July 1936 that enabled Susannah to meet and speak with over 20 of the men who had been involved in the Frontier War of the 1890s. Their signatures, particularly of those in the lower ranks, are sometimes quite laboured and scratched, indicating the advanced age of these old soldiers as well as a different era when literacy was less easy to come by. The recollections that they record often refer to their company and their officer, giving a real sense of the comradeship that still held their memories together.

Susannah always managed to find people with interesting tales to tell. Texas Ranger B.M. 'Manny' Gault certainly had notoriety. He was one of the six law enforcement officers who ambushed the bank robbing lovers Bonnie Parker and Clyde Barrow in May 1934. He was struggled to prevent the curious from gawping at the bodies in the hours afterwards.[84] Above all, the name that inspired these veterans can be found standing alongside them. Captain John R. Hughes was a living legend to the Texas Rangers, the man who had embodied the spirit and grit of law enforcement in Texas, initially as a captain in the Frontier Battalion and from 1901, in the same role in the State Rangers.[85]

Alongside these men are veterans of the more recent Great War such as Captain Julian Gillespie and Lieutenant Leist who had been part of the American Expeditionary Force.[86] Major C.B. Fullerton took the trouble to make an extensive note with his signature, having already served in Company 'B' of the Frontier Battalion from 1893-95, the Texas Rangers, and had been recalled to serve in the Great War in the 36th Division of the US Army. His son, Hal B. Fullerton, had served in the 29th Division.[87] Two generations had faced conflict over three decades, serving together at the same time in Europe. Susannah captured them as comrades together.

Susannah was treated with great hospitality by the Texas Rangers when she visited their exhibition stand. M.T. 'Lone Wolf' Gonzaullas, as the senior captain of the Texas Rangers, was head of the Bureau of Intelligence. He added this message to the *Album* which read: 'Welcome to the Department of Public Safety State of Texas Exhibit at the Texas Rangers [Building] Texas Centennial Central Exposition at Dallas Texas August 11th 1936'.[88] The Director of the committee for Public Safety himself, H. Carmichael, as well as his assistant, both give their autographs.[89] Beneath the signature of the veterans is that of E.A. Muret, the Project Superintendent and builder of the Rangers Station, the Centennial Park and the National Exhibition Building exhibiting 'the best of the 48 states' in Dallas.[90]

The Centennial featured celebratory entertainment as well as stalls to inform visitors or to sell the state. It included dramatised recreations of great moments in Texas history. These were performed on gigantic stage areas with full wagon trains and pursuits by horsemen. They captured the Wild Western ideal which had inspired a spirit of adventure in her youth. It must have been in the context of the Centennial exhibition performance that she met Tex Cooper on 25 August 1936. Cooper had performed in a show for some years as a skilled rider and marksman and had even had some small appearances in films.

Mistaking a connection with Buffalo Bill, for they looked alike, Susannah spent a good deal of time talking with Cooper and he passed a photograph of himself to her.[91] He wrote a long passage about his adventures on the reverse of a page in the *Album* and his signature is accompanied by two other performers who recreated the adventures of the Wild West 'The Original Cheyenne Joe' and Dudley White Jr. It is clear that Susannah was recalling the Buffalo Bill show she had seen in Liverpool in 1891 and though Cooper was an actor who did feature in several 'Western' films in the 1930s, he had never performed with Buffalo Bill. It is worth noting that the Liverpool Mercury refers to Fenimore Cooper, the novelist, in both articles on Buffalo Bill's visit in 1891. It may be that Susannah was grasping at an incomplete recollection of these very same articles four decades after the event.[92]

Susannah made some very unlikely associations while she was in Dallas. The fact that she recorded the signature of the Chief of Police, R.L. James, is something one might take for granted by this stage.[93] To find the immaculately laid-out autographs of the management and staff of the *The Dallas Morning News, The Dallas Journal, The Semi-Weekly Farming News* and the *WFAA* radio station is rather more surprising. Each media organisation had arranged for its corporate masthead to be printed on each respective page of the *Album*. The signatures are neatly ranged across full pages. Though other newspapers are represented in the volumes, all four of these enterprises were part of the Belo business empire.[94] Many of the signatures are repeated two or even three times across different pages for people that had overlapping roles. These pages appear to be a bespoke undertaking and the staff to have dedicated a great deal of time and care to the presentation.[95]

Susannah returned to Fort Worth at the end of the month, probably to stay with Bob and Nora Barker, before pursuing her next adventure. On 31 August she offered the *Album* to George D. Fairtrace, the City Manager of Fort Worth. The City Manager of Austin had already signed this very page and perhaps in an effort to outdo a rival, Fairtrace added: 'The Frontier City where the West begins', promoting Fort Worth's own celebratory contribution to the Texas Frontier Centennial.[96]

Susannah did not stay long and was in Dallas two weeks later. Gene Autry, the contemporary film star known as the 'Singing Cowboy', was given a whole page of the *Album* to place his autograph. He was filming *The Big Show* in the city between 15 and 19 September and the crew used the spectacular exhibition areas of the Centennial Exposition for the film's location. The buildings provided a stunning set on which to play out the Hollywood drama and the scenes give a great sense of the excitement of the Centennial itself. The storyline allowed Autry to pursue his trademark horsemanship, with romance and law enforcement thrown in for good measure. It may have been through her meeting with the Texas Rangers that Susannah was put in the company of Autry and they indeed feature on parade and in action in the film's background.

From the wording of his contribution it seems that he must have spent some time in Susannah's company and warmed to her. The eye is caught by the signed photograph of Autry on horseback and his written contribution opens with the greeting: 'To my friend from England, always wishing you the best of luck and success', signing his name, adding a list of eight of the songs that had made his name in Hollywood, and then scribing his name again. Beneath his signature are those of Audrey Davis and Frankie Marvin from the management of Republic Pictures.[97] Susannah's curious relationship with the culture of the Wild West may well have reached its zenith at this point. She had left America by the time 'The Big Show' was released in mid-November but the picture included the song 'Ride, Ranger, Ride' which might well have been familiar to Susannah as it also featured as the headline song to the eponymous Autry movie which was released on 30 September 1936.

Susannah had met the State Reclamation Engineer McMahon in April and had cause to recall him when September came.[98] Texas suffered even more significant floods in July and September than it had in the previous May when the land reclamation systems had been put to the test at Dallas. Three bodies had already been recovered from the Colorado River between Austin and San Antonio in July and houses had been washed away. A train had been wrecked when it had attempted to cross a bridge that had been swept away, and there had been two further fatalities. The *Standard-Times* of

20 September 1936 reported '… the Colorado River rose to the highest flood stage on record; lives and property were menaced in its wild sweep through several hundred miles of the richest farming country in Texas'.[99]

This catastrophe made a huge impression on Susannah and she deliberately marked the *Album* on several occasions, annotating the smear that crossed the account of Cheyenne Joe with 'the Colorado marked this page'.[100] This is not the only instance, as the Board of Water Engineers page has a similar note which has been slurred beyond recognition.[101] Moreover, on the stunningly illustrated page on which Governor James Allred and his Secretary of State, R.B. Stamford, placed their names, there is a slew across the 'six flags' of Texas and Susannah has written 'The marks below have been caused by the Mighty Colorado River which overflowed its banks, 1936' [*sic*] (Plates 19 and 20).[102] These were no souvenirs, but relics of remembrance for the devastation this natural disaster had wrought on the ordinary folk. The deliberate marking of the *Album* in this way cannot be fully explained.

In June, Susannah had told Eleanor Roosevelt that she was going to visit Houston and Galveston. She had been quite definite about this point. She set out on her final excursion on 9 October 1936.[103] She had had a busy morning meeting Oscar Holcombe, the Mayor of Houston, bringing the *Album* and its story to his attention.[104] Later that day Susannah spoke with Miss May in the city's Airway ticket office. It was a fleeting moment, a transaction and a chat, but Susannah obtained two photographs of aeroplanes which she pasted into the *Album*. The first photograph is of an American Airlines DC3, which flew out of Houston. Miss May's annotation beneath is inconclusive for establishing whether Susannah boarded a plane there: 'Transcontinental and Western Service American Airlines 'Coast to Coast' 1936' is a frustratingly imprecise caption. The second photograph is of a Pan American Airways flying boat, the *Caribbean Clipper*. The company flew out of Houston with routes heading towards the Pacific and across the Gulf of Mexico. Miss May's annotation for this photograph, too, is similarly brief, noting that the aeroplane was 'used from San Francisco to the Orient'.[105] Susannah's cousin, Anne Crewes, was certainly a possible port of call as she neared the end of her year-long journey. Her cousin lived at 233 Olmstead Street in the city. The fact that Susannah includes the photographs may suggest that she did fly. It might even have been her first air flight as she had only been a spectator at Croydon Aerodrome in 1924.

If Susannah travelled briefly to the West coast, it is possible that she visited California in a very short excursion which occasioned another curious happenstance. Susannah knew that she was reaching the end of her adventure and her associations became more outlandish. One unorthodox individual to place his name in the *Album*, incongruent, perhaps, with the purpose Susannah had set upon, was Peter Howard. He was sometimes known as 'Peter the Hermit', but Susannah gives him the moniker the 'Shakespeare of Hollywood' adding that he 'came from the Emerald Isle and taught Shakespearean plays'. Susannah's supplemental comments become almost mystical, fitting for such an ascetic individual who held sway amongst the more earthly stars of the movies. He was somewhat of a tourist attraction on Broadway and certainly made an impression on Susannah.[106] His entry in the *Album* is heavily annotated in Susannah's own words:

> He lived in a wood house and adopted the dress of a hermit so that he could preach to the drunkards and worldlings. He was not a religious by profession. He kept reminding sinners that they had an immortal soul for which they had to render an account.[107]

The photograph of Howard pasted alongside the account makes him appear slightly ordinary in comparison with the text and Susannah seems to have been much taken by him, perhaps feeling that his spiritual sensibilities were not too distant from her own. [108] She had lived through war, austerity and depression and Peter Howard's asceticism amongst the glitz and glamour of Hollywood may have struck a chord with the stern retired school mistress.

Within ten days of her visit to the Airway Ticket Office in Houston Susannah was in Oklahoma. The evidence of her route seems to suggest that she was travelling by train at this stage. Her contacts in Oklahoma were very different from those she had in Texas. Worthy as their roles were, the signature of L.D. Rikey, the Oklahoma State Game Warden was hardly on a par with the signatures Susannah obtained in Texas to represent civic responsibilities.[109] Rikey's signature is supported by his Assistant Game Warden, George Bailey and a Game Ranger M.G. Goodwin.[110] There is no context to explain their inclusion, other than that they locate themselves in Oklahoma City. They probably signed the *Album* before 18 October.

The other Oklahoma signatures are more intriguing, indicating that Susannah was pursuing a rather specific line of interest. All seem to date from 19 October 1936. There are several members of the Choctaw, Cherokee, Sac and Fox tribes who have given their names in the *Album*. Some were clearly in a position of authority, such as Andy Payne, the Chief of Supreme Court, George D. Bushyhirch, the Assistant Chief of Supreme Court and Mary Elizabeth Hammett, the Deputy Clerk of Supreme Court. Their civic roles seem less important than their own backgrounds and they define themselves by their tribal roots. Payne does not even feel the need to mention that he had been winner of the Trans-American Footrace staged in 1928. He ran the 3,423.5 mile route from Los Angeles to New York City along the famous Route 66 in 573 hours, four minutes, 34 seconds averaging six miles per hour over an 84-day staged run.[111]

The emphasis on a common thread of Native American heritage continues in this phase of the *Album*. The Governor of the Chickasaw Nation, Douglas H. Johnston is given a full page for his signature.[112] On the preceding page his daughter, Juanita Johnston Smith, gives an extended account of the brave conduct of the tribe in warfare and its role in forging the American nation: 'They made it possible for the English speaking race'.[113] The words written by the various members of the tribes are more strident than those of Two Eagles when he wrote at the Centennial, though there is still an aching sadness. They echo the words that Mary Jourdan Atkinson wrote earlier in the year to describe the experiences of the Comanche and Tiguas of Texas as they faced the wave of colonists in the 19th century.[114] One of Susannah's Oklahoma contributors was Juanita Mahaffey, who was one quarter Sac and Fox, being the grand-daughter of Alex Connolly who was once prominent in tribal affairs. She wrote: 'The tribe is now mainly extinct, there only being 150 or 200 full bloods left'.[115] This history of brave resistance and the decline of a society fascinated Susannah.

Susannah's interest in the welfare of veterans continued to help her to connect with the people she met whilst she was in Oklahoma and in all her interactions, it was foremost in her thoughts. The name of Lutie Hailey Walcote can be found on the same page as that of Juanita Mahaffey. Walcote was Secretary of the Confederate Pensions Department, She was well-placed to appreciate the welfare issues that had affected veterans of the American Civil War as the youngest of its veterans reached their final years. The department had then taken responsibility for men returning from more recent wars and had a particular role in the years of the Depression. Walcote celebrated her distant Choctaw heritage and wrote proudly that there were 'More Choctaw Indians in the Confederate Army of the War Between the States than any other State according to population'.[116] Walcote seems to have been moved by a similar spirit as Susannah and was in a stronger financial position to make her purpose a reality.

Still to this day the Oklahoma Veterans Centre is at 1015 South Commerce in Southwest Ardmore in the grounds of the former Oklahoma Confederate Home. Lutie donated the land for this Veterans Centre and there is still a plaque recalling her dedication to these ex-servicemen.[117] When Walcote retired in 1943, she had become the Commissioner for the Confederate Pensions. She clearly wished to preserve a record of the work of the Confederate Pensions Board and presented the Oklahoma Historical Society with minutes and memorabilia for the sake of preservation.[118] Susannah had much to share in conversation with her. This phase of the *Album* includes people with a civic role, guiding society through the years of the Depression and there is a broader issue of Susannah recalling the people that were responsible for the care of veterans as well as the veterans themselves.

There are two further explanations for the presence of so many Native Americans clustered in the Oklahoma pages. Dettie Galdsby Dickens provides one possibility in the *Album* itself: 'We have in Oklahoma City an Indian Club called the India-Okla Club. It is comprised of the different Indians residing in Oklahoma City. Once a year, the Club invites other Indians, and Indian Clubs over the state to participate with them at a yearly banquet held at one of the city's leading Hostelries. The object is to promote all things cultural'. Dickens was the Business Manager for the Club and also the Financial Secretary in Douglas H. Johnston's Office.[119]

A more surprising and seemingly unlikely opportunity appears possible. Remarkably, Susannah was probably present at a singular, if obscure, moment of history on the previous day. On Sunday, 18 October 1936 an eight-foot memorial was dedicated to Will Rogers at Oologah, in northwest Oklahoma. Rogers had been an actor, comedian, satirist and to some a philosopher. He was killed in air accident in August 1935. He had a significant place in the nation's popular culture. Moreover, the Texas Centennial had incorporated a Will Rogers Memorial Centre in Fort Worth. Rogers had Cherokee heritage on both sides of his family and the October memorial ceremony attracted closer friends and family from the community in which he had been brought up. About 600 people were in attendance. On that same day the *Rogers Flyer* brought a variously reported 3,000 to 8,000 people to the Frisco railway station in Claremore on its maiden trip. Claremore and Tulsa were the only stops from St Louis to Oklahoma City. Susannah made a connection with this event and acquired associated signatures on this and the following day. On the page stamped with the gold seal of the Supreme Court of Oklahoma, underwritten by a Chief and Assistant Chief of the Court, is an unsigned statement:

> The Cherokee were the first Indians to have a written language, Saquoyah, a member of the tribe and inventor of the Cherokee alphabet is now honored with a statue in the Hall of Fame in Washington, Oklahoma's foremost citizen and America's most loved countryman the late Will Rogers was a Cherokee Indian, the Cherokee are a proud and stable people.[120]

Will Rogers was clearly in the minds of those who signed the *Album* too.[121]

Susannah moved on, probably by train again, to Missouri. By 21 October, she was in St James. This was a particularly small community. It is not clear how she met Woodrow Byington, but it was a point of call on the railway. Byington, probably from farming stock as many of the Byingtons of Phleps and Sainte Genevieve Counties seem to have been, made a first-hand account of life in the West:

> The Cowboys are of several different nationalities & different in looks as well as ideas they often have rodeos where they all meet to match their skill in riding wild horses also to rope calves & tie them they differ now as 40 years ago they all carried guns & knew how to use them they had to be fast drawing a gun. [*sic*][122]

Susannah ended her American tour with the fast, furious and unpunctuated words of a man who lived the reality of the West that she had dreamed of as a child. Now 68 years old, and she made the journey of a lifetime but time, physically necessity and emotional exhaustion were bringing her project to an end.

Susannah boarded *Samaria* at New York on 2 November 1936, a stop on its route to Liverpool via Boston. She made some well-rehearsed approaches to the Master, J. McRostie and his First Officer, E.M. Fall. She does not appear to have engaged with her fellow passengers as she might have done in her earlier years and even recycled the navigation chart from San Francisco to record the liner's senior officers. This may have been a curiosity, a souvenir, or a deliberate plan to extend the capacity for signatures. 'All paper was finished chart used', she added, presumably after McRostie and Fall had placed their autographs.[123] She had reached the limit of her paper supply and had concluded her quest.

12 AT DUSK

SUSANNAH broke her ties with Chorley when she returned to Britain, having completed her final pilgrimage for peace. She gave her half-sister Mary's address of Church Road, Freshfield in Crosby on the passenger list of *Samaria*. This might have been a matter of convenience for if she was in rented accommodation she would have had no formal address whilst she was abroad. When she moved from Chorley the *Album* remained in the town, disconnected from its compiler.

Susannah seems to have been in lodgings from August 1939. An envelope is addressed to her the care of Mrs Digon at 65 Merton Road, Bootle.[1] At the point at which another World War was about to rage, Susannah was living seven doors away from her brother's *Huascar*, where Mary Louisa still lived. At some point Susannah moved further along to number 69 Merton Road in her last years of independence.[2]

There is scant evidence to describe her activities from 1936 to 1945 and her mobility must have become increasingly restricted as a consequence of her damaged leg. Her reasoning probably became less sharp and it is entirely possible that the onset of war in Europe in 1939 broke her spirit. The allied friendship she had worked so hard to foster in the years after the Great War were now to be tested by another conflict. The enduring peace that she had fought for slipped away as another generation prepared to fight again for their country. The favourite nephew of the Knight and McInnes girls, young Angus Dickinson, joined the RAF.

Susannah's mission had come to a close but there was one last battle to fight. She had described to Eleanor Roosevelt how she expected the *Album* to be presented to the nation on its completion but despite the promise made by the Borough Council in October 1921 it was still out of public view. She was too frail to revive the determination she had had when she was younger.

It was on 18 May 1945 that the *Chorley Guardian* began to ask questions about the location of the 'Golden Book'.[3] The closing stages of the Second World War prompted thoughts of how to remember those who had lost their lives in the most recent and recalled memories of the Great War. The Mayor of Chorley in that year was Alderman J. Green, a former pupil of Miss Knight at Weld Bank School. He was determined not let her service go unrecognised as her life drew to a close and acted quickly, within two weeks of the *Chorley Guardian* raising the issue. He had searched in Bootle with no success but had eventually been able to visit her in Nazareth House, Great Crosby. She was being well-tended by the Sisters of Nazareth but was in deteriorating health. Susannah told Alderman Green that money was owed for the binding, perhaps because she had been unable to raise sufficient funds to pay the bill when she left Chorley. She was able to help him locate the discarded volumes. Their rediscovery as three volumes was reported by the end of the June.[4]

The *Album* seems to have been in the possession of Ethel Leach, the daughter of W.J. Sandiford, the printer and stationer who had a shop at 22 Chapel Street. According to the *Chorley Guardian*, the it had been kept in a room at the print works in Byron Street when Susannah had left Chorley and when Sandiford's firm closed they resided in the dining room at Leach's home at 4 Harrington Road.[5] Ethel Leach's daughter recalls that the *Album* was in the format of a single volume at this stage.[6] Though Leach was praised for her connection with the preservation of the *Album* in a *Chorley Guardian* article in 1969, there has to be a question as to how much the Sandiford family withheld the volumes from the public until they were recompensed for the binding.

The newspaper announced that the sum of £40 was owed on the binding and that when the money had been raised 'the Town Council should be asked to provide a room for the books in either Astley hall itself or a war memorial or the Public Library which was a gift to the town'. The newspaper estimated that £20 was sufficient for the *Album* to be housed in a suitable cabinet and contributions were to be made to the Mayor or to the *Chorley Guardian*.[7] It was reported that there had been little public response in the newspaper's next edition but it announced that the Soroptomists of Chorley intended to raise the necessary amount.[8] It is significant that three volumes are referred to. Contemporaries frequently referred to a single volume, only two of the volumes were eventually displayed and the third volume was largely forgotten until the present. The Soroptomists gave momentum to the campaign that the mayor had set in motion, having already decided to set up a public subscription at their meeting on 3 July and devised a programme of events to raise money. They made the project their own and became Susannah Knight's final champions.

Susannah had much in common with the goals of the Soroptomists. They were, and still are, an organisation of professional women making a difference to society through charitable work with a social conscience. The President of the Preston branch reminded 30 or so women who were at the inauguration of the Chorley Branch on 24 November 1943 that their aim was to offer 'service' and 'friendship' to the community. Miss Knight's era was receding and the Second World War was framing the context of the meetings. Their early initiatives included raising money for the needy in formerly occupied countries and plans for post-war relief.[9] In July 1945 they were discussing a 'Reconstruction Fund' to repair the physical and emotional damage wreaked by the war. These were far-sighted and thoughtful women and worthy successors to the women who had supported Susannah's project immediately after the Great War.[10]

Miss Littlewood, a teacher at Chorley Secondary School, spoke on the progress of the 'Golden Book' fund at the recital and 'suggested that presentation of the book in the Town should be proceeded with at the earliest possible moment in view of the failing health of Miss Knight'. At the meeting of 18 September, the members agreed to organise a Snowball Tea, a Bring and Buy Sale, a raffle of foodstuffs and a social evening in order to raise the necessary funds. [sic][11]

By October the Soroptomists were confident that their work was reaching a conclusion. Miss Littlewood 'gave an assurance from the Town Clerk that the Golden Book would after presentation to the town by the Soroptomists be housed in Astley Hall'. They had raised £34. The committee was so sure that the *Album* was about to be presented and displayed that they decided that Miss Fairer should be chosen to represent them if there was limited space on the occasion.[12]

By the meeting on 6 November 1945 the members were given a report on the progress of their 'Golden Book' project. They were also able to discuss sending clothing and shoes 'to the Dutch people to help them this winter'. It was a terrible time for people in Europe as they struggled to cope with an infrastructure shattered by the war. Many starved to death. The Soroptomists' fund-raising drive was formalised as support for the 'Holland Fund Subscription' at the meeting on 4 December. It was reported that 'the Mayor had seen the Town Clerk and that it was definitely decided that the

Golden Book should go in to Astley Hall. The Mayor agreed to write to the publishers who had the Book in their possession'. There had clearly been concerns raised already if assurances needed to be given and it may be that at this stage there was some re-sequencing of pages, putting Susannah's intended order in disarray.

There was an increasing sense of anticipation through the Soroptomist minutes of 1946. On 8 January 'agreements were made to view the 'Golden Book' in the Mayor's Parlour on 9 January'. On 21 May it was reported that '... the 'Golden Book' has been accepted by the Town Council and placed in Astley Hall'. It may have been transferred there, but no cabinet had been made to house it, despite the fund-raising efforts of the Soroptomists. The Soroptomists' enthusiasm was not enough to overcome the weight of bureaucracy and the lack of interest within the Council.[13]

Susannah's health had deteriorated significantly and she was removed to Newsham Hospital in Liverpool towards the beginning of 1946.[14] Newsham largely cared for geriatric patients and at Nazareth House she had been in a Roman Catholic environment, but her new location was more disorientating.

In early 1947 the Council began to prevaricate. It will be remembered that the impetus for acknowledging the importance of the *Album* in 1945 was the failing health of Miss Knight and, thus far, their response had been sluggish. The minutes of the Soroptomists give a detailed narrative of the Council's inaction. On 4 February 1947 the correspondence from the Town Clerk assured them that 'suitable cases were being made for the Golden Book'. By 3 June the committee had word that 'the Golden Book was being proceeded but would not be ready for exposition in Astley Hall by 14 June'. The exchange between the Soroptomists and the Town Council degenerated into acrimony on 2 September over the provision of a table to support the books:

> 'Mr Lowe of the office of works insisted on the provision of a suitable table to hold the boxes containing the Golden Book before the latter could be placed in Astley Hall. This would cost approximately £60 approx. i.e. £80 including the boxes. Miss Yates proposed that the boxes with supports be made the whole costing not more than £25'.[15]

At the committee meeting on 4 November the Secretary had not received a reply to her enquiry about the boxes for the books and Miss G. Mercer (a town councillor) said that it was unlikely that the work would be completed before Christmas. The protracted negotiations became farcical and at the meeting of 2 December the President was able to state that 'Mr Lowe said that the boxes for the Golden Book were not yet made through lack of wood'. Mrs Fairer responded quirkily by offering to 'provide wood from an old piano if it were suitable'. The President promised to investigate the possibility of this.[16]

In May 1948 Miss Mercer was able to report that the cases were ready. Miss Davy, as President, was commissioned to meet representatives from the Town Council and press for official presentation of the Memorial to take place as soon as possible. But, yet again, the Council let Susannah Knight down. On 1 June Miss Mercer reported that 'no further progress had been made in the instillation of the Golden Book in Astley Hall'. As a consequence it was proposed that the committee refuse to pay for the cabinet holding the books until it had definitely been placed in the Hall. Their anger was incandescent. This resolution was carried unanimously and a letter of was sent to the Town Council to protest about the continued delay. This pressure seems to have spurred the Council to take a little more interest in the matter and a letter was sent to Miss Knight to gain her consent for the books to be handed over officially.[17]

Finally, on 1 November 1948, the *Chorley Memorial Album* was presented to the mayor, the post now being held by Alderman E. Warburton. They were displayed in the Drawing Room of Astley Hall just in time for the 30th anniversary of the Armistice. At the meeting of the Soroptomists on the following day, the members were given a full account. The Misses Mercer had purchased the velvet lining for the bottom of the case containing the books. An inscription plate recording Miss Knight's work was to be inserted on the 'handsome show-case'. Miss Ethel Davy thanked the Misses Mercer for purchasing the velvet and for all the time and effort they had expended in getting the books housed at last in Astley Hall.[18] Susannah Knight's life's work was now to be shared with the people of Chorley. The men who had given their lives in service to their country could now be remembered with the dignity Susannah had intended.

On 14 November 1949 Liverpool's *Daily Dispatch* gave a final glimpse of Susannah. She is photographed lying in her hospital bed with her head supported, half-turned towards the camera. The article is headlined 'Fairy Godmother, 80, tells her secret'. It portrays her as a lonely and forgotten women whose 'Golden Books' were considered anonymous. The article summarised her efforts in the Great War, the achievements in recording the biographies of Chorley's casualties and her pursuit of the signatures. The journalist took the view that Miss Knight 'would hardly be recognised by her friends in Chorley'. This was, perhaps, an exaggeration, but may have reflected Susannah's sense of being rejected by the town to which she had devoted so much of her life. The journalist wrote that Miss Knight said she had 'burnt herself out in the service of others' and perhaps she felt that, at the end of her days, at least some recognition might be made for the *Album*. Dedicated to the end, she gave her last public words: 'I hate to feel that I am not doing my share'.[19]

Her friends in Chorley were well aware of her condition and it is known that two veterans of the East Lancashire Regiment visited Susannah on a weekly basis and Alderman Green had visited her too. Her family came to her bedside regularly, as did members of the Chorley Branch of the Soroptomists. The Soroptomists of Chorley were keeping Susannah informed of their progress. On 6 December 1949 Miss Fairer's sister, a Miss Gray, who lived in Liverpool, visited Susannah to give her news. The committee even sent two bed jackets to Susannah as a Christmas gift.[20] The Soroptomists had made it possible for Susannah's work to be given public recognition. Not for the first time, the 'work of women' had helped secure the *Album*. Miss Littlewood, Dr Derbyshire, Miss L.G. Mercer, Miss G. Mercer, Miss Davy and Miss Fairer had worked together to succeed against the more local obstacles which Susannah had faced repeatedly since 1916.

The display of the *Album* had been achieved with little time to spare. Susannah Mary Crossley Knight died in Newsham Hospital on the evening of 13 August 1950. She was 82 years old. The cause of death was recorded as terminal broncho-pneumonia.[21] The family had sensed that the end of her life was near. Her half-sister, Ada Maxwell, had already travelled from London and was able to sign the death certificate the following day. The burial at Anfield Cemetery was arranged quickly, performed by Father Patrick O'Sullivan at 11.30am on the 16 August.[22] Father O'Sullivan was an assisting priest at St James' Roman Catholic Church of Marsh Lane in Bootle.[23] The parish of her childhood was there at her committal and she was returned to God by the community that had given her unfailing faith and compassion.

The Liverpool *Daily Dispatch* gave a fitting obituary soon after her death and before her burial, outlining her teaching career. It recalled not only her compilation of the 'Golden Book' but also her tireless commitment to those who survived the war and her travels to collect signatures. The article gently dispelled Susannah's own imaginings that she had been forgotten, referring to the relatives, ex-servicemen and friends who visited her regularly. The report noted that Susannah was to be buried with her parents.[24]

Whatever family rifts had existed in the 1920s and 1930s were in the past. Mary Louisa Knight kept a notebook which seems to suggest that she was responsible for coordinating some of the arrangements. Susannah's death and burial are recorded, as is the payment to Les Humphreys, the funeral director. Susannah's half-sister, Mary Dickinson, reimbursed Mary Louisa with the sum of £32 2s 6d.[25] Ada's name appears in the Anfield Burial Order Register, suggesting that she was the informant for arrangements. All the women of the family worked together to see that Susannah was buried with dignity. The gravestone fell into disrepair some years ago and has been removed. Her grave is now an unmarked scrub of grass. There is no public remembrance of her quest for allied friendship, peaceful reconciliation and dignity for the victims of war.

The people of Chorley learned of Susannah's death in the *Chorley Guardian* when it placed an article on the front page of its very next edition on 18 August. Though the local paper reused the headline given by the *Daily Dispatch*, it gave a creditable account of Susannah's life and work, largely building upon previous articles that had been published in 1920 and 1948. The *Chorley Guardian* praised the efforts of Alderman Green and the Soroptomists in bringing the *Album* to public display.[26] There must have been widespread awareness of her death even before the newspaper's publication, as there is a contribution in the letters column of the same edition from the anonymous correspondent 'Cold Facts' which took issue with earlier portrayals of Susannah as lonely and abandoned. 'Cold Facts' wanted to give credit to those who had kept her in mind and visited her regularly, but also reflected that there was a truth in the view that she had been largely unrecognised by the town as a whole. The correspondent reported the words of someone who knew her well who had said: 'Why an old lady who should die in such tragic circumstances after doing so much for her country is a puzzle to me'.[27]

The Soroptomists discussed the announcements of Susannah's death and were keen to correct the *Lancashire Evening Post* for crediting the Corporation of Chorley for presenting the books to the town.[28] They also contributed a letter in the following edition of the *Chorley Guardian* which replied to 'Cold Facts'. Miss Fairer is known to be the author of the anonymous letter. She pointed out that it was the Soroptomists who had 'rescued from oblivion' the *Album*: 'Forgetfulness of past service is a common trait in human nature, but some of us are glad to have been amongst those who during her lifetime showed their appreciation of Miss Knight's work for the servicemen'.[29]

The September edition of the town's *Catholic Bulletin* mourned the loss of Susannah too. It expressed 'genuine regret' at her passing, and believed that the 'Golden Books' would be an enduring remembrance of Susannah as well as those who died in the Great War. It recalled that there were 'many who have cause to revere her memory by her charitable acts. Generous to a fault, she literally gave all she had to those considered less fortunate'.[30]

Forgetfulness is indeed a common trait in human nature. Susannah's work was not completely forgotten, but nearly two decades passed before it the *Album* was given further attention. In May 1969 a room in Astley Hall was dedicated as a memorial to the men who fought and died in the Great War. The panels showing the names of those who died were transferred from the Town Hall and a small display began to evolve. In July, the cabinet housing the *Album* was moved from the Drawing Room to this Memorial Room, though the room was often missed as visitors searched out some of the Hall's more popular attractions.[31] In 2013 the third volume was rediscovered in an audit of the hall's acquisitions. In the same year a new cabinet was constructed to house all three volumes, but the contents of the books remain inaccessible to the relatives of the men who gave the ultimate sacrifice to the nation.

This is the final chapter of the present work, but should serve as the penultimate chapter of Susannah's life and work. Susannah met the promise in her original appeal in April 1919 that 'no name, from the humblest to the greatest, may be omitted, so that our heroes may never be forgotten, and their names may be revered and honoured throughout the future generations'. How will future generations respond to the demands that conflicts past, present and yet to come place upon those of us who have not the opportunity, courage, or misfortune to take up arms? There has been no end to the suffering wrought by war on servicemen and civilians. The peace Susannah sought and the recovery she witnessed descended into a second world conflict. The scourge of war has never ebbed away and soldiers still return from fields of combat carrying wounds both visible and invisible. Susannah Mary Crossley Knight acted independently to leave a permanent legacy of peace not only for the people of Chorley but a world scarred by war. Despite her promise to Eleanor Roosevelt in 1936, the 'Golden Books' were never presented to the nation or to the reigning monarch. Susannah's final chapter will need to be written by a future generation.

At Dusk

I saw three women enter a church
At dusk, one summer eve,
One was gold, and one was grey,
One wore a nun's black weave!
(What desire was in each heart
Thus from the world to draw apart?)
One begged her saint for a lover true,
One prayed for a soul's secret rest.
The nun, for all impartially
To her lips a crucifix pressed.
(So faint the gleam from the altar light
It could not make the place so bright!)
For lo! In the dusk of the summer eve
If here knelt these women three,
Like radiant stars, three virtues shone,
Faith, Hope, and Charity!

At Dusk - a poem from *Panorama* (1926) by Theresa M. Hunter which was chosen by the poet and written in her hand for Susannah Mary Crossley Knight in Austin, Texas, probably in 1936. It can be found on page 144 of the third volume of the *Chorley Memorial Album*. It serves as a most fitting epitaph to a woman who gave so much of her life for others through her faith, her hope and charity.

ENDNOTES

Preface

[1] *Chorley Guardian (CG)*, 5 April 1919, p. 1.
[2] *CG*, 25 August 1950, p. 5.

1 Beginnings

[1] Dublin Register Office, Register of Marriages, 27 April, 1867, nos. 71 and 228.
[2] Greenock Register Office, Registers of Births, 28 February, 1868, no. 207.
[3] Walmsley Archive (WA), Correspondence, passim
[4] 1841 Census, HO107, 578, Folio 33, p. 19.
[5] 1841 Census, HO107, 578, Folio 33, p. 19. His siblings were William H (b.1831), Edwin (b.1836), John
   (b.1836), Eliza (b.1838), John (b.1834) and Sarah Ann (b.1839).
[6] WA, Correspondence, letter from Anne Crewes to John Knight, 1 July 1909.
[7] WA, Correspondence, letter from Anne Crewes to John Knight, 1 July 1909.
[8] WA, fragment of a family history and anecdotal references.
[9] WA, Correspondence, letter from Anne Crewes to John Knight, 1 July 1909.
[10] *Slater's Lancashire Directory* (1848)
[11] 1861 Census, RG 9, 2953, Folio, 7, p. 7.
[12] WA, Correspondence, letter from Anne Crewes to John Knight, 1 July 1909.
[13] 1861 Census, RG 9, 2953, Folio, 7, p. 7.
[14] Dublin Register Office, Register of Marriages, 27 April, 1867, nos. 71 and 228.
[15] Greenock Register Office, Registers of Births, 28 February, 1868, no. 207.
[16] Tradeston Register Office, Registers of Births, 20 July, 1869, no. 1090.
[17] WA Correspondence, letter from Anne Crewes to John Knight, 1 July 1909.
[18] 1881 Census, RG11, 3689, Folio 39, p. 4.
[19] http://www.rshm.org/History/England_1872
[20] 1881 Census, RG11, 3691, Folio 93, p. 36.
[21] *The Messenger* (The Parish Magazine St Mary's Roman Catholic Church, Chorley), May 1916 and October 1916.
[22] 'Fairy Godmother, 79, tells her secret', *Liverpool Daily Dispatch*, 14 November 1949.
[23] WA Letter from Elizabeth (Knight) McInnes to Susannah Knight 24 March 1904.
[24] Obituary for John Knight 'Commodore of Convoys', *Bootle Times* 30 November 1934.
[25] 1891 Census, RG11, 3689, Folio 39, p. 4.
[26] Register of Marriages July-September 1881 vol 8b, p 884.
[27] 1891 Census, RG12, 2970, Folio 105, p. 2.

2 Teacher and Traveller 1888 - 1914

[1] *Chorley Standard*, 8 June 1895.

2 1891 Census, RG12, 3421, Folio 37, p. 5.

3 1891 Census, RG12, 2970, Folio 105, p. 2.

4 CMB, III, Page 124.

5 *Liverpool Mercury*, 3 July 1891.

6 Gallop, Alan *Buffalo Bill's British Wild West* (The History Press: Stroud, 2001), pp. 168-171.

7 CMB, III, p. 124.

8 CMB, III, passim.

9 CMB, III, Page 124; CMB, III, Page 104; CMB, III, p. 98.

10 *Liverpool Mercury*, 7 July 1891.

11 'A Presentation to an Euxton School Mistress', *Chorley Standard*, 8 June 1895.

12 French Military Records.

13 'Euxton - Presentation to a School Mistress', *CG*, 6 June 1895.

14 'Commodore of Convoys', *Times*, 30 November 1934, Obituary for John Knight.

15 Ibid.

16 WA, Jack Knight writing to Susannah from *Elbe* in Calcutta, 6 April [1896].

17 WA, brochure of fees for Notre Dame Day School, Southport, date not known.

18 WA, Jack Knight writing to Susannah from *Elbe* in Calcutta, 6 April [1896].

19 *Nourse Line*, https://en.wikipedia.org/wiki/Nourse_Line Accessed 5/4/2016

20 WA, Jack Knight writing to Elizabeth McInnes from *Elbe* in Calcutta, 14 September 1897.

21 ibid.

22 WA, Jack Knight writing to Susannah from *Huascar* in Madeira on route to Brazil, Sunday 19 March 1900.

23 Recollection of Jan Walmsley, granddaughter of Jack Knight.

24 WA, Jack Knight writing to Susannah from *Huascar* in Madeira, Sunday 19 March 1900.

25 WA, John Knight writing to Susannah from *Huascar* in Para, 5 February [probably 1901].

26 WA, Jack Knight writing to Susannah from *SS Basil* in Manoâs [no date given for letter but probably between Feb 1896 and 1901 when Ilha Grande operated as a quarantine station].

27 WA, Jack Knight writing to Susannah from *Huascar* in Manoâs, 15 July 1901.

28 Ibid.

29 WA, Continuous Discharge Book, 1 June 1901 to May 1915, pp. 5-26.

30 WA, Jack Knight writing to Susannah from *Huascar* in Manoâs, 15 July 1901.

31 1901 Census, RG13, 3458, Folio 94, Page 54.

32 WA, Jack Knight writing to Susannah from his lodgings at 14 Park Street, Stanley Park [date not given but probably September 1901].

33 1901 Census, RG13, 3938, Folio 12, p. 16.

34 WA, Jack Knight writing to Susannah from *Huascar* in Madeira on route to Brazil, 19 March 1900.

35 Weld Bank School Log Book (WBSLB), passim.

36 Gillett, T. (Chorley, 1974) *Weld Bank School 1913*, Lancashire Record Office S3/WEL/WEL.

[37] *Lancashire Historic Town Survey Programme Chorley Historic Town Assessment* Report (Preston, 2006).

[38] WA, Jack Knight writing to Susannah from *Huascar* in Madeira on route to Brazil, 19 March 1900.

[39] WA, Jack Knight writing to Susannah, Sunday 21 April 1901.

[40] WA, Continuous Discharge Book (1902), Marriage Banns and marriage certificate (1902).

[41] Liverpool Record Office; Reference Number: 283 SPK/2/2.

[42] Family recollections and photographs of Janice Walmsley, Mary Louisa's granddaughter

[43] Anne Crewes writing to Jack Knight establishes the residence at Litherland Road (1909)

[44] WA, Continuous Discharge Book, *passim.*

[45] Helen Foreshaw, ed., *History of the Society of the Holy Child Jesus* (Washington, 1988), Issue II, p. 28.

[46] WA, Continuous Discharge Book (1903-4).

[47] Elizabeth (Bryan) McInnes writing to Susannah from 106 Benedict Street (24 May 1905).

[48] Death Index, West Derby, Lancashire 8b 255 and Anfield Burial Order Book reference 44189 gives internment on 18/8/1905, aged 57.

[49] Anfield Burial Order Book reference 45114 gives internment 18/8/1905, aged 51.

[50] *CG*, 19 September 1914. Kelly's Trade Directories (1905) gives the proprietor of the business at 57 Bolton Road as Peter Catterall. Kelly's Trade Directory (1924) gives the proprietor as Harry Mander. The residential portion of the address is occupied by James and Harriet Blackburn 1918 (Chorley Library, Electoral Register, 1918).

[51] Gillett, Tom *Weld Bank School 1816-1913* (Nelson Brothers: Chorley, 1974), Lancashire Record Office S3/WEL/WEL.

[52] 'Their Majesties' Tour In Lancashire'. *Times* [London, England] 11 July 1913, p. 6. *The Times Digital Archive*. Web. 30 Dec. 2014.

[53] Duffy, Michael *The Sacred Heart* (Brewer's Print: Chorley, 1993), p. 86.

[54] Passenger Records, Source Situation: Year: 1913; Microfilm Serial: T715; Microfilm Roll: T715_2131; Line: 1; Page Number: 84.

[55] 'Royal Review In The Mersey'. *Times* [London, England] 12 July 1913, Page 8. *The Times Digital Archive*. Web. 30 Dec. 2014.

[56] *New York Times*, 17 July 1913.

[57] Passenger Records, *Source Citation:* Year: 1913; Arrival: New York, New York; Microfilm Serial: T715; Microfilm Roll: 2131; Line: 1; Page Number: 84 (extended page) and Source Citation: Year: 1913; Arrival: New York, New York; Microfilm Serial: T715; Microfilm Roll: 2131; Line: 19; p. Number 173.

[58] Passenger Records, BT26; Piece 553; Item: 67.

[59] Ibid.

[60] WBSLB (unnumbered introductory pages).

[61] Ibid, p. 59.

[62] Ibid, p. 9.

[63] ibid, p. 9.
[64] Ibid, pp. 4, 64, 80 and 133.
[65] Ibid, passim.

3 Pupils and Pals 1914 - 15

[1] 'Chorley People in Switzerland' *CG* (22 August 1914), p. 5.
[2] WBSLB, pp. 1-2.
[3] Clark, Christopher *The Sleepwalkers* (Penguin: London, 2013).
[4] 'Stranded on the Continent, Chorley Teacher's Experience', *CG*, 5 September 1914, p. 8.
[5] 'Schoolmaster Returns from Switzerland', *Chorley and District Weekly News*, 5 September 1914, p. 4.
[6] 'Holidaymakers' Experiences Abroad - Chorley Party in Belgium', *CG*, 8 September 1914, p. 5.
[7] The *Chorley Guardian* article for 8 September 1914 describes his two teenage daughters but in 'A Rush From The Continent' the *Chorley and District Weekly News*, 8 August 1914, Page 5, names his sisters Misses Annie and Hettie Leech.
[8] 'Chorley Secondary School Students Return From Paris', *Chorley and District Weekly News*, 8 August 1914, p. 5.
[9] CMB, II, p. 148b.
[10] WBSLB, pp. 1-2.
[11] CMB, I, p. 190a; CMB, I, p. 184b; CMB, I, p. 191b; CMB, I, p. 192b; CMB, I, p. 193b; CMB, I, p. 196b; CMB, I, p. 186b; CMB, I, p. 198b; CMB, I, p. 199a.
[12] List of enlistments by church membership, *CG*, 19 December 1914.
[13] CMB, passim.
[14] CMB, I, p. 246a.
[15] http://www.memoiredeshommes.sga.defense.gouv.fr/en/ark:/40699/m005239f7057022c
[16] CMB, I, p. 235a.
[17] CMB, II, p. 58a
[18] CMB, II, p. 193a.
[19] *CG*, 27 September 1914.
[20] CMB, II, p. 69a and http://www.worldwar1.co.uk/cressy.htm
[21] WA, Jack Knight writing to Mary Louisa from the *SS Boniface*, Naval Rio Grande De Norte, Brazil, 1 September 1914.
[22] *CG* (19 September 1914), p. 5.
[23] Williams, Steve & Garwood, John *Chorley Pals* (Chorley Pals Memorial: Chorley, 2009), p. 90.
[24] *CG*, 21 November 1914, p. 8.
[25] Jackson, Andrew *Accrington's Pals* (Pen and Sword: Barnsley, 2013), p. 17.
[26] *CG*, 29 August 1914, p. 8.
[27] *CG*, 22 August, Page 5 and *CG*, 29 August, p. 4.
[28] WBSLB, p. 3.
[29] WBSLB, p. 6.

[30] WBSLB, November to October 1914, p. 4.

[31] CMB, I, p. 211b; CMB, II, Page 45a; CMB, II, p. 21b; CMB, II, p. 35a.

[32] CMB, II, p. 45a.

[33] CMB, I, p. 114a.

[34] List of enlistments by church membership, *CG*, 19 December 1914.

[35] 'German Raid in Home Waters.' *Times* [London, England] 4 Nov. 1914, p. 9. *The Times Digital Archive*. Web. 25 Mar. 2014.

[36] CMB, I, p. 102a.

[37] *CG*, 21 November 1914, p. 8.

[38] *CG*, 19 December, and *CG*, 26 December 1914.

4 Home and Front 1915 - 18

[1] *Chorley and District Weekly News*, 13 February 1915.

[2] *CG*, 21 November 1914, p. 8.

[3] *CG*, 13 February 1915, p. 5.

[4] CG, 23 February 1935, p. 7.

[5] WBSLB, p. 7.

[6] WBSLB, p. 7

[7] *CG*, 24 and 31 October 1914, p. 4.

[8] *CG*, 17 October 1914.

[9] *CG*, 26 October 1914.

[10] Garwood, John *Chorley Pals* (Neil Richardson: Radcliffe, Manchester, 1998) pp. 18-26.

[11] CMB, II, Page 174a and 'How The Bayano Went Down.' *Times* [London, England] 15 Mar. 1915: 6. *The Times Digital Archive*. Web. 25 Mar. 2014.

[12] CMB, I, p. 84a.

[13] CMB, I, p. 67b.

[14] CMB, I, p. 167a.

[15] CMB, I, p. 166a.

[16] CMB, I, p. 234a.

[17] 1901 Census RG13, 3668, Folio 66, p. 32; 1911 Census, RG14, 25214; Parish records for St Laurence Church, Chorley for marriage between Robert Jackson and Elizabeth Ann Young 26 April 1890, Army Service Record in WO363 , and CMB, I, p. 65b.

[18] *CG*, 9 December 1916, p. 5.

[19] *CG*, 5 June 1915, p. 5.

[20] WBSLB, February, March and April 1915, pp. 7-8.

[21] CMB, II, p. 111b.

[22] WA, Jack Knight writing to Mary Louisa from the *SS Boniface*, Ceara, 1 September 1914.

[23] Continuous Discharge Book, pp.23-24.

[24] 'Fairy Godmother, 79, Tells Her Secret', *Daily Dispatch*, Liverpool, 14 November 1949.

[25] 'Chorley Territorials at the Front', *CG*, 5 June 1915, p. 5.

[26] CMB, II, p. 127a.

[27] CMB, I, p. 44a.

[28] 1901 Census sate: Class: *RG13*; Piece: *3935*; Folio: *29*; p.: *11*.

[29] CMB, I, p. 65a.

[30] CMB, I, p. 45a, CMB, I, p. 59b, CMB, I, p. 66a, CMB, I, p. 49a, CMB, I, p. 78b and CMB, I, p. 71a

[31] CMB, I, p. 197b.

[32] WBLB, 25 June to 9 July 1915, pp. 12-13.

[33] Lancashire Record Office, Leaders' Minutes – Chorley Methodist Circuit, Trinity Methodist Church, Chorley. MCH/1/10.

[34] Trinity Manse was at 14 Rawcliffe Road on the 1911 Census, though eventually it occupied 78 Gillibrand Walks in the gift of the Sellers family at a later date. Probate and Wills adds that he was living at 57 Munster Road, Nottingham by 1917. His property of £120 2s 2d reverted to his father. John Williams, Wesleyan Minister. CWGC notes he was the 'Son of the Rev. John Williams, of 205, Waterloo Rd., Burslem, Stoke-on-Trent. Enlisted Aug 1914. A London News Agency Journalist'.

[35] CMB, I, p. 138, Commonwealth War Graves Commission, Probate and Wills and Medal Rolls Index all confirm. His memorial is at Tyne Cot Cemetery Panel 154 to 159 and 163A.

[36] WBSLB, 9 November 1915, p. 13.

[37] WBSLB, 10 September 1915, p. 14 and WBSLB, 4 November 1915, p. 16.

[38] WA, Jack Knight writing to Mary Louisa, New York, over the period 19-21 November 1915.

[39] Passenger Records, *Source Citation:* Year: 1913; Arrival: New York, New York; Microfilm Serial: T715; Microfilm Roll: 2131; Line: 1; Page Number: 84 (extended page) and Source Citation: Year: 1913; Arrival: New York, New York; Microfilm Serial: T715; Microfilm Roll: 2131; Line: 19; p. Number 173.

[40] WA, undated list of addresses belonging to Mary Louisa Knight.

[41] WA, Jack Knight writing to Mary Louisa, New York (over period 19-21 November 1915)

[42] WBSLB, 12 and 19 November 1915, p. 16

[43] CMB, I, p. 75a, CMB, I, p. 72b, p., II, p. 105b, CMB, I, p. 68a

[44] Interview on 2 September 2013 by A Cree with M.B. (b1927-), a member of St Gregory's Church who was taught by Susannah Knight.

[45] Interview by J Cree with the daughter of N.G., November 2014.

[46] *CG*, adverts for 'Cotton Ball', 27 September and 4 October 1919.

[47] Monthly enlistment reports, *CG*, passim.

[48] *CMB*, passim.

[49] *St Mary's Messenger*, May 1916.

[50] WBSLB, May and June 1916, pp. 22-23.

[51] *CG*, 29 July 1916, p. .

[52] *CMB*, II, p. 184b, CMB, II, p. 190a and CMB, I, p. 190b.

[53] *CMB*, I, p. 190a.

[54] Family recollection by Pauline Critchley, daughter of Joseph Critchley.

[55] WBSLB, 7 July 1916, p. 24.

[56] 'Tokens of Gratitude, *CG*, 9 September 1916.

[57] Outgoing Passenger Records: Class: *BT26*

[58] WA, Jack Knight writing to Mary Louisa from hospital in Barbados, 27 September 1916.

[59] *The Messenger,* May 1916 and *CMB*, I, p. 229a.

[60] French Army Service Records

[61] *The Messenger,* October 1916.

[62] *CMB*, I, PAGE 229a

[63] *CG,* 21 October 1916, p. 1

[64] *CG,* 28 October 1916, p. 1

[65] Lancashire Record Office, Leaders' Minutes – Chorley Methodist Circuit, Trinity Methodist Church, Chorley. MCH/1/10.

[66] *CG,* 4 November 1916, p. 8.

[67] *CG,* 11 November 1916, p. 4.

[68] *CG,* 11 November 1916, p. 8.

[69] Ibid.

[70] *CG,* 18 November 1916.

[71] UK Incoming Passenger Records: Class: BT26; Piece: 628; Item: 3.

[72] *CG,* 25 November 1916, p. 8.

[73] *CG,* 2 December 1916, p. 5.

[74] WA, Letter from Jack to Mary Louisa, 4 July 1917 from the *SS Benedict* makes reference to recuperation.

[75] Letter from the Admiralty War Staff, Trade Division dated 27 March, 1917.

[76] *Bootle Times,* 30 November 1934, 'Commodore of Convoys'.

[77] CMB, I, p. 43b.

[78] WA, Letter from Jack to Mary Louisa, 4 July 1917 from the *SS Benedict* makes reference to recuperation.

[79] *CG,* 10 November 1917.

[80] WBSLB November 1917, p. 39.

[81] WBSLB January 1918, pp. 41-42.

[82] *CG,* 19 January 1918.

[83] *CG,* 19 January 1918.

[84] WBSLB, 25 January and 1 February 1918, p. 41.

[85] *CG,* 16 February 1918, p. 1.

[86] *CG,* 11 May 1918, p. 3.

[87] Ibid.

[88] CMB, I, p. 136b

[89] CMB, I, p. 42a and Census Record Class: RG14; Piece: 25200.

[90] *CG,* 11 May 1918, p. 3.

[91] CMB, I, p. 168a.

[92] WBSLB, 16 August 1918, p. 46.

[93] WBSLB, 14 October 1918, pp. 47-8.

[94] 'Dawn of Peace'. *CG,* 13 November 1920, p. 5.

[95] CMB, I, p. 142b.

5 Compiling the Memorial 1918 - 20

1 CMB, I, p. 139a, CMB, I, p. 193b, CMB, I, p. 158a, CMB, II, p. 113b, CMB, I, p. 195a

2 CMB, I, p. 53b, CMB, I, p. 246b, CMB, II, p. 43b, CMB, II, p. 47b, CMB, I, p. 83b (Henry Parker had enlisted in June 1918, CMB, I, p. 50a (Herbert Marsden's brothers Harry [CMB, I, p. 50b] and Edwin [CMB, I, p. 51a] had also been killed) and CMB, I, p. 148a.

3 WBSLB, 19 March 1919 p. 51.

4 Death Index January, February, March 1919.

5 WBSLB, 19 March 1919, p. 51.

6 *CG*, 19 April 1919.

7 *CG*, 5 April and 17 May 1919.

8 *CG*, 17 May 1919.

9 *CG*, 28 January 1922.

10 *CG*, advertisement, 2 December 1916, p. 5.

11 David Crane, *Empires of the Dead* (London, 2013), pp. 203-204.

12 De Groot, Gerard J. *Blighty: British Society in the era of the Great War* (Longman: London and New York, 1996), *passim*.

13 Kelly's Lancashire Directory, 1924, pp. 430 and 434, expands the detail on the helpers identified in the CG advertisement of 5 April 1919.

14 *CG*, 11 November 1916, p. 8.

15 *CG*, 27 September and 8 October 1919.

16 *CG*, 13 March 1920, p. 1.

17 CMB, I, p. 108b.

18 *CG*, 26 April 1919.

19 CMB, I, p. 95b

20 Family memorabilia held by Stephanie Robinson, 2013.

21 Stuart A. Clewlow, *In Memoriam*, (Stuart Clewlow: Chorley, 2011), *passim*.

22 CMB, I, p. 45b.

23 Some men would live out a longer lifetime but retain the physical or emotional scars of war. Such was a man, unnamed, who lived on Lyons Lane: 'One veteran, the victim of serious wounds, could be seen trundling his way through the streets in the southern part of [Sacred Heart's] parish for years after the war. As a result of his injuries, both legs were amputated close to the hip but apart from the occasional bad day, he kept up a cheerful front. He propelled his wheel chair along by hard manual effort ... Pulling up to the 'Red House' or the 'Green Man Still', a glass of beer would soon be thrust into his hand'. - Michael Duffy, *The Sacred Heart* (Chorley 1998), pp. 93-94.

24 *CG*, 4 December 1920, front page.

25 *CG*, 11 December 1920.

26 Ibid.

27 Programme for the Presentation of Paintings and Photographs, December 1920, Astley Hall Museum and Art Gallery, Chorley, (AHMAG).

28 *CG*, 11 December 1920.

29 AHMAG.

30 CMB, I, 40b.

[31] CMB, I, page 39a; CMB, I, page 40a; CMB, I, 133a; CMB, I, page 155a; CMB, II, page 136a.

[32] AHMAG.

[33] CG, 11 December 1920.

[34] AHMAG.

[35] CG, 11 December 1920.

[36] Father William Joseph Carroll has been difficult to identify. His initials are given as 'W.T.' in the *Chorley Guardian*, 'T.W.' on the frame of the painting and 'W.J.' in the burial registers for funerals that he performed between May 1914 and November 1915. He was in East Africa by October 1916 and a letter he had sent appeared in the *St Mary's Messenger* apprising the congregation of his activities. Significantly, he seems to have become a chaplain to the Irish Republican Army after returning to parish responsibilities in 1919. He is said to have been involved in at least one ambush at Grange in 1920, the very year that his portrait was displayed with such ceremony in Chorley. This adds complications to Susannah's character and outlook. It is extremely unlikely that Susannah would have condoned any connection with violence. Carroll gained the Military Cross and was proud to have received it for the spiritual care he had given to his fellow men. The fact that he reversed his British War Medal and Victory Medal to obscure the King's image demonstrates his political opposition. Susannah was supremely British, born in Scotland with to an Irish mother and an English father, but her connections with Irish Roman Catholic could have aroused her sympathies for Irish independence. The complicated tangle of Irish politics may well have precipitated a breach with her brother later in the 1920s. What can be certain is that Susannah searched out other chaplains who had given their care to servicemen during the war.

[37] Programme for the Presentation of Paintings and Photographs, December 1920, AHMAG.

[38] Diary of the 27th Earl of Crawford and Balcarres. My thanks to The Rt Hon. The Earl of Crawford and Balcarres for his insight on this matter – Correspondence 14 January 2014

[39] Arnander, Christopher *Private Lord Crawford's Great War Diaries* (Barnsley: P and Sword, 2013).

[40] Programme for the Presentation of Paintings and Photographs, December 1920, AHMAG.

[41] My thanks to The Rt Hon. The Earl of Crawford and Balcarres for his insight on this matter – Correspondence 14 January 2014.

[42] CG, 11 December 1920.

[43] Programme for the Presentation of Paintings and Photographs, December 1920, AHMAG - Thanks to Steve Bellis for enlightening me on this.connection.

[44] CG, 11 December 1920.

[45] Ibid.

[46] W J Sandiford operated from Byron Street according to a CG article from 17th July 1948. A later address,22 Chapel Street is given in the 1920s but had moved to 62 Market Street by the 1954. It may be that that the printing works was

separate from their public office. They are no longer in business. Kelly's Directory 1924 and Blackburn, Burnley, Preston, Barrow Directory1954-5

[47] CMB, I, p. 2.

[48] *CG*, July 1969.

[49] *CG*, 5 April 1919, p. 1

[50] *CG*, 11 December 1920.

[51] *CG*, 5 April 1919, p. 1

[52] CMB, I, p. 38.

[53] CMB, I, p. 129.

[54] Crane, David. *Empires of the Dead* (William Collins: London, 2014) p. 200.

[55] *CG*, 16 February 1918, front page.

[56] Psalm 129 (Douay version) [Psalm 130 (Authorised version)].

[57] The appending of the Roman Catholic churches of St Mary's Leyland and Mary's Euxton to their Chorley namesake seems a little out of place, so it is possible that Susannah was reflecting on her association with St Mary's school in Euxton earlier in her career. They are awkward contributions because they fall further from the geographical core of the memorial's remit. There is a strong possibility that a less assured hand such as that of Susannah's friend Ethel Leach was at work sequencing the pages after Susannah became too frail to undertake the editing of the *Album* herself.

[58] CMB, I, p. 181.

[59] Mark Robinson appears at CMB, I, p. 246b and CMB, I, p. 246b.

[60] CMB, I, p. 247a and CMB, I, p. 247b.

[61] CMB, I, p. 246-8.

[62] CMB, II, p. 88b, CMB, II, p. 215b

[63] Paul de Méhérenc de St Pierre, born 27 February 1889 in Versailles, 33rd Infantry Regiment, died 11 September 1914

[64] CMB, I, p. 78a and CMB, II, p. 107b.

[65] CMB, III, p. 118 (Reverse)

[66] *Daily Dispatch* (Liverpool) 14 November 1949.

6 Underwriting the Losses 1921

[1] F. D. Roosevelt Library, Washington, letter from Susannah Knight to Eleanor Roosevelt, Eleanor Roosevelt Papers, box 860, folder '110 ER Autographs 1936 I-L', 4 June 1936 and CMB, I, p 2.

[2] CMB, I, p. 2.

[3] CMB, I, p. 14 and CMB, I, p. 9.

[4] The sample of American Bar Association signatures collected in the *Album* represents a gender balance in proportion to the full listing provided in their 1924 commemorative programme.

[5] CMB, I, p. 2; CMB, I, p. 15; CMB, I, p. 18; CMB, I, p. 24; CMB, I, p. 30; and CMB, I, p. 34.

[6] CMB, II, p. 4. Benedict XV died 22nd January 1922 so the printing of the pages must predate this event.

[7] CMB, I, p. 30.

[8] CMB, II, p. 6.

[9] 'Bemersyde, The Ancestral Home Of Earl Haig'. *Times* [London, England] 22 June 1921: 12. *The Times Digital Archive*. Web. 25 Mar. 2014.

[10] 'Court Circular'. *Times* [London, England] 5 July 1921: 13. *The Times Digital Archive*. Web. 25 Mar. 2014.

[11] 'King Albert In The City'. *Times* [London, England] 6 July 1921: 12+. *The Times Digital Archive*. Web. 25 Mar. 2014.

[12] *CG*, 13 March 1920, p. 1.

[13] Graham Wooton, *The Official History of the British Legion* (London, 1958), *passim*. No names from the *Album* figure in the text. match in the *Album*.

[14] *CG*, 28 June 1930.

[15] CMB, II, p. 6. Douglas Haig's biography is well known. Henry Wilson represented the British Mission in France during the war, chief of Imperial General Staff in 1918 and was promoted to Field Marshal in July 1919. Blamey was an Australian general of the First and Second World Wars, and the only Australian ever to attain the rank of field marshal.

[16] CMB, I, p. 4 and CMB, I, p. 12.

[17] CMB, I, p. 6.

[18] CMB, I, p. 4.

[19] *CG*, 9 July 1921.

[20] Duffy, Michael *The Sacred Heart* (Brewer's Print: Chorley, 1993), p. 86.

[21] *CG* 2 July 1921, p. 2.

[22] WBSLB, 7 July 1921, p. 83

[23] *CG*, 9 July 1921.

[24] Ibid.

[25] CMB, II, p. 111b.

[26] Local un-attributable stories persist of Edward being inebriated at Euxton. The evidence of his signature and the stilted conversation might well support this.

[27] CMB, I, p. 3.

[28] *CG*, 9 July 1921.

[29] CMB, I, p. 4.

[30] Ibid.

[31] http://hansard.millbanksystems.com/people/dr-christopher-addison/ accessed 6/4/2006.

[32] WBSLB, 23 March 1921, p. 77 and WBSLB, 7 July 1921, p. 83.

[33] CMB, I, p. 4.

[34] Ibid.

[35] WBSLB, 24 February 1922, p. 93.

[36] Ibid.

[37] *CG*, 8 October 1921, p. 8.

[38] My thanks to The Rt Hon. The Earl of Crawford and Balcarres for his insight on this matter – Correspondence 14 January 2014.

7 The European Adventure 1921

[1] WBSLB, 10 August 1914, 1.

[2] CMB, II, p. 5.

[3] CMB, I, p. 246a.

[4] Rennes Archives: 257FI7 – Thanks to Laurence Prod'homme Conservatrice au musée de Bretagne

[5] Laughlin, Clara E. *Foch the Man – A Life of the Supreme Commander of Allied Armies* (Fleming H. Revell Company: New York, 1918), Chapter VI

[6] *L'Ouest-Éclair*, 18 July 1921, p. 1.

[7] *L'Ouest-Éclair*, 19 July 1921, p. 8.

[8] Ibid, p. 8.

[9] Rennes Archives 350Fi47 - Thanks to Romain Joulia, Director of Rennes Archives Office

[10] CMB, I, p.16.

[11] *L' Ouest Éclair*, 19 July 1921, p. 3, 'Le Parti En L' Honneur De Duguesclin et Argentré '.

[12] CMB, I, p. 16.

[13] *L' Ouest Éclair*, 19 July 1921, p. 3, 'Le Parti En L' Honneur De Duguesclin et Argentré '.

[14] CMB, I, p. 16.

[15] http://fr.wikipedia.org/wiki/Jean-Baptiste_Langlet, accessed 6/4/2016.

[16] CMB, I, p. 16.

[17] CMB, I, p. 17.

[18] CMB, I, p. 15.

[19] Study of the President's itinerary of public engagements places him in northern France in this period.

[20] *L'Ouest-Éclair*, 23-30 July 1921, passim.

[21] *The Messenger,* May and October 1916.

[22] CMB, I, PAGE 229a

[23] CMB, I, p. 16.

[24] http://fr.wikipedia.org/wiki/Constant_Blaqui%C3%A8 re accessed 6/4/1916.

[25] CMB, I, p. 16.

[26] WBSLB, 12 August 1921, pp. 83-84.

[27] CMB, II, p. 4. Letter from the Secretary of State to the Vatican, Cardinal Gasparri dated Wednesday 10 August 1921.

[28] Ibid.

[29] WA, Letter from Mary de Navarro to Angus 'Bubbles' Dickinson 13/10/1932.

[30] CMB, II, p. 4. Letter from the Secretary of State to the Vatican, Cardinal Gasparri dated Wednesday 10 August 1921.

[31] CMB, I, p. 181.

[32] CMB, III, p. 15 (Reverse).

[33] CMB, I, p. 30.

[34] CMB, I, p. 26.

[35] WBSLB 12 August 1921, pp. 83-84.

[36] *CG,* 8 October 1921, p.8.

[37] Ibid, p.8.

[38] Ibid, p 8.

8 The Washington Conference 1921

1 *CG*, 8 October 1921, p.8.

2 Council and Education Committee Minutes 1921, Schools Management Sub-Committee paragraphs 12 and 13, p. 15.

3 WBSLB, 28 October 1921, p. 88.

4 Ibid.

5 WBSLB, 28 October 1921, p. 88; Passenger Records, Source Citation: Year: 1921; Arrival: New York, New York; Microfilm Serial: T715, 1897-1957; Microfilm Roll: Roll 3048; Line: 23; Page Number: 16.

6 F. D. Roosevelt Library, Washington, letter from Susannah Knight to Eleanor Roosevelt, Eleanor Roosevelt Papers, box 860, folder '110 ER Autographs 1936 I-L', 6 June 1936.

7 *New York Times* 28 August 1921.

8 CMB, I, p. 11.

9 CMB, I, p. 13.

10 *New York Times* 9 November 1921.

11 WA, Jack writing to Mary Louisa, 19-21 November 1915 Pier 56 Cunard, New York.

12 *New York Times*, 9 November 1921.

13 *New York Times*, 10 November 1921.

14 *New York Times*, 12 November 1921.

15 *New York Times*, 15 November 1921.

16 CMB, I, p. 11.

17 Borden, Robert Laird, *Conference for the Limitation of Armaments Held at Washington – Report of the Canadian delegate* (Ottawa: F.A. Acland, printer, 1922) pp. 8-9 has been on particular use http://archive.org/stream/conferenceonlimi00cana#page/28/mode/1up and https://archive.org/details/conferenceonlimi00cana

18 CMB, I, p. 23 and CMB, I, p. 33.

19 CMB, I, p. 6.

20 CMB, I, p. 25. Thanks also to William de Baets of the Belgian Embassy in Washington DC for his assistance on this matter.

21 CMB, I, p. 16.

22 CMB, I, p. 16 and Papers Relating to the Foreign Relations of the United States: 1922, Vol. 1, pp. 247-266. Page 247 Treaty Series NO. 671 at http://www.ibiblio.org/pha/pre-war/1922/nav_lim.html

23 CMB, I, p. 19 and CMB, I, p. 20.

24 CMB, I, p. 6.

25 CMB, I, p. 36.

26 CMB, I, p. 37.

27 CMB, I, p. 34 and CMB, I, p. 31.

28 CMB, I, p. 35.

29 CMB, I, p. 35 and CMB, I, p. 37 (Reverse).

30 CMB, I, p. 32 and p., I, p. 33. Danby, as Secretary for the Navy, had been persuaded by Fall to transfer responsibility of the oil field at Teapot Dome,

Wyoming, to the Department of the Interior. This was one of the areas which had been protected as the US Navy's oil reserve to ensure sufficient supplies of fuel as the fleets moved from using coal to oil. Now under Albert B. Fall's authority, oil production rights at Teapot Dome were given over to associates of Fall who showed their gratitude with no-interest loans and gifts. Fall briefly became a very rich man but Thomas J Walsh exposed his corruption with dogged determination. Danby resigned office in 1924. Fall was given a 12-month prison sentence in 1929, the first US Cabinet Secretary to be incarcerated. Harding's term of office was to be curtailed by his death in August 1923, which was just as well. He had exposed himself to the tune of $170 000, by investing in stocks and shares. As Head of State this was not only injudicious but also illegal.

[31] http://www.senate.gov/artandhistory/history/minute/Senate_Investigates_the_Teapot_Dome_Scandal.htm Accessed 6/4/2016.

[32] Thanks to L. Cohick Library Tech, USAHEC.

[33] CMB, I, p. 35.

[34] CMB, I, p. 32 and CMB, I, p. 33.

[35] CMB, I, PAGE 35 (Reverse).

[36] CMB, I, p.37 (Reverse).

[37] 'Men of the Month', *The Crisis*, Vol 12, No 2, p 67-68, 1916. Article and photograph.

[38] CMB, I, p. 37 (Reverse). Also see *The Crisis* (July 1916) page 16 with a short article on Powell. https://www.marxists.org/history/usa/workers/civil-rights/crisis/0600-crisis-v12n02-w068.pdf accessed on 6/4/1916.

[39] CMB, I, p. 37.

[40] CMB, I, p. 36.

[41] CMB, I, p. 27.

[42] CMB, I, p. 28.

[43] CMB, I, p. 12 and CMB, I, p. 4.

[44] CMB, I, p. 377 (Reverse). Also see *The Crisis* (July 1916) p. 16 with a short article on Powell.

[45] CMB, I, p. 36 (reverse) and http://www.sixtyninth.net/duffy.html

[46] *New York Times*, 29 June 1936

[47] F. D. Roosevelt Library, Washington, letter from Susannah Knight to Eleanor Roosevelt, Eleanor Roosevelt Papers, box 860, folder '110 ER Autographs 1936 I-L', 4 June 1936.

[48] Ibid.

[49] *New York Times* 1 December 1921

[50] *New York Times* 13 December 1921

[51] CMB, I, p. 11.

[52] CMB, I, p. 11.

[53] CMB, III, p. 12.

[54] Information provided by the grandson of Daniel Dow.

[55] 'Merrymaking At Sea'. *Times* [London, England] 21 Dec. 1921: 9. *The Times Digital Archive*. Web. 25 Mar. 2014.

[56] Ibid.

[57] CMB, I, p. 9

58 *Dictionary of National Biography* http://www.oxforddnb.com/view/article/39011
59 *New York Times 13* December 1921 - Article - Print Headline: 'SAIL FOR EUROPE TODAY'; Lord Arlington Among Passengers on *Aquitania* -The Arrivals'.
60 Ibid.
61 CMB, I, p. 9.
62 CMB, I, p. 4.
63 *New York Times* 13 December 1921 and also 'Japanese Mission'. *Times* [London, England] 20 Dec. 1921:-10. *The Times Digital Archive*. Web. 25 Mar. 2014.
64 WBSLB, 21 December 1921, p. 91 and Shipping'. *Times* [London, England] 20 Dec. 1921: 2. *The Times Digital Archive*. Web. 25 Mar. 2014.

9 The Recovery 1922 - 33

1 Interview with A.H., March 2015. Her father was killed at the end of June 1915 and Susannah gave enduring support to A.S. mother over a long period of time, helping with the her three siblings.
2 CMB, I, p. 30.
3 *CG*, 9 October 1921, p. 8.
4 WBSLB, 12 April 1922, p. 96.
5 CMB, II, p. 4.
6 CMB, II, p. 4.
7 CMB, I, p. 18.
8 WBSLB, 24 and 28 April 1922, p. 96.
9 CMB, III, pp. 16, 18, 19, 26-28 and CMB, III, p. 18.
10 CMB, III, p. 16.
11 CMB, I, p. 36 (Reverse).
12 CMB, III, pp. 75-77.
13 CMB, I, p. 13.
14 CMB, I, p. 36 (Reverse).
15 CMB, I, p. 20.
16 CMB, III, p. 20 and CMB, I, p. 7.
17 CMB, II, p. 6.
18 CMB, II, p. 5.
19 Strong, David *Australian Dictionary of Jesuit Biography* (Melbourne University Press: Broadway, Australia, 1998), pp. 294-5.
20 Costello, Peter Clongowes Wood (Dublin: Gill and Macmillan, 1989), passim.
21 Joyce. James, *Portrait of an Artist as a Young Man* (New York, 1916).
22 CMB, II, p. 75.
23 Coop, James Ogden *The Story of the 55th (West Lancashire) Division* (Liverpool Daily Post: Liverpool, 1919). Republished by Naval and Military Press: Uckfield, 2002) and Steve Bellis
24 CMB, I, p. 14.
25 CMB, I, p. 37.
26 CMB, II, p. 5.

[27] Harris, J.P. Douglas *Haig and the First World War* (Cambridge University Press: Cambridge, 2008).

[28] CMB, I, p. 9.

[29] F. D. Roosevelt Library, Washington, letter from Susannah Knight to Eleanor Roosevelt, Eleanor Roosevelt Papers, box 860, folder '110 ER Autographs 1936 I-L', 4 June 1936.

[30] CMB, I, p. 4.

[31] CMB, I, p. 9 (Reverse).

[32] CMB, I, p. 35 (Reverse).

[33] CMB, I, p. 9 and CMB, I, p. 8.

[34] CMB, I, p. 4 and CMB, I, p. 6

[35] CMB, I, PAGE 40a

[36] CMB, I, p. 9.

[37] CMB, I, p. 35 (Reverse).

[38] CMB, I, PAGE 32 and http://bioguide.congress.gov/scripts/biodisplay.pl?index=C000138 accessed 7/4/2016.

[39] Electoral Rolls, 1918-1937 consulted in Chorley Library

[40] CMB, I, p. 9.

[41] CMB, I, p. 8.

[42] John, A.H. *A Liverpool Merchant House* (George Allen & Unwin: London, 1959).

[43] CMB, I, p. 8 (Reverse).

[44] CMB, I, p. 9 (Reverse).

[45] CMB, I, p. 10.

[46] CMB, I, p. 26.

[47] CMB, I, p. 35.

[48] http://afleetingpeace.org/index.php/business-pleasure/14-business-and pleasure/167-the-pilots-of-imperial-airways

[49] CMB, I, p. 6.

[50] 'American Airmen At Croydon'. *Times* [London, England] 17 July 1924: 11. *The \ Times Digital Archive*. Web. 25 Mar. 2014.

[51] CMB, I, p. 35.

[52] There is a coincidence here, for Joyce and Davidson appear beneath the columns including of the Secretaries of State, Labor, War and Commerce, and both attachés were likely to have been in Washington at the time when the earlier signatures were obtained. It seems likely that they penned their names in July 1924, but is possible that Susannah was renewing a connection.

[53] 'American Airmen At Croydon'. *Times* [London, England] 17 July 1924: 11. *The Times Digital Archive*. Web. 25 Mar. 2014.

[54] 'American Airmen At Croydon'. *Times* [London, England] 17 July 1924: 11. *The Times Digital Archive*. Web. 25 Mar. 2014.

[55] 'American Bar Visit'. *Times* [London, England] 21 July 1924: 10. *The Times Digital Archive*. Web. 25 Mar. 2014.

[56] Ibid.

[57] Ibid.

[58] Ibid.

[59] CMB, III, pp. 22-25, 29, 30-31, 33-35, 39, 42-45.

[60] CMB, III, p. 123.

[61] American Bar Association visit to England, Scotland and Ireland 1924 Memorial Volume.

[62] CMB, I, p.35.

[63] 'Mr Hughes In London'. *Times* [London, England] 21 July 1924: 12. *The Times Digital Archive*. Web. 25 Mar. 2014.

[64] CMB, III, p. 31.

[65] CMB, III, p. 15.

[66] CMB, III, p. 15 (Reverse).

[67] Anne Jensen, Assistant Archivist, Archive & Record Office, Group Publishing Services.

[68] CMB, III, p. 42.

[69] The periods of individuals were in or out of office seems to determine a range of dates in which this could have taken place.

[70] WBSLB, 13 July 1926 p. 154

[71] CMB, III, pp. 2-5.

[72] CMB, III, pp. 2-4.

[73] WBSLB, 16 February 1923, p. 109.

[74] Ibid, 16 March 1923, 110.

[75] Ibid, 25 April 1923, p. 112.

[76] Ibid, 28 May 1923, p. 113.

[77] WA, Letter from John Knight to Mary Louisa, undated.

[78] Recollection of Jack's granddaughter, Jan Walmsley 25 February 2012.

[79] F. D. Roosevelt Library, Washington, letter from Susannah Knight to Eleanor Roosevelt, Eleanor Roosevelt Papers, box 860, folder '110 ER Autographs 1936 I-L', 4 June 1936 and M.B. (b1927-), a member of St Gregory's Church who was interviewed by A Cree 2 September 2012.

[80] *CG*, 15 August, 1920.

[81] WBSLB, 17 December 1920, p. 73.

[82] Ibid, 6 February 1925, p. 136 and 16 October 1925, p. 144.

[83] Ibid, 16 April 1928, p. 172.

[84] Reynolds, David *The Long Shadow* (Simon and Schuster: London, 2014), pp. 180-185 and Crane, David. *Empires of the Dead* (William Collins London, 2014), *passim.*

[85] *CG*, 26 August 1928, p. 8.

[86] *Chorley Standard*, 28 June, 1930.

[87] Ibid, 9 January 1931, p. 192.

[88] M.B. (b1927-), a member of St Gregory's Church who was interviewed by A Cree 2 September 2012.

[89] Ibid, 13 September 1927, p. 165.

[90] Ibid, 22 June 1932, p. 204.

[91] Ibid, 28 June 1932, p. 204.

[92] Ibid, 10 February, 1933, pp. 209-10.

[93] Ibid, 1 March 1933, p. 210.

[94] Ibid, 30 June 1933 pp. 214-5.

10 Retirement 1933-35

[1] F. D. Roosevelt Library, Washington, letter from Susannah Knight to Eleanor Roosevelt, Eleanor Roosevelt Papers, box 860, folder '110 ER Autographs 1936 I-L', 4 June 1936.
[2] CMB, II, p. 2 and CMB, II, p. 3.
[3] *Bootle Times*, 30 November, 1934.
[4] Probate Records, 1934.
[5] WA, Recollections and photographs.
[6] *CG*, 9 February 1935.
[7] *CG*, 23 February, 1935, p. 7.
[8] CMB, I, p. 8.
[9] Article by George Birtill, *CG*, 11 December 1980, p. 14.
[10] *CG*, 15 December 1934, p. 3.
[11] *CG*, 9 February 1935.
[12] F. D. Roosevelt Library, Washington, letter from Susannah Knight to Eleanor Roosevelt, Eleanor Roosevelt Papers, box 860, folder '110 ER Autographs 1936 I-L', 4 June 1936.
[13] Passenger Records: *Source Citation: Year:* 1935: Roll 5728 from www.ancestry.co.uk
[14] F. D. Roosevelt Library, Washington, letter from Susannah Knight to Eleanor Roosevelt, Eleanor Roosevelt Papers, box 860, folder '110 ER Autographs 1936 I-L', 4 June 1936
[15] Lloyd George, David *War Memoirs Volume 2* (Odham's Press: London, 1936).
[16] Passenger Records: *Source Citation: Year:* 1935: Roll 5728 from www.ancestry.co.uk

11 The Last American Adventure 1935-16

[1] 'Mails and Shipping'. *Times* [London, England] 28 Oct. 1935: 22. *The Times Digital Archive.* Web. 25 Mar. 2014. Also 'Shipping'. *Times* [London, England] 23 Oct. 1935: 2. *The Times Digital Archive.* Web. 25 Mar. 2014.
[2] Passenger Records: *Source Citation:* Year: 1935; Arrival: New York, New York; Microfilm Serial: T715; Microfilm Roll: 5728; Line: 3; Page Number: 152.
[3] Passenger Records: *Source Citation:* Year: 1935; Arrival: New York, New York; Microfilm Serial: T715; Microfilm Roll: 5728; Line: 3; Page Number: 152.
[4] US Federal Census: Year: *1930*; Census Place: *Fort Worth, Tarrant, Texas*; Roll: *2394*; Page: *18B*; Enumeration District: *0036*; Image: *168.0*; FHL microfilm: *2342128*.
[5] US WW1 Draft Registration Cards: Registration State: *Texas*; Registration County: *Tarrant*; Roll: *1953360*; Draft Board: *3*.
[6] CMB, III, p. 64.
[7] http://www.buffalobill.org/PDFs/Buffalo_Bill_Visits.pdf

[8] 'TEXAS CENTENNIAL,' *Handbook of Texas Online* m http://www.tshaonline.org/handbook/online/articles/lkt01, accessed September 26, 2013. Published by the Texas State Historical Association.

[9] CMB, III, p. 70 and http://en.wikipedia.org/wiki/Charley_Lockhart and http://www.texasarchive.org/library/index.php?title=Smallest_Treasurer accesses 7/4/2016.

[10] Dick Smith, 'BOARD OF CONTROL,' *Handbook of Texas Online* http://www.tshaonline.org/handbook/online/articles/mdb02, accessed March 25, 2014. Uploaded on June 12, 2010. Published by the Texas State Historical Association.

[11] CMB, III, p. 70.

[12] CMB, III, p. 105 and CMB, III, p. 110.

[13] http://www.lib.utexas.edu/taro/utcah/00630/cah-00630.html

[14] CMB, III, p. 129.

[15] CMB, III, p. 130.

[16] CMB, III, p. 146.

[17] National Archives and Records Administration. *U.S. World War II Army Enlistment Records, 1938-1946* [database on-line]. Provo, UT, USA: Ancestry.com Operations Inc, 2005. Original data: Electronic Army Serial Number Merged File, 1938-1946 [Archival Database]; ARC: 1263923. World War II Army Enlistment Records; Records of the National Archives and Records Administration, Record Group 64; National Archives at College Park. College Park, Maryland, U.S.A.

[18] CMB, III, p. 130.

[19] Correspondence with Mel Oakes, September 2013.

[20] CMB, III, p. 138.

[21] 'PATTERSON, CALEB PERRY,' *Handbook of Texas Online* http://www.tshaonline.org/handbook/online/articles/fpa51, accessed October 02, 2013. Published by the Texas State Historical Association.

[22] CMB, I, p. 32.

[23] Texas War Records Collection, 1916-1919, 1940-1951, Dolph Briscoe Center for American History, The University of Texas at Austin.

[24] 'GUTSCH, MILTON RIETOW,' *Handbook of Texas Online* http://www.tshaonline.org/handbook/online/articles/fgu12, accessed October 02, 2013. Published by the Texas State Historical Association.

[25] CMB, III, p. 138.

[26] CMB, III, p. 138.

[27] J. Horace Bass, 'RAMSDELL, CHARLES WILLIAM,' *Handbook of Texas Online* http://www.tshaonline.org/handbook/online/articles/fra25, accessed October 02, 2013. Published by the Texas State Historical Association

[28] CMB, II, p. 9.

[29] Mayellen Bresie, 'FOIK, PAUL JOSEPH,' *Handbook of Texas Online* http://www.tshaonline.org/handbook/online/articles/ffo02, accessed October 11, 2013. Published by the Texas State Historical Association

[30] CMB, III, p. 140.

[31] Francis E. Abernethy, 'DOBIE, JAMES FRANK,' *Handbook of Texas Online* http://www.tshaonline.org/handbook/online/articles/fdo02, accessed October 11, 2013. Published by the Texas State Historical Association.

[32] Quoted from Southwest Review, Volume XXI N°1

[33] CMB, III, p. 144.

[34] CMB, III, p. 139.

[35] CMB, III, p. 142.

[36] Mayellen Bresie, 'FOIK, PAUL JOSEPH,' *Handbook of Texas Online* http://www.tshaonline.org/handbook/online/articles/ffo02, accessed December 04, 2013. Published by the Texas State Historical Association.

[37] CMB, III, p. 133.

[38] Atkinson, Mary Jourdan *The Texas Indians* (The Naylor Company: San Antonio, Texas 1935).

[39] CMB, II, p. 8.

[40] CMB, III, p. 74.

[41] CMB, III, p. 75.

[42] CMB, III, p. 57 and CMB, III, p. 58.

[43] CMB, III, p. 59.

[44] CMB, III, p. 60.

[45] CMB, III, p. 58.

[46] CMB, III, p. 61-62; CMB, III, p. 65-69. Further amplification is available at: Texas Almanac and State Industrial Guide 1936, Book, 1936; digital images, http://texashistory.unt.edu/ark:/67531/metapth117161/ : accessed October 13, 2013), University of North Texas Libraries, The Portal to Texas History, http://texashistory.unt.edu; crediting Texas State Historical Association, Denton, Texas.

[47] CMB, III, p. 130.

[48] CMB, III, p. 71.

[49] Railroad Commission of Texas Docket No. 4824-R 18th August 1942, Austin Texas http://www.thehistorycenteronline.com/uploads/resources/tse_passenger_service_termination_testimony.pdf

[50] CMB, III, p. 88.

[51] CMB, III, p. 87.

[52] CMB, III, p. 85 and CMB, III, p. 86

[53] CMB, III, p. 73.

[54] CMB, III, PAGE 72

[55] CMB, III, p. 92 and CMB, III, p. 93

[56] CMB, III, p. 94.

[57] CMB, III, p. 102.

[58] CMB, III, p. 81 and CMB, III, p. 82.

[59] CMB, III, p. 83.

[60] F. D. Roosevelt Library, Washington, letter from Susannah Knight to Eleanor Roosevelt, Eleanor Roosevelt Papers, box 860, folder '110 ER Autographs 1936 I-L', 4 June 1936.

[61] Ibid.

[62] Ibid.

[63] CMB, III, p. 48.

[64] CMB, III, p. 49 (Reverse).

[65] F. D. Roosevelt Library, Washington, letter from Susannah Knight to Eleanor Roosevelt, Eleanor Roosevelt Papers, box 860, folder '110 ER Autographs 1936 I-L', 4 June 1936

[66] CMB, III, p. 148.

[67] CMB, III, p. 94 and CMB, III, p. 127.

[68] CMB, I, p. 36 (Reverse).

[69] 'Veterans Dip Flag for Father Duffy', *The New York Times*, 29 June 1936.

[70] CMB, III, p. 148.

[71] CMB, III, p. 55.

[72] 'TEXAS CENTENNIAL,' *Handbook of Texas Online* http://www.tshaonline.org/handbook/online/articles/lkt01, accessed December 04, 2013. Published by the Texas State Historical Association.

[73] Texas Almanac and State Industrial Guide 1936, Book, 1936; digital images, http://texashistory.unt.edu/ark:/67531/metapth117161/ : accessed December 04, 2013, University of North Texas Libraries, The Portal to Texas History, http://texashistory.unt.edu; crediting Texas State Historical Association, Denton, Texas. p. 375.

[74] CMB, III, p. 126.

[75] CMB, III, p. 121.

[76] CMB, III, p. 89.

[77] CMB, III, PAGE 122, Texas Almanac and State Industrial Guide 1936, Book, 1936, digital images, http://texashistory.unt.edu/ark:/67531/metapth117161/ accessed December 05, 2013, University of North Texas Libraries, The Portal to Texas History, http://texashistory.unt.edu; crediting Texas State Historical Association, Denton, Texas. Also 'TEXAS CENTENNIAL,' *Handbook of Texas Online* http://www.tshaonline.org/handbook/online/articles/lkt01, accessed December 05, 2013. Published by the Texas State Historical Association.

[78] Jim Parsons and David Bush, *Chicago Art Deco Magazine*, Fall 2011, p. 22.

[79] Texas Almanac and State Industrial Guide 1936, Book, 1936; digital images, http://texashistory.unt.edu/ark:/67531/metapth117161/ : accessed December 03, 2013, University of North Texas Libraries, The Portal to Texas History, http://texashistory.unt.edu, crediting Texas State Historical Association, Denton, Texas, p. 373.

[80] Texas Almanac and State Industrial Guide 1936, Book, 1936, digital images, http://texashistory.unt.edu/ark:/67531/metapth117161/ : accessed December 04, 2013), University of North Texas Libraries, The Portal to Texas History, http://texashistory.unt.edu, crediting Texas State Historical Association, Denton, Texas, p. 373.

[81] Cullen F Thomas, President, Texas Centennial Commission, 2 June 1935.

[82] Jim Parsons and David Bush, *Chicago Art Deco Magazine*, (Fall 2011), pp. 21-25.

[83] CMB, III, p. 90.

[84] CMB, III, p. 98.

[85] CMB, III, p. 125 and http://www.texasranger.org/halloffame/ Hughes_John.htm accessed 7/4/2016.

[86] CMB, III, p. 99.

[87] CMB, III, p. 97.

[88] CMB, III, p. 125.

[89] CMB, III, p. 100.

[90] CMB, III, p. 98.

[91] CMB, III, p. 124.

[92] *Liverpool Mercury* (Liverpool, England), Tuesday, 7 July 1891, Issue 13572

[93] CMB, III, p. 121.

[94] Texas Almanac and State Industrial Guide 1936, Book, 1936; digital images, http://texashistory.unt.edu/ark:/67531/metapth117161/ : accessed December 05, 2013), University of North Texas Libraries, The Portal to Texas History, http://texashistory.unt.edu; crediting Texas State Historical Association, Denton, Texas, p 40.

[95] CMB, III, p. 106; CMB, III, p. 107; CMB, III, p. 109; CMB, III, p. 108.

[96] CMB, III, p. 88.

[97] CMB, III, p. 104.

[98] CMB, III, pp. 81-82.

[99] Dalrymple, Tate etc. *Major Texas Floods of 1936* (Government Print Office: Washington D.C, USA, 1937) to be found at http://pubs.usgs.gov/wsp/0816/report.pdf

[100] CMB, III, p. 124.

[101] CMB, III, p. 183.

[102] CMB, III, p. 58.

[103] The American practise of recording dates by mm/dd/yy has been applied here.

[104] CMB, III, p. 91.

[105] CMB, III, p. 84.

[106] 'Peter the Hermit, Once Hollywood Attreaction, Dies Unmourned at 90', *Gettysburg Times*, 20 March, 1969, p. 24.

[107] CMB, III, p. 11.

[108] CMB, III, p. 124.

[109] CMB, III, p. 120.

[110] CMB, III, p. 119

[111] http://en.wikipedia.org/wiki/Andy_Payne accessed 7/7/2016

[112] CMB, III, p. 115.

[113] CMB, III, p. 114.

[114] CMB, III, p. 143.

[115] CMB, III, p. 111.

[116] CMB, III, p. 111.

[117] http://www.oklahomahistory.net/CarterCountyHistoricalMarkers.htm

[118] *Minutes of the Board of Directors of the Oklahoma Historical Society*, 29 July 1943 at http://digital.library.okstate.edu/chronicles/v021/v021p315.pdf accessed 7/4/2016.

[119] CMB, III, p. 114.

[120] CMB, III, p. 112.

[121] Thanks to Carolyn Krumanocker, of the Oklahoma Historical Association, for her guidance on the Will Rogers connection to 18-19 October 1936.
[122] CMB, III, p. 112.
[123] CMB, III, p. 11.

12 At Dusk

[1] WA.
[2] Probate Records for 1950.
[3] *CG*, 18 May 1945.
[4] *CG*, 29 June 1945.
[5] *CG*, 17 July 1969.
[6] Interview with Margaret Bailey, 31 May, 2017
[7] *CG*, 29 June 1945, p. 4.
[8] *CG*, 6 July 1945, p. 4.
[9] *Soroptomists of Chorley Minute Book*, November 1943, Lancashire County Records DDX 1796/1.
[10] Ibid, July 1945.
[11] Ibid, July to September 1945.
[12] Ibid, October 1945.
[13] Ibid, 1946.
[14] *Daily Dispatch*, 14 August 1950.
[15] *Soroptomists of Chorley Minute Book* - 1946 Lancashire County Records DDX 1796/1.
[16] Ibid.
[17] Ibid, 1948.
[18] Ibid, 2 November 1948.
[19] *Daily Dispatch*, 14 November 1949.
[20] *Soroptomists of Chorley Minute Book*, December 1950 Lancashire County Records DDX 1796/1
[21] Liverpool Register Office, Register of Deaths, 14 August, 1950, no.186. The age of death supplied by the family as 81 is incorrect when cross-referenced with the registration of her birth.
[22] Burial Records, Liverpool Archives. Microfilm 352 CEM/6/3/13, Burial Registration number 77128. The Burial Records give her address as 79, Merton Road – her sister in law's house.
[23] Thanks to Dr Meg Whittle, Archdiocesan Archivist, Liverpool and Jim Lancaster for narrowing this down.
[24] *Daily Dispatch*, 14 August 1950.
[25] WA, Mary Louisa's notebook.
[26] *CG*, 18 August 1950, p. 1.
[27] *CG*, 18 August 1950, p. 5.
[28] *Soroptomists of Chorley Minute Book*, 22 August 1950 Lancashire County Records DDX 1796/1.
[29] *CG*, 25 August 1950, p. 5.
[30] *Catholic Bulletin*, Chorley, September 1950.

31 *CG*, 17 July 1969, p. 5.

APPENDIX

The Names of the Men recorded in the Chorley Memorial Album

Private James Gifford Abbott 6th Bn The Loyal North Lancashire Rgt
Private John Abram 105th Field Ambulance Royal Army Medical Corps
Private Peter Abram 1st/4th Bn The Loyal North Lancashire Rgt
Private Thomas Abram 1st Bn The Loyal North Lancashire Rgt
Private James Henry Adams 11th Bn Manchester Rgt
Lance Corporal John Henry Adams 3rd Bn The Loyal North Lancashire Rgt
2nd Lieutenant Henry Ainscough 1st/5th Bn Border Rgt
2nd Lieutenant Thomas Ainscough 303rd Siege Bty Royal Garrison Artillery
Private Thomas Ainscough 8th Bn King's Own Royal Lancaster Rgt
Private William Henry Ainscough 9th Bn The Loyal North Lancashire Rgt
Driver Charles Ainsworth 88th Brigade Royal Field Artillery
Corporal Eli Ainsworth 11th Bn East Lancashire Rgt
Private Henry Ainsworth 5th Bn Connaught Rangers
Private Joseph Ainsworth 1st/4th Bn The Loyal North Lancashire Rgt
Rifleman William Ainsworth 11th Bn King's Royal Rifle Corps
Sapper Leonard Alker 529th Field Coy Royal Engineers
Private William Alker 21st Bn Manchester Rgt
Private Amos Allen 9th Bn The Loyal North Lancashire Rgt
Private Thomas Allsup 2nd Bn Royal Scots Fusiliers
Driver John William Alston 1st Coy. 37th Div. Train Army Service Corps
Private Leo Alston 18th Bn Canadian Infantry (Western Ontario Rgt)
Private Robert Anglezarke 1st Bn The Loyal North Lancashire Rgt
Corporal William Archer 10th Canadians
Private Harold Armstrong 11th Bn The Loyal North Lancashire Rgt
Private Samuel Arrowsmith 3rd Bn The Loyal North Lancashire Rgt
Private John Thomas Ashton 10th Bn The Loyal North Lancashire Rgt
Gunner John Ashworth 15th Brigade Royal Field Artillery
Private Patrick Asleford 1st Bn The Loyal North Lancashire Rgt
Private Joseph Aspinall 6th Bn The Loyal North Lancashire Rgt
Private Walter Aspinall 2nd/6th Bn Lancashire Fusiliers
Lance Corporal Robert Astley 11th Bn East Lancashire Rgt
Private Robert Astley 2nd Bn King's Own Royal Lancaster Rgt
Lance Corporal Thomas Atkinson 1st Bn King's Own Royal Lancaster Rgt
Private Thomas Bagan 11th Bn The Loyal North Lancashire Rgt
Private John William Baines 8th Bn The Loyal North Lancashire Rgt
Private Alfred Frederick Baker 6th Bn The Loyal North Lancashire Rgt
Lance Corporal William Baker 6th Bn The Loyal North Lancashire Rgt
Private Thomas Baldwin 11th Bn South Wales Borderers
Private William Baldwin 16th Bn Royal Scots Rgt
Private Eli Ball 1st/4th Bn The Loyal North Lancashire Rgt
Private James Roger Ball 1st/4th Bn The Loyal North Lancashire Rgt

Private Richard Ball 10th Bn Lancashire Fusiliers
Corporal Thomas Balshaw 2nd Bn Gordon Highlanders
Private Walter Bamber 10th Bn The Loyal North Lancashire Rgt
Private Harold Banks 10th Bn Lancashire Fusiliers
Private Herbert Banks 7th Bn The Loyal North Lancashire Rgt
Private Robert Banks 10th Bn The Loyal North Lancashire Rgt
Private William Barker Mechanical Transport Coy. Army Service Corps
Private Fred Barnes 10th Bn The Loyal North Lancashire Rgt
Lance Corporal John Barnes 16th Bn Royal Welch Fusiliers
Private John Evans Barron 1st/5th Bn Manchester Rgt
2nd Lieutenant James Barton yet to be identified Royal Garrison Artillery
Private Giles Baxendale 6th Bn South Wales Borderers
Private James Baxendale 1st/4th Bn The Loyal North Lancashire Rgt
Private Jesse Baxendale 1st/4th Bn The Loyal North Lancashire Rgt
Private Philip Baxendale 15th Bn West Yorkshire Rgt
Private Robert Bracken Baxendale 10th Bn South Wales Border Rgt
Private Albert Beardsworth 10th Bn The Loyal North Lancashire Rgt
Private Frederick Beardsworth 6th Bn York and Lancaster Rgt
Private Joseph Beardsworth 61st Coy Machine Gun Corps (Infantry)
Private Robert Beardwood 1st Bn The Loyal North Lancashire Rgt
Private John Harrison Beesley 3rd Bn The Loyal North Lancashire Rgt
Private William Beesley 1st/12th Bn The Loyal North Lancashire Rgt
Acting Bombardier Thomas Bennett 235th Royal Field Artillery
Private William Bennison 12th Reserve Cavalry Rgt
Private Edward Berry 1st Bn Lancashire Fusiliers
Private Edward Berry 8th Bn The Loyal North Lancashire Rgt
Private James Berry 9th Bn Welsh Rgt
Private Thomas Berry 11th Bn East Lancashire Rgt
Private Charles Bibby 1st Bn King's (Liverpool Rgt)
Driver Leo Bibby 100th Brigade Royal Field Artillery
Private Thomas Bibby 1st/4th Bn The Loyal North Lancashire Rgt
Private Joseph Bilsborrow 2nd/4th Bn The Loyal North Lancashire Rgt
Private Nathan Birchall 8th Bn The Loyal North Lancashire Rgt
Sergeant Thomas Birchall 8th Bn The Loyal North Lancashire Rgt
Private Oliver Blackburn 17th Bn Lancashire Fusiliers
Trooper Richard Henry Blackburn N/A Household Bn
Private William Blackburn 5th Bn King's Own Shropshire Light Infantry
Sergeant Thomas Blackhurst 9th Bn The Loyal North Lancashire Rgt
Lance Corporal Alfred Blackledge 1st/4th Bn The Loyal North Lancashire Rgt
Private Wass Blakeley 1st/4th Bn The Loyal North Lancashire Rgt
Private Richard Bland 1st/4th Bn The Loyal North Lancashire Rgt
Corporal Herbert A. Bleakledge 1st/4th Bn The Loyal North Lancashire Rgt
Private Thomas Bleasdale 18th Bn Lancashire Fusiliers
Leading Seaman Wright Boardman D5 Royal Navy
Private Charles Bolton 1st/4th Bn The Loyal North Lancashire Rgt
Lance Corporal Ernest Bolton 1st Bn Scots Guards
Private James Bolton 1st Bn King's Own Royal Lancaster Rgt

Private Wilfred Bolton 6th Bn The Loyal North Lancashire Rgt
Private William Bolton 11th Bn East Lancashire Rgt
Sapper John Booth 171st Tunnelling Coy Royal Engineers
Senior Reserve Attendant George H. Bortfield HMS Crescent , RN
Signaller John Willie Bottomley 9th Bn East Surrey Rgt
Private Edward Bradley 1st/4th Bn The Loyal North Lancashire Rgt
Private Hugh Bradshaw 1st/4th Bn The Loyal North Lancashire Rgt
Private John Brennan 3rd Bn The Loyal North Lancashire Rgt
Private Patrick Brennan 1st Bn The Loyal North Lancashire Rgt
Private Thomas Brennan 6th Bn The Loyal North Lancashire Rgt
Private William Bretherton 11th Bn East Lancashire Rgt
Private James Bretland 10th Bn The Loyal North Lancashire Rgt
Private Albert Brindle 9th Bn East Lancashire Rgt
Private Charles Richard Brindle 1st Bn Coldstream Guards
Private Francis Brindle 11th Bn East Lancashire Rgt
Private Frank Rawlinson Brindle 15th Bn Durham Light Infantry
Lance Corporal James Richardson Brindle 5th Bn Manchester Rgt
Private John Brindle 19th Bn Lancashire Fusiliers
Private John Edward Brindle 3rd Bn Dragoon Guards
Captain John Lawrence Brindle 1st/4th Bn The Loyal North Lancashire Rgt
Private Nathaniel Brindle 2nd Bn South Wales Borderers
Corporal William Brindle 56th Coy Machine Gun Corps
Private John Bromiley 2nd Bn The Loyal North Lancashire Rgt
Private David Bromley 6th Bn The Loyal North Lancashire Rgt
Private Joseph Bromley 9th Bn The Loyal North Lancashire Rgt
Private Christopher Brooks 2nd Bn Lancashire Fusiliers
Lance Corporal Richard Broome 9th Bn The Loyal North Lancashire Rgt
Signaller Herbert Brown 15th Bn Durham Light Infantry
Lance Corporal Richard Brown 2nd/4th Bn The Loyal North Lancashire Rgt
Private Thomas Brown 1st Bn King's Own Royal Lancaster Rgt
Signaller Thomas Brown 13th Field Ambulance Royal Army Medical Corps
Lance Corporal Thomas Henry Brown 8th Bn King's Own Royal Lancaster Rgt
Private Harry Burgess 1st Bn Border Rgt
Sergeant John Thomas Burke 2nd Bn King's Royal Rifle Corps
Private Henry Calderbank 7th Bn East Lancashire Rgt
Private John Calderbank 6th Bn The Loyal North Lancashire Rgt
Private Joseph Campbell 94th Coy Machine Gun Corps (Infantry)
Private Albert Carr 8th Bn King's Own Royal Lancaster Rgt
Private John William Carr 8th Bn King's Own Royal Lancaster Rgt
Private Tom Carr 2nd Bn Border Rgt
Private William Carr 11th Bn East Lancashire Rgt
Private George Carrington 9th Bn The Loyal North Lancashire Rgt
Private John Carter 1st/5th Bn The Loyal North Lancashire Rgt
Private Richard Carter 9th Bn West Riding Rgt
Sergeant Herbert Catterall 8th Bn King's Own Royal Lancaster Rgt
Private John Catterall 4th/5th Bn The Loyal North Lancashire Rgt
Private Leo Catterall 1st/5th Bn The Loyal North Lancashire Rgt

Lance Corporal Percy Catterall 1st/4th Bn The Loyal North Lancashire Rgt
Private Michael Cavanagh 2nd Bn Leinster Rgt
Sapper Cecil Chadwick 54th Field Coy Royal Engineers
Private Joseph Chadwick 1st/4th Bn The Loyal North Lancashire Rgt
Private Walter Chadwick 10th Bn Training Reserve
Private William Chamberlain 6th Bn The Loyal North Lancashire Rgt
Lance Corporal Joseph Robert Chappell 1st Bn Scots Guards
Corporal Frederick Charlson 25th Bn Cheshire Rgt
Lance Corporal Richard Charnley 17th Bn Lancashire Fusiliers
Corporal George Charnock 2nd/4th Bn The Loyal North Lancashire Rgt
Fireman Thomas Christie HMS Hannibal RN Reserve
Private John Henry Christopher 11th Bn East Lancashire Rgt
Lance Corporal Albert Henry Clarkson 1st Bn King's Own Royal Lancaster Rgt
Corporal Leonard Clarkson 11th Bn The Loyal North Lancashire Rgt
Corporal William Clarkson 11th Bn East Lancashire Rgt
Private Sidney Clayton 1st/4th Bn The Loyal North Lancashire Rgt
Lance Corporal William Clegg 8th Bn The Loyal North Lancashire Rgt
Private John Clemmy 11th Bn Lancashire Fusiliers
Signaller James Cliffe 9th Bn Cheshire Rgt
Corporal Norman Cliffe 15th Bn Lancashire Fusiliers
Corporal Herbert Clitheroe 7th Bn The Loyal North Lancashire Rgt
Lance Corporal William Clubb 2nd/7th Bn Manchester Rgt
Private Leonard Cobham 1st Bn South Wales Borderers
Sergeant Edmund Cocker 8th Bn The Loyal North Lancashire Rgt
Sergeant George Collier 11th Bn East Lancashire Rgt
Private Edward Commons 1st/4th Bn The Loyal North Lancashire Rgt
Driver Edward Henry Connolly 2nd MT Coy Australian Imperial Forces
Corporal Herbert John Connolly 3rd Bn The Loyal North Lancashire Rgt
Private William Connolly 1st/4th Bn The Loyal North Lancashire Rgt
Private William Cooper 6th Bn South Wales Borderers
Private Richard Corless 5th Bn South Wales Borderers
Corporal Frank A. Cornwall Railway Operating Division Royal Engineers
Private John Cottam 9th Bn The Loyal North Lancashire Rgt
Private James Counsell 1st/4th Bn Royal Sussex Rgt
Private Walter Counsell 9th Bn The Loyal North Lancashire Rgt
Sergeant Albert Cowell 8th Bn The Loyal North Lancashire Rgt
Private John William Cowell 11th Bn East Lancashire Rgt
Private Robert Henry Critchley 2nd/4th Bn The Loyal North Lancashire Rgt
Private Richard Crook 1st/4th Bn The Loyal North Lancashire Rgt
Private William Crook 13th Bn East Lancashire Rgt
Sergeant Edward Cross 1st/4th Bn The Loyal North Lancashire Rgt
Private William Culshaw 12th Bn Manchester Rgt
Private William Harrison Culshaw 202nd Coy Machine Gun Corps
Private James Edward Cuncannon 1st Bn Border Rgt
Sergeant Ernest Cutler 11th Bn East Lancashire Rgt
Private James Dawson 8th Bn Border Rgt
Lieutenant Paul de Méhérenc de St Pierre 33rd Artillery Rgt, Aremée Française

Private Joseph Derbyshire 7th Bn East Kent Rgt
Private Samuel Derbyshire 1st/4th Bn The Loyal North Lancashire Rgt
Private Thomas Desoer 6th Bn The Loyal North Lancashire Rgt
Private Henry Dewhurst 9th Bn The Loyal North Lancashire Rgt
Private James Dickinson 11th Bn East Lancashire Rgt
Private John Dickinson 17th Bn Manchester Rgt
Private Richard (Dick) Dickinson 1st/5th Bn The Loyal North Lancashire Rgt
Private Fred Diggles 37th Bn Australian Infantry, AIF
Private Richard Ditchfield 6th Bn The Loyal North Lancashire Rgt
Private Thomas Dixon 1st Bn East Lancashire Rgt
Private Fred N Dobson 8th Bn East Lancashire Rgt
Private Sydney Bramwell Dobson 1st/4th Bn The Loyal North Lancashire Rgt
Private James Douglas 1st Bn The Loyal North Lancashire Rgt
Corporal Thomas Downs 10th Bn The Loyal North Lancashire Rgt
Sergeant Michael Duffy 10th Bn The Loyal North Lancashire Rgt
Private Frank Dunlop 12th Bn The Loyal North Lancashire Rgt
Private John James Dunlop 12th Bn The Loyal North Lancashire Rgt
Private James Durkin 9th Bn The Loyal North Lancashire Rgt
Private William Durkin 1st Bn The Loyal North Lancashire Rgt
Private Herbert Duxbury 4th/5th Bn The Loyal North Lancashire Rgt
Private Charles Eccles 1/5th Bn The Loyal North Lancashire Rgt
Corporal Gordon Edgerley 1st Canadian Div. Signal Coy
Private George Edwards 12th Bn Lancashire Fusiliers
Private James Edwards 10th Bn The Loyal North Lancashire Rgt
Private James Willoughby Elliott 149th Coy Machine Gun Corps (Infantry)
Private John Ellis 4th Bn Canadian Mounted Rifles (Central Ontario Rgt)
Corporal of Horse Abraham Ellison 2nd Life Guards
Private Wilfred Ellison 11th Bn East Lancashire Rgt
Private Joseph Enderby 11th Bn East Lancashire Rgt
Private William Enderby 1st/4th Bn The Loyal North Lancashire Rgt
Lance Corporal Carswell Entwistle 11th Bn East Lancashire Rgt
Private Ernest Entwistle Machine Gun Corps (Infantry)
yet to be identified George Evans yet to be identified yet to be identified
Lance Corporal Robert Thomas Evans 14th Bn Royal Welch Fusiliers
Corporal Michael Fadden 11th Bn East Lancashire Rgt
Private John Fairclough 2nd Bn Border Rgt
Private Robert Isaac Fairclough 1st/5th Bn The Loyal North Lancashire Rgt
Serjeant William Fairclough King's Own Royal Lancaster Rgt
Private John Farnworth 53rd Cheshire Rgt
Private Richard Farnworth 2nd Bn Welsh Rgt
Private William Farnworth 1st Bn The Loyal North Lancashire Rgt
Senior Reserve Attendant William Farnworth HMS Bayano RN
Private Arthur Farrar 1st Bn The Loyal North Lancashire Rgt
Corporal James Feeney 1st Bn The Loyal North Lancashire Rgt
Leading Signalman Thomas Feeney HMS Hogue RN
Private John Edward Felton 1st Bn The Loyal North Lancashire Rgt
Sapper Thomas Taylor Felton 202nd Royal Engineers

Private James Edward Finch 9th Bn The Loyal North Lancashire Rgt
Private John Finch 1st Bn King's Own Royal Lancaster Rgt
Private Henry Fishwick 21st Bn Welsh Rgt
Lance Corporal William Fishwick yet to be identified Royal Engineers
Private William Fishwick 2nd/4th Bn The Loyal North Lancashire Rgt
Private Harold Fletcher 4th/5th Bn The Loyal North Lancashire Rgt
Serjeant William Foley 1st/4th Bn The Loyal North Lancashire Rgt
Private Jesse Forsyth 1st/4th Bn The Loyal North Lancashire Rgt
Gunner Harry Fowler 110th Brigade Royal Field Artillery
Private Harry Fowler 10th Bn The Loyal North Lancashire Rgt
Private Herbert Fowler 10th Bn The Loyal North Lancashire Rgt
Private John Fowler 1st/4th Bn The Loyal North Lancashire Rgt
Sergeant Richard Fowler 10th Bn The Loyal North Lancashire Rgt
Private William Fox 9th Bn Canadian Infantry (Western Ontario Rgt)
Pioneer George Edward Foy 4th Labour Bn Royal Engineers
Private John Foy 1st Bn The Loyal North Lancashire Rgt
Private Timothy Foy 7th Bn The Loyal North Lancashire Rgt
2nd Lieutenant John Cecil Frankland 5th Bn The Loyal North Lancashire Rgt
Corporal Thomas Worswick Gabbott B Coy Canadian Cyclist's Corps
Colour-Sergeant Frank Gartside 3rd Bn Monmouthshire Rgt
Driver Henry Gaskell yet to be identified Royal Field Artillery
Private Herbert Gaskell 2nd Bn South Wales Borderers
Private Thomas Gaskell 11th Bn East Lancashire Rgt
Private Richard Geldeard 1st/4th Bn The Loyal North Lancashire Rgt
Private William Geldeard 8th Bn Seaforth Highlanders
Private David Allison Gent 1st/4th Bn The Loyal North Lancashire Rgt
Gunner Tom Gent 39th Royal Garrison Artillery
Private Louis Cleghorn George 1st Bn The Loyal North Lancashire Rgt
Sergeant William R Gilbert [Callan] 8th Bn King's Own Royal Lancaster Rgt
Lance Corporal Charles Gillett 8th Bn The Loyal North Lancashire Rgt
Lance Corporal Nicholas Gillett 1st/4th Bn The Loyal North Lancashire Rgt
Sapper Robert Gillett 4th Signal Coy Royal Engineers
Private William Gillett 2nd Bn Lincolnshire Rgt
Private William Gillibrand 1st/4th Bn The Loyal North Lancashire Rgt
Private Thomas Glossop 9th Bn The Loyal North Lancashire Rgt
Sergeant William Glover 2nd/4th Bn The Loyal North Lancashire Rgt
Private Benjamin Graves 1st Bn The Loyal North Lancashire Rgt
Private John William Gray 15th Bn Lancashire Fusiliers
Private Alfred Gray 8th Bn The Loyal North Lancashire Rgt
Private Harry Stock Green 6th Bn The Loyal North Lancashire Rgt
Private Richard Green 8th Bn The Loyal North Lancashire Rgt
Private William Green 11th Bn East Lancashire Rgt
Lance Corporal Gilbert Greenhalgh 1st/4th Bn Loyal North Lancashire Rgt
Private William Greenwood 11th Bn East Lancashire Rgt
Private Richard Grime 73rd Coy Machine Gun Corps (Infantry)
Private Thomas Grime 1st/4th Bn The Loyal North Lancashire Rgt
Corporal Frank Grimshaw 10th Bn The Loyal North Lancashire Rgt

Private Robert Rigby Grimshaw 1st Bn Coldstream Guards
Private Thomas Grimshaw 8th Bn Border Rgt
Sergeant Thomas Grimshaw 11th Bn East Lancashire Rgt
Sergeant Percy Grundy 8th Bn Northumberland Fusiliers
Private John Hacking 10th Bn The Loyal North Lancashire Rgt
Private Francis Haddon 6th Bn The Loyal North Lancashire Rgt
Private Joseph Hagan 1st Bn Lancashire Fusiliers
Private Walter Hailwood 1st Bn The Loyal North Lancashire Rgt
Private Henry Hall 1st/4th Bn The Loyal North Lancashire Rgt
Corporal John (Jack) Hall 5th Trench Mortar Battery Royal Field Artillery
Private Joseph Hall 75th Field Ambulance Royal Army Medical Corps
Private Nicholas Hall 1/4th Bn Royal Welch Fusiliers
Sergeant Robert Hall 21st Bn Manchester Rgt
Private Tom Victor Hall 1st/4th Bn The Loyal North Lancashire Rgt
Private Gerald Raymond Hallatt yet to be identified Royal Army Medical Corps
Private Frank Halliwell 1st Bn Lancashire Fusiliers
Lance Corporal Herbert Halton 1st/5th Bn The Loyal North Lancashire Rgt
Sapper John Halton 94th Field Coy Royal Engineers
Private Lawrence Hammond 1st/4th Bn The Loyal North Lancashire Rgt
Private Alfred Edward Handley 4th/5th Bn The Loyal North Lancashire Rgt
Private Arthur Herbert Handley 1st Bn Scots Guards
Private Edward Hardman 1st/4th Bn The Loyal North Lancashire Rgt
Corporal James Holt Hargreaves Military Foot Police Military Police Corps
Private Harry Harling 58th Canadian Expeditionary Force
Corporal John Harling 1st/5th Bn The Loyal North Lancashire Rgt
Private Michael Harlow 7th Bn South Lancashire Rgt
Acting Bombardier Arthur Harper 255th Siege Bn Royal Garrison Artillery
Private Benjamin Harper 2nd/5th Bn The Loyal North Lancashire Rgt
2nd Lieutenant Thomas Harper 10th Bn Lancashire Fusiliers
Sapper William Heald Harper 80th Field Coy Royal Engineers
Private Edwin Harrison 7th Bn The Loyal North Lancashire Rgt
Airman 2nd Class John Harrison 66th Wing Royal Flying Corps
Sergeant-Instructor John Harrison 15th Bn Cheshire Rgt
Private Thomas Harrison 1st Bn The Loyal North Lancashire Rgt
Private William Harrison 4th Bn Canadian Infantry (Central Ontario Rgt)
Private Edmund Hart 1st/4th Bn The Loyal North Lancashire Rgt
Lance Corporal James Hart 2nd Bn The Loyal North Lancashire Rgt
Gunner Robert Hart 51st Brigade Royal Field Artillery
Private Thomas Hart 6th Bn The Loyal North Lancashire Rgt
Quartermaster John Ellis Harvey 10th Bn Lancashire Fusiliers
Private Robert Hatton 1st/4th Bn The Loyal North Lancashire Rgt
Driver John Allan Haworth 73rd Brigade Royal Field Artillery
Private John Haydock 1st/5th Bn The Loyal North Lancashire Rgt
Private Alexander Heald 22nd Bn Northumberland Fusiliers
Acting Coy Sergeant Austin R. Heald 8th Bn King's Own Royal Lancaster Rgt
Private Eli James Heald 2nd/6th Bn Manchester Rgt
Private Frederick Heald 6th Bn The Loyal North Lancashire Rgt

Private Harry Heald 2nd/5th Bn King's (Liverpool Rgt)
Private Thomas Sisson Heald 10th Bn The Loyal North Lancashire Rgt
Serjeant James Heaps 18th Bn Welsh Rgt
Sergeant John Heaps 1st/4th Bn The Loyal North Lancashire Rgt
Private William Hennerley 4th Bn South Wales Borderers
2nd Lieutenant John Hesketh 1st/6th Bn West Yorkshire Rgt
Private John W Hewitt 9th Bn The Loyal North Lancashire Rgt
Private Henry Heyworth 1st/5th Bn The Loyal North Lancashire Rgt
Captain Cyril G.R. Hibbert 1st/4th Bn The Loyal North Lancashire Rgt
Lance Corporal Albert Higgins 7th Bn Welsh Rgt
Private John Higgins 7th Bn The Loyal North Lancashire Rgt
Private Ernest Higham 1st Bn King's Own Royal Lancaster Rgt
Private Walter Higson 1st/7th Bn Lancashire Fusiliers
Lance Corporal Harold Hill 9th Bn The Loyal North Lancashire Rgt
Private William Hilsley 9th Bn The Loyal North Lancashire Rgt
Private Christopher Henry Hilton 2nd Bn Royal Welch Fusiliers
Lieut. Colonel Ralph Hindle 1st/4th Bn The Loyal North Lancashire Rgt
Lance Corporal William Hindle 1st/7th Bn Royal Warwickshire Rgt
Lance Corporal Fred Hitchen 1st Bn The Loyal North Lancashire Rgt
Private Herbert Hitchen 8th Bn The Loyal North Lancashire Rgt
Private Richard Hitchen 13th King's (Liverpool Rgt)
Private Robert Hitchen 15th Bn Welsh Rgt
Private Thomas Hodges 9th Bn Australian Imperial Forces
Private John Hodgon 9th Bn The Loyal North Lancashire Rgt
Private Herbert Hodgson 10th Bn The Loyal North Lancashire Rgt
Private Ernest Hodkinson 2nd/4th Bn York and Lancaster Rgt
Signaller Peter Hodson 1st Bn Scots Guards
Private William Holbrook 6th Bn The Loyal North Lancashire Rgt
Coy Quartermaster Sergeant Arthur Holden 9th Bn Lancashire Fusiliers
Private James Holden 2nd/4th Bn The Loyal North Lancashire Rgt
Driver Peter Holden 94th Royal Field Artillery
Corporal James Holding 2nd Bn King's Own Royal Lancaster Rgt
Corporal Alfred Holland 21st Coy Machine Gun Corps (Infantry)
Lance Corporal Roland L. Holland 1st Bn King's Own Royal Lancaster Rgt
Private Samuel Holland 8th Bn King's Own Royal Lancaster Rgt
Corporal William Holland yet to be identified yet to be identified
Private Hubert Holme 12th Bn Lancashire Fusiliers
Private Charles Holmes 98th Coy Machine Gun Corps (Infantry)
2nd Lieutenant Herbert Holmes 97th Royal Air Force
Private Joseph William Holmes 6th Bn The Loyal North Lancashire Rgt
Private John Holt 3rd Bn Grenadier Guards
Rifleman George Hoolton 1st Bn Royal Irish Rifles
Private John Hooper 3rd Bn Royal Welch Fusiliers
Private Robert John Hope 3rd Bn East Lancashire Rgt
Rifleman Alfred Hopwood 1st/5th Bn South Lancashire Rgt
Sergeant Harry Hopwood 7th Bn The Loyal North Lancashire Rgt
Pioneer Walter Horrocks Base Signal Depot (EEF) Royal Engineers

Private Walter Hough 10th Bn The Loyal North Lancashire Rgt
Deckhand James Edward Houghton 524 Royal Naval Reserve
Private Frank Howard 2nd Bn King's Own Royal Lancaster Rgt
Private Thomas Howard 6th Bn The Loyal North Lancashire Rgt
Private Thomas Howard 1st Bn Notts and Derby Rgt (Sherwood Foresters)
Private Ellis Howarth 1st Bn The Loyal North Lancashire Rgt
Private Harry Howarth 16th Bn Lancashire Fusiliers
Sergeant Thomas Howarth 10th Bn The Loyal North Lancashire Rgt
Private Robert William Hughes 1st/4th Bn King's Own Royal Lancaster Rgt
Private Jack Hull 11th Bn East Lancashire Rgt
Private Jesse Hull 2nd/4th Bn The Loyal North Lancashire Rgt
Private George Hunter 1st Bn Northumberland Fusiliers
Private James Hunter 9th Bn The Loyal North Lancashire Rgt
Rifleman James Hunter 1st/6th Bn King's (Liverpool Rgt)
Private Richard Hunter 10th Bn The Loyal North Lancashire Rgt
Private Thomas Hunter 2nd/4th Bn The Loyal North Lancashire Rgt
Private Henry Hunter 11th Bn East Lancashire Rgt
Sergeant Joseph Hurley 1st/4th Bn The Loyal North Lancashire Rgt
Private John Hurst 11th Bn East Lancashire Rgt
Corporal Albert Ince 17th Bn King's (Liverpool Rgt)
Private George Irving 1st/4th Bn The Loyal North Lancashire Rgt
Lance Corporal George Isherwood 1st Bn The Loyal North Lancashire Rgt
Captain Harold Jackman 7th Bn King's Royal Rifle Corps
Private John Jackman 1st/4th Bn The Loyal North Lancashire Rgt
Private Joseph Jackson 2nd Bn Coldstream Guards
Private Robert Jackson 2nd Bn Northumberland Fusiliers
Private Robert Jackson 3rd Bn The Loyal North Lancashire Rgt
Private Samuel Jackson 1st/4th Bn The Loyal North Lancashire Rgt
Private William Jameson 1st/4th Bn King's Own Royal Lancaster Rgt
Private Edward Jenkins 4th Bn King's Own Royal Lancaster Rgt
Private Stephen Johnson 6th Bn The Loyal North Lancashire Rgt
Private Fred Jolly 10th Bn The Loyal North Lancashire Rgt
Private John Jolly 2nd Bn Royal Sussex Rgt
Driver John Jones Horse Transport Army Service Corps
Private Joseph Edward Jones 9th Bn King's Own Yorkshire Light Infantry
Private William Justice Jones 3rd Bn Bedfordshire Rgt
Sergeant Drum Major James Jordan 9th Bn The Loyal North Lancashire Rgt
Private Edwin Joyce 8th Bn The Loyal North Lancashire Rgt
Private John Joyce 3rd Bn Suffolk Rgt
Private Thomas Kelleher 1st Bn The Loyal North Lancashire Rgt
Private Robert Henry Kellock 8th Bn Black Watch (Royal Highlanders)
Private John Kelly 12th Bn King's (Liverpool Rgt)
Lance Corporal Herbert Kelsall 10th Bn Lancashire Fusiliers
Private Albert Kenyon 9th Bn The Loyal North Lancashire Rgt
Private Henry Kenyon 1st/5th Bn The Loyal North Lancashire Rgt
Private Frederick Kerfoot 9th Bn East Lancashire Rgt
Lance Corporal John Kerfoot 1st/4th Bn The Loyal North Lancashire Rgt

Private William Kerfoot 1st Bn The Loyal North Lancashire Rgt
Private John Kettle 7th Bn The Loyal North Lancashire Rgt
Sergeant Francis Joseph Kevill 7th Bn The Loyal North Lancashire Rgt
Corporal John King 2nd Bn King's Own Royal Lancaster Rgt
Signaller William Robson Kirby 2nd/4th Bn The Loyal North Lancashire Rgt
Private James Ward Kirkman 6th Bn Yorkshire Rgt
Sapper John Dawson Knight yet to be identified Royal Engineers
Private Joseph Knight 2nd Bn South Wales Borderers
Private James Lancaster 11th Bn East Lancashire Rgt
Gunner John Lancaster 330th Royal Field Artillery
Private Joseph Lancaster 1st/7th Bn King's (Liverpool Rgt)
Private Richard Lancaster 7th Bn The Loyal North Lancashire Rgt
Private Thomas Lancaster 13th King's (Liverpool Rgt)
Sergeant Austin Lang 11th Bn East Lancashire Rgt
Private Henry Latham 17th Australian Imperial Forces
Private John Lawrenson 11th Bn East Lancashire Rgt
2nd Lieutenant George Leach 17th Bn Manchester Rgt
Private Joseph Leach 1st Bn The Loyal North Lancashire Rgt
Lance Corporal John C. Leigh 1st/4th Bn The Loyal North Lancashire Rgt
Private Wallace Leigh 1st Bn The Loyal North Lancashire Rgt
Private Arthur Leighton 10th Bn The Loyal North Lancashire Rgt
Private Wilfred Leyland 1st Bn Royal Welch Fusiliers
Rifleman Herbert Lightbown 2nd Bn King's Royal Rifle Corps
Sapper William Montgomery Lister 108th Field Coy Royal Engineers
Private Harold Livesey 1st Royal Marine Light Infantry
Private James Livesey 19th Bn King's (Liverpool Rgt)
Private Nicholas Livesey 6th Bn The Loyal North Lancashire Rgt
Private Percy Livesey 1st/4th Bn East Yorkshire Rgt
Private Edward Lofthouse 1st Bn King's Own Royal Lancaster Rgt
Lance Corporal John Lofthouse 29th Australian Infantry, AIF
Corporal Robert Longton 1st/4th Bn The Loyal North Lancashire Rgt
Private Joseph Ellis Longworth 8th Bn The Loyal North Lancashire Rgt
Private Alfred Hopkinson Lord 11th Bn East Lancashire Rgt
Private John Lord 1st Bn The Loyal North Lancashire Rgt
Private Harold Lowe 1st Bn The Loyal North Lancashire Rgt
Private James Lowe 11th Bn East Lancashire Rgt
Lance Corporal John Thomas Lowe 7th Bn South Wales Borderers
Private Robert Hesketh Lucas 1st/4th Bn The Loyal North Lancashire Rgt
Sapper Lawrence Lupton 13th Royal Engineers
Drummer Stephen Lupton 1st/4th Bn The Loyal North Lancashire Rgt
Sapper John Lythgoe 183rd Tunnelling Coy Royal Engineers
Private Andrew Magrath 11th Bn East Lancashire Rgt
Private William Alexander Donald MacKay Preston Army Pay Corps
Private John MacNamara 2nd Division Royal Marine Light Infantry
Gunner Joseph Makin 133rd Siege Bn Royal Garrison Artillery
Private James Makinson 11th Bn East Lancashire Rgt
Private Nicholas Makinson 1st/4th Bn The Loyal North Lancashire Rgt

Private William Mariner 2nd Bn King's Royal Rifle Corps
Private Daniel Marsden 2nd Bn Border Rgt
Driver Joseph Marsden 311th Brigade Royal Field Artillery
Private Robert Marsden 8th Bn King's Own Yorkshire Light Infantry
Private Septimus Marsden 25th Bn Australian Infantry, AIF
Private Edwin Marsden 6th Bn The Loyal North Lancashire Rgt
Private Harry Marsden 6th Bn The Loyal North Lancashire Rgt
Lance Corporal Herbert Marsden Motor Transport Coy RAMC
Private Isaac Marshall 6th Bn The Loyal North Lancashire Rgt
Private James Martin 1st/5th Bn Norfolk Rgt
Private Moses Martindale 8th Bn King's Own Royal Lancaster Rgt
Private George Mather 2nd/10th Bn Middlesex Rgt
Private Thomas Mawdsley 1st/4th Bn The Loyal North Lancashire Rgt
Steward Fred Mayoh HMS Theseus RN Reserve
Lance Corporal Robert McClellan 10th Bn The Loyal North Lancashire Rgt
Lance Corporal Hugh McDade 21st Bn Manchester Rgt
Private Harold McGinty 11th Bn Manchester Rgt
Sergeant Anthony McGowan 1st (Garrison) King's (Liverpool Rgt)
Private William McGowan 2nd Bn Royal Irish Rgt
Sergeant Peter McGuinness 1st Bn East Lancashire Rgt
Private George McIver 14th Bn Gloucester Rgt
Private Thomas McIver 1st Bn Duke of Cornwall's Light Infantry
Gunner William John McLoughlin 96th Brigade Royal Field Artillery
Private Francis McNally 6th Bn The Loyal North Lancashire Rgt
Private William McNally 2nd Bn Royal Scots Rgt
Private Edward McPartlin 10th Bn The Loyal North Lancashire Rgt
Private Harry Miller 19th Bn King's (Liverpool Rgt)
Corporal Henry Miller 1st Bn The Loyal North Lancashire Rgt
Gunner Herbert Miller 148th Brigade Royal Field Artillery
Private John Miller 7th Bn The Loyal North Lancashire Rgt
Private Joseph Miller 9th Bn The Loyal North Lancashire Rgt
Private Joseph Miller 9th Bn The Loyal North Lancashire Rgt
Lance Sergeant William Miller 1st/4th Bn King's Own Royal Lancaster Rgt
Private George Milton 11th Bn East Lancashire Rgt
Lance Serjeant Charles Mitchell 10th Bn The Loyal North Lancashire Rgt
1st class Stoker Daniel Mitchinson HMS Anchusa RN
Private Albert Mitton 1st Bn The Loyal North Lancashire Rgt
Ordinary Seaman Harry Molyneux HMS Terrible RN
Private Edward Monks 1st/4th Bn The Loyal North Lancashire Rgt
Private James Monks 2nd/4th Bn The Loyal North Lancashire Rgt
Private James Leo Moon 2nd Bn The Loyal North Lancashire Rgt
Private Charles Moorcroft 25th Coy Machine Gun Corps
Private James Moore 1st/4th Bn The Loyal North Lancashire Rgt
Private James Emmett Moore 1st Bn Duke of Cornwall's Light Infantry
Gunner John Joseph Moore 6th Bn Tank Corps
Coporal Leon Moreau 139th Rgt d'Infanterie 11th Cie, 1re Section
Corporal John Egan Morgan 1st/5th Bn The Loyal North Lancashire Rgt

Private Jones Morris 1st Bn Border Rgt
Private Lancelot Morris 1st/4th Bn The Loyal North Lancashire Rgt
Private Richard Morris 9th Bn East Lancashire Rgt
Lance Sergeant William Edward Moss 12th Bn Lancashire Fusiliers
Sergeant Thomas Mullen 10th Bn The Loyal North Lancashire Rgt
Private Martin Murray 8th Bn The Loyal North Lancashire Rgt
Private Robert Myerscough 4th Bn South Wales Borderers
Lance Corporal Thomas Myerscough 1st Bn The Loyal North Lancashire Rgt
Private Austin Naylor 1st/4th Bn The Loyal North Lancashire Rgt
Gunner John William Naylor 20th Bn Manchester Rgt
Gunner Thomas Harold Naylor 56th Royal Field Artillery
Private Joseph Nelson 1st/4th Bn The Loyal North Lancashire Rgt
Private Thomas Newsham 142nd Coy Machine Gun Corps (Infantry)
Private Henry Nightingale 10th Bn The Loyal North Lancashire Rgt
Private James Albert Nightingale 1st/4th Bn The Loyal North Lancashire Rgt
Sergeant Reginald Nixon 1st/4th Bn The Loyal North Lancashire Rgt
Gunner Peter Nolan 196th Heavy Battery Royal Garrison Artillery
Private Jonas Norminton 3rd Bn King's Own Royal Lancaster Rgt
Private James Norris 2nd/4th Bn The Loyal North Lancashire Rgt
Sapper John Henry Norris 201st Royal Engineers
Private Samuel Ashton Norris 9th Bn The Loyal North Lancashire Rgt
Driver Thomas Ogden 17th Division Royal Field Artillery
Private Peter O'Malley 8th Bn King's Own Royal Lancaster Rgt
Private Edward O'Neill 1st/4th Bn The Loyal North Lancashire Rgt
Rifleman Patrick Joseph O'Neill 1st Bn Royal Irish Rifles
Private Philip O'Neill 1st/4th Bn The Loyal North Lancashire Rgt
2nd Lieutenant Fred Openshaw 8th Bn King's (Liverpool Rgt)
Lance Corporal William Owen 2nd/5th Bn East Lancashire Rgt
Private William Owens 12th Coy Machine Gun Corps
Sergeant Harry Parker 170th Brigade Royal Field Artillery
Sergeant Henry Parker 1st Bn East Lancashire Rgt
Sergeant Major Alexander Cuthbert Parkinson 90th Wininpeg Rifles
Corporal Frederick Henry Parkinson 164th Coy Machine Gun Corps (Infantry)
Private Harry Parkinson HMS Glory Royal Marines Light Artillery
Acting Corporal Owen Thomas Parry 11th Bn East Lancashire Rgt
Private James Pearce 1st/4th Bn The Loyal North Lancashire Rgt
Private James Pearson 9th Bn The Loyal North Lancashire Rgt
Private Alfred Peers 6th Bn The Loyal North Lancashire Rgt
Private Richard Pendlebury 11th Bn East Lancashire Rgt
Lance Corporal John Perrigo 6th Bn The Loyal North Lancashire Rgt
Private Arthur Pilkington 9th Bn The Loyal North Lancashire Rgt
Private George Pilkington 1st/4th Bn The Loyal North Lancashire Rgt
Private George William Pilkington 11th Bn East Lancashire Rgt
Private James Pilkington 1st Bn Duke of Cornwall's Light Infantry
Chief Engineer James Fred Platt HMS Wellholme RN Volunteer Reserve
Private Robert Polding 1st/12th Bn The Loyal North Lancashire Rgt
Private Tom Pollard 72nd Canadian Infantry

Private Joseph Porter 7th Bn The Loyal North Lancashire Rgt
Private Richard Prescott 1st Bn The Loyal North Lancashire Rgt
Drummer John Preston 1st/4th Bn The Loyal North Lancashire Rgt
Sapper Charles Quinn 250th Royal Engineers
Private Wilfred Rainford 11th Bn King's Own Royal Lancaster Rgt
Lance Corporal Charles Ratcliffe 4th/5th Bn The Loyal North Lancashire Rgt
Private Herbert Ratcliffe 4th/5th Bn The Loyal North Lancashire Rgt
Lance Corporal John L. Ratcliffe 4th/5th Bn The Loyal North Lancashire Rgt
Private Joseph Ratcliffe 20th Bn Lancashire Fusiliers
Private Thomas Ratcliffe 9th Bn The Loyal North Lancashire Rgt
Private William Ratcliffe 11th Bn East Lancashire Rgt
Sapper Francis Rawcliffe 436th Field Coy Royal Engineers
Lance Corporal Thomas Rawcliffe Military Foot Police Military Police Corps
Lance Serjeant Jack Read 1st Bn The Loyal North Lancashire Rgt
Private James Francis Reed 1st Bn The Loyal North Lancashire Rgt
Captain E.M. Rennard 1st/4th Bn The Loyal North Lancashire Rgt
Private William Riding 1st/4th Bn The Loyal North Lancashire Rgt
Lance Corporal Albert Rigby 10th Bn The Loyal North Lancashire Rgt
Private Arthur Rigby 11th Bn Suffolk Rgt
Lance Corporal John T. Rigby 1st/4th Bn The Loyal North Lancashire Rgt
Private Norman Rigby 1st/4th Bn The Loyal North Lancashire Rgt
Private William Rigby 1st Bn Lincolnshire Rgt
2nd Lieutenant William Geoffrey Morris Rigby 1st Machine Gun Section
Private John Rigby 1st/2nd Bn Monmouthshire Rgt
Private Edward Riley 22nd Bn Manchester Rgt
Private Ernest Riley 1st Bn King's Own Royal Lancaster Rgt
Private John Riley 1st/4th Bn The Loyal North Lancashire Rgt
Private Robert Riley 75th Training Reserve
Private Thomas Rimmer 1st Bn The Loyal North Lancashire Rgt
Private Charles Robinson 1st Bn Grenadier Guards
Private John Robinson 8th Bn King's (Liverpool Rgt)
Corporal John Dennis Robinson 5th Bn Border Rgt
Gunner Mark Robinson 14th Brigade Royal Horse Artillery
Private Richard Preston Robinson 1st Bn East Lancashire Rgt
Lance Corporal Robert Robinson 10th Bn Lancashire Fusiliers
Private Thomas Robinson 249th Coy Machine Gun Corps (Infantry)
Private Walter Robinson 73rd Coy Machine Gun Corps
Bombardier Edgar Rogers 95th Brigade Royal Field Artillery
Private James William Rogerson 2nd Bn Lancashire Fusiliers
Sergeant John William Rogerson 9th Bn The Loyal North Lancashire Rgt
Private Seth Rollins 11th Bn East Lancashire Rgt
Lance Corporal William Rooney 1st/4th Bn The Loyal North Lancashire Rgt
Private William Roper 6th Bn The Loyal North Lancashire Rgt
Bombardier George Roscoe 77nd Brigade Royal Field Artillery
Private James Roscoe 10th Bn The Loyal North Lancashire Rgt
Private Peter Roscoe 1st Bn Scots Guards
Private Francis Rostron 2nd/5th Bn East Lancashire Rgt

Lance Corporal George Rostron 1st/5th Bn King's Own Royal Lancaster Rgt
Private William Rothwell 1st Bn The Loyal North Lancashire Rgt
Private George Roughsedge 15th Bn Highland Light Infantry
Rifleman Stephen Roughsedge 1st/7th Bn County of London Rgt
Private Edwin Sanderson 1st Bn The Loyal North Lancashire Rgt
Private Robert Sanderson 1st/10th Bn King's (Liverpool Rgt)
2nd Lieutenant Wilfred Sanderson 1st/7th Bn West Yorkshire Rgt
Private Gilbert Sandiford 1st Bn The Loyal North Lancashire Rgt
Lance Corporal Leonard Saunders 11th Bn East Lancashire Rgt
Private William Saunt 3rd Bn The Loyal North Lancashire Rgt
Lance Corporal George Scott 8th Bn The Loyal North Lancashire Rgt
Private John Scott 1st/5th Bn The Loyal North Lancashire Rgt
1st Class Stoker Herbert Seager HMS Tiger RN
Sergeant George Seddon 1st/4th Bn The Loyal North Lancashire Rgt
Serjeant Edward Seward 28th Coy Machine Gun Corps (Infantry)
Private James Sharples 3rd Bn Royal Sussex Rgt
Private Leo Sharples 8th Bn King's (Liverpool Rgt)
Private Levi Sharples 21st Bn Manchester Rgt
Private Robert Sharples 7th Bn East Kent Rgt
Lance Serjeant Thomas Sharples 18th Bn Cameronians (Scottish Rifles)
Private William Sharples 17th Bn Lancashire Fusiliers
Private Ernest Shaw 2nd (Garrison) King's (Liverpool Rgt)
Lance Corporal John Shaw 2nd/4th Bn The Loyal North Lancashire Rgt
Private Allan Shepherd 100th Coy Machine Gun Corps (Infantry)
Private John Shepherd 10th Bn The Loyal North Lancashire Rgt
Private Jack Sherburne 2nd/5th Bn The Loyal North Lancashire Rgt
Private Robert [Ernest] Shipcot 11th Bn The Loyal North Lancashire Rgt
Private John Sibbald 1st Bn King's Own Royal Lancaster Rgt
Private William Simm 1st/4th Bn The Loyal North Lancashire Rgt
Signaller James Simmons 90th Coy Machine Gun Corps
Private George Skelton 2nd Bn Lancashire Fusiliers
Gunner Helion Slater 1st Depot Royal Garrison Artillery
Private Joseph Slater 1st/4th Bn The Loyal North Lancashire Rgt
Private William Thomas Slater 1st Bn Grenadier Guards
Private John Robert Smalley 6th Bn The Loyal North Lancashire Rgt
Private Richard Smalley 76th Coy Machine Gun Corps (Infantry)
Lance Corporal James Smethurst Military Foot Police Military Police Corps
Lance Corporal Frank Smith 10th Bn The Loyal North Lancashire Rgt
Private Thomas Alfred Smith 1st Bn The Loyal North Lancashire Rgt
Private Walter Smith 1st/4th Bn The Loyal North Lancashire Rgt
Private William Edward Smith 10th Bn Lancashire Fusiliers
Lance Corporal William Henry Smith 10th Bn The Loyal North Lancashire Rgt
Gunner Henry Smith 881st Battery Royal Field Artillery
Corporal James Smith 1st/4th Bn The Loyal North Lancashire Rgt
Corporal George Snape 2nd Bn East Lancashire Rgt
Private John Snape 2nd Bn South Wales Border Rgt
Private Thomas Snape 52nd Coy Machine Gun Corps

Private Thomas Snape 15th Bn Lancashire Fusiliers
Private John Southworth 1st/4th Bn The Loyal North Lancashire Rgt
Private William Southworth 8th Bn Border Rgt
Sapper William Henry Speak 126th Field Coy Royal Engineers
Lance Corporal Daniel Speakman 10th Bn The Loyal North Lancashire Rgt
Private James Speakman 11th Bn East Lancashire Rgt
Private John Spencer 3rd Ambulance Train Royal Army Medical Corps
2nd Petty Officer William Spencer Marmion Royal Navy
Private Herbert Stables 2nd Bn King's Own Royal Lancaster Rgt
Lance Corporal Sam Stead 10th Bn The Loyal North Lancashire Rgt
Private Mossetse Stephenson 7th Bn Royal Sussex Rgt
Private Samuel Stirzaker 19th Bn Durham Light Infantry
Private James Stockley 9th Bn King's Own Royal Lancaster Rgt
Private William Strickland 6th Bn The Loyal North Lancashire Rgt
Private Edward Stringfellow 2nd/7th Bn Manchester Rgt
Private Henry Sturgess 19th Bn Manchester Rgt
Private Frank Sumner 10th Bn Lancashire Fusiliers
Private Harry Sumner Royal Army Medical Corps
Private John Sumner 1st Bn The Loyal North Lancashire Rgt
Lance Corporal Joseph Sutcliffe 1st Bn King's Own Royal Lancaster Rgt
Lance Corporal William Suter 4th Bn Seaforth Highlanders
Private Alexander Taylor 11th Bn The Loyal North Lancashire Rgt
Private Daniel Taylor 2nd/4th Bn The Loyal North Lancashire Rgt
Private Herbert Taylor 25th Australian Imperial Forces
Drummer James Edward Taylor 1st/4th Bn The Loyal North Lancashire Rgt
Corporal Lee Taylor 17th Bn King's (Liverpool Rgt)
Private Robert Taylor 3rd Bn Cameronians (Scottish Rifles)
Private Thomas Taylor 1st/4th Bn The Loyal North Lancashire Rgt
Private William Taylor 1st/4th Bn The Loyal North Lancashire Rgt
Private William Fielden Taylor 1st/4th Bn East Lancashire Rgt
Private Sidney Thexton 1st/4th Bn The Loyal North Lancashire Rgt
Private Harold Cecil Thom 2nd Bn Border Rgt
Lance Corporal Arthur J. Thomas 1st/4th Bn The Loyal North Lancashire Rgt
Private Frederick Henry Thomas 1st Bn The Loyal North Lancashire Rgt
Lance Sergeant Henry Thomas 5th Bn Royal Highlanders of Canada
Private James Thompson 7th Bn Royal West Kent Rgt
Lance Corporal John Thompson 12th Bn Manchester Rgt
Sergeant Joseph Thompson 4th Bn The Loyal North Lancashire Rgt
Private Joseph Alexander Thompson 11th Bn East Lancashire Rgt
Private Harry Thornley 10th Bn The Loyal North Lancashire Rgt
Private William Thornley 87th Coy Machine Gun Corps
Lance Corporal John Thorpe The Loyal North Lancashire Rgt
Private Harold Tindall 9th Bn The Loyal North Lancashire Rgt
Private Thomas Tomlinson 18th Bn King's (Liverpool Rgt)
Lance Corporal John Tootell 1st/4th Bn The Loyal North Lancashire Rgt
Private William Tootell 11th Bn East Lancashire Rgt
Private William Edward Tootell 9th Bn Royal Welch Fusiliers

Private Edward Tootill 2nd/7th Bn Manchester Rgt
Gunner William Trought 160th Brigade Royal Field Artillery
Private Frederick Jones Turner 1st Bn The Loyal North Lancashire Rgt
Corporal Henry Turner 1st Bn King's Own Royal Lancaster Rgt
Trooper Horace Turner 1st Bn Life Guards
Private William Turner 2nd Bn King's Own Royal Lancaster Rgt
Private Richard Tyrer 9th Bn The Loyal North Lancashire Rgt
Private Herbert Unsworth 11th Bn East Lancashire Rgt
Private Nathan Pilkington Urmston 9th Bn East Surrey Rgt
Private Edward John Vaughan Mechanical Transport Army Service Corps
Private John James Waddington 11th Bn East Lancashire Rgt
Private Horace Waine 6th Bn The Loyal North Lancashire Rgt
Private Robert Wallbank 9th Bn The Loyal North Lancashire Rgt
Private Robert Walmsley 149th Brigade Royal Field Artillery
Lance Corporal Stephen Walmsley 313th Royal Defence Corps
Private William Thomas Walmsley 136th Royal Army Medical Corps
Private James Walsh 1st/6th Bn Lancashire Fusiliers
Private William Walsh 14th Bn Welsh Rgt
Private Albert Wane 2nd Bn The Loyal North Lancashire Rgt
Driver Charles William Wane 186 Brigade Royal Field Artillery
Private Robert Warburton 1st Bn East Surrey Rgt
Private Thomas Warburton 2nd/6th Bn Sherwood Foresters
Private David Waring 2nd/4th Bn The Loyal North Lancashire Rgt
2nd Lieutenant Frank Waring 5th Bn York and Lancaster Rgt
Private James Waring 1st Bn South Wales Borderers
Private Thomas Waring 17th Bn Lancashire Fusiliers
Private Sydney Waterworth 1st/4th Bn The Loyal North Lancashire Rgt
Private Richard Watmaugh 11th Bn East Lancashire Rgt
Private James Watson 7th Bn The Loyal North Lancashire Rgt
Private Thomas Welsby 10th Bn King's (Liverpool Rgt)
Private John Westby 10th Bn The Loyal North Lancashire Rgt
Senior Reserve Attendant Albert Whalley HMS Garth Castle RN
Sergeant George Harold Whalley 165th Brigade Royal Field Artillery
Private Herbert Whalley 1st/8th Bn Durham Light Infantry
Private Thomas Whalley 10th Bn The Loyal North Lancashire Rgt
Private Adam Wharton 1st/4th Bn The Loyal North Lancashire Rgt
Private Harold Wheatcroft 19th Bn Royal Welch Fusiliers
Private Ernest Whitehead 1st Bn Royal Welch Fusiliers
Private Joseph Whitehouse 6th Bn East Lancashire Rgt
Captain John L Whitfield 1st/4th Bn The Loyal North Lancashire Rgt
Private George Whittle 1st/5th Bn The Loyal North Lancashire Rgt
Private Henry Whittle 1st Bn King's Own Royal Lancaster Rgt
Private James Whittle 2nd/4th Bn The Loyal North Lancashire Rgt
Private William Whittle 1st Bn East Lancashire Rgt
Private Clarence Widdop 11th Bn East Lancashire Rgt
Private Robert Wiggans 8th Bn King's Own Royal Lancaster Rgt
Private James Wildman 11th Bn Lancashire Fusiliers

Lieutenant [Alfred] Richard Williams 49th Coy Machine Gun Corps
Private James Wilson Not yet identified Not yet identified
Private Percy Wilson 1st Bn North Staffordshire Rgt
Private Robert Wilson 1st/4th Bn The Loyal North Lancashire Rgt
Private Michael Winn 1st/4th Bn The Loyal North Lancashire Rgt
Private Percy Withnell 1st Bn King's Own Royal Lancaster Rgt
Private John Wilson Wood 1st/10th Bn Liverpool Scottish Rgt
Lance Corporal George Woodcock 6th Bn The Loyal North Lancashire Rgt
Private John Woodcock 6th Bn The Loyal North Lancashire Rgt
Lance Corporal William Woodruff 1st/4th Bn The Loyal North Lancashire Rgt
Private Stephen Woods 11th Bn East Lancashire Rgt
Private William Woods 10th Bn The Loyal North Lancashire Rgt
Corporal William Worsfold HMS Laurentic Royal Marine Artillery
Private Thomas Worsley 3rd Bn Canadian Infantry (Central Ontario Rgt)
Private Albert Worthington 1st/4th Bn The Loyal North Lancashire Rgt
Driver Joshua Worthington Mechanical Transport Army Service Corps
Private Albert (Harry) Yates 2nd./8th Bn Royal Warwickshire Rgt
Private Thomas Yates 4th Bn South Staffordshire Rgt
Private James Young 8th Bn The Loyal North Lancashire Rgt

Bibliography

Note on Principal Sources

The *Chorley Memorial Album* is comprised of three books. Each facing page has been denoted by a referencing system which identifies the book within the *Album* its page. As an example CMB, II, p. 5 refers to Chorley Memorial Book II and identifies the fifth facing page. The *Album* is held by Astley Hall Museum and Art Gallery in Chorley.

The *Walmsley Archive* is the family collection comprises the letters, photographs and personal effects of Susannah and Jack Knight, contributed by Jack's granddaughter, Jan Walmsley. This includes Jack Knight's Continuous Discharge Book.

The *Weld Bank School Log Book* (St Gregory's School, Chorley, 1914 to 1953).

Soroptomists of Chorley Minute Book (Lancashire County Records DDX 1796/1).

Other Archival Sources

Astley Hall Museum and Art Gallery, Chorley
Chorley Library
F. D. Roosevelt Library, Washington DC, USA
Lancashire Record Office, Preston
Liverpool Roman Catholic Archdiocesan Archives
National Library of Scotland, Edinburgh
Rennes Archives, France

Newspapers and Periodicals

Catholic Bulletin (Chorley)
Liverpool Mercury (Liverpool)
L'Ouest-Éclair (Ille et Vilaine)
New York Times (New York)
Texas Almanac and State Industrial Guide 1936 (Dallas, 1936).
The Chorley and District Weekly News (Chorley)
The Chorley Guardian (Chorley)
The Chorley Standard (Chorley)
The Daily Dispatch (Liverpool)
The Messenger (Chorley)
The Times (London)

Books

Costello, Peter *Clongowes Wood* (Dublin: Gill and Macmillan, 1989).
Arnander, Christopher *Private Lord Crawford's Great War Diaries* (Barnsley:

Pen and Sword, 2013).

Atkinson, Mary Jourdan *The Texas Indians* (The Naylor Company: San Antonio, Texas 1935).

Battalion History Committee *The War History of the 1st/4th Battalion the Loyal North Lancashire Regiment* (Preston: G. Toulmin & Sons, Limited, 1921). Republished in *The Lancashire Lads at War* (Driffield, Yorkshire: Leonaur, 2015).

Blades, Barry *Roll of Honour, Schooling & The Great War* (Barnsley: Pen and Sword, 2015).

Bolwell, F.A. *With a Reservist in France* (London: Routledge, 1918). Republished in *The Lancashire lads at War* (Driffield, Yorkshire: Leonaur, 2015).

Borden, Robert Laird, *Conference for the Limitation of Armaments Held at Washington – Report of the Canadian delegate* (Ottawa: F.A. Acland, printer, 1922).

Clark, Christopher *The Sleepwalkers* (Penguin: London, 2013).

Clewlow, Stuart A. *In Memoriam* (Stuart Clewlow: Chorley, 2011).

Coop, James Ogden *The Story of the 55th (West Lancashire) Division* (Liverpool Daily Post: Liverpool, 1919). Republished by Naval and Military Press: Uckfield, 2002).

Crane, David. *Empires of the Dead* (William Collins: London, 2014).

Dalrymple, Tate etc. *Major Texas Floods of 1936* (Government Print Office: Washington D.C, USA, 1937).

De Groot, Gerard J. *Blighty: British Society in the era of the Great War* (Longman: London and New York, 1996).

Dictionary of National Biography (Oxford).

Duffy, Michael *The Sacred Heart* (Brewer's Print: Chorley, 1993).

Gallop, Alan *Buffalo Bill's British Wild West* (The History Press: Stroud, 2001).

Gillett, Tom *Weld Bank School 1816-1913* (Nelson Brothers: Chorley, 1974).

Harris, J.P. *Douglas Haig and the First World War* (Cambridge University Press: Cambridge, 2008).

Garwood, John *Chorley Pals* (Neil Richardson: Radcliffe, Manchester, 1998).

Jackson, Andrew *Accrington's Pals* (Pen and Sword: Barnsley, 2013).

John, A.H. *A Liverpool Merchant House* (George Allen & Unwin: London, 1959).

Laughlin, Clara E. *Foch the Man – A Life of the Supreme Commander of Allied Armies* (Fleming H. Revell Company: New York, 1918)

Lloyd George, David *War Memoirs Volume 2* (Odham's Press: London, 1936).

MacDonald, Lynn *Somme* (Penguin: London, 2003).

Middlebrook, Martin *The First Day of the Somme* (Penguin: London, 1971).

Reynolds, David *The Long Shadow* (Simon and Schuster: London, 2014).

Strachan, Hew *The First World War* (Simon and Schuster: London, 2014).

Williams, Steve & Garwood, John *Chorley Pals* (Chorley Pals Memorial: Chorley, 2009).

Wooton, Graham *The Official History of the British Legion* (Macdonald & Evans,. Ltd: London, 1958).

Wylly, Colonel H.C. *The Loyal North Lancashire Regiment* (The Royal United Service Institution: London, 1933). Republished by Naval and Military Press: Uckfield, 2007).

INDEX

A

ABOUT THE AUTHOR

Adam Cree studied History and History of Science at the University of Lancaster. He is a teacher of History at St Michael's CE High School in Chorley, Lancashire. He is a volunteer at Astley Hall, a Tudor mansion in the town where the *Chorley Memorial Album* is displayed.

Printed in Great Britain
by Amazon

54034943R00122